What Has Religion Done for Mankind?

"There is not a fine tree
producing rotten fruit;
again there is not a rotten
tree producing fine fruit.
For each tree is known
by its own fruit."

Luke 6: 43, 44, *NW*.

PUBLISHERS

WATCHTOWER BIBLE AND TRACT SOCIETY, INC.
INTERNATIONAL BIBLE STUDENTS ASSOCIATION
Brooklyn, New York, U. S. A.

2,000,000 Edition

DEDICATED to the peace and unity of all people of good will of whatever race or nation, by the exposure of the false religion and the vindication of the true.

Abbreviations of Bible versions quoted or cited in this book

AS   – American Standard Version, by the American Committee of Revision

AT   – An American Translation, by J. M. P. Smith and E. J. Goodspeed

CB   – The Holy Bible, translated by the Catholic Biblical Association of America

Da   – The 'Holy Scriptures', a New Translation, by J. N. Darby

Dy   – Translation of the Latin Vulgate made at Douay and Rheims

Fn   – The Holy Bible in Modern English, by Ferrar Fenton

Kx   – The Holy Bible, translated by Monsignor Ronald A. Knox

LXX – The Septuagint Version of the Hebrew Scriptures, translation published by S. Bagster and Sons Limited

Ly   – The New Testament in the Westminster Version, by Cuthbert Lattey, S.J.

Mo   – A New Translation of The Bible, by James Moffatt

Mk   – The Syriac New Testament, by James Murdock

NW   – New World Translation of the Christian Greek Scriptures, 2d edition

Ro   – The Emphasised Bible, a New Translation, by J. B. Rotherham

RS   – Revised Standard Version of the New Testament, by the International Council of Religious Education

Sp   – The New Testament, a New Translation, by Francis A. Spencer, O.P.

Yg   – The Holy Bible, translated by Robert Young

Any quotation not followed by any specific abbreviation should be understood to be made from the Authorized or King James Version.

CONTENTS

What Has Religion Done for Mankind?

CHAPTER I

RELIGION or no religion—what shall it be for me? That is the question every full-grown, intelligent person must decide today. Upon each one's personal decision depends his everlasting destiny. It is as serious as all that. We have to face the question and answer it, because religion, all religion, is on judgment in this most trying time.

[2] Now, for the first time in human history, all the civilizations that have survived till today are in turmoil at the same time. This is most unusual. It must be very significant. Religion cannot be divorced from responsibility for the situation, for from the beginning religion has been connected with every civilization that has arisen on the face of the earth. That is why it is sorely feeling the effects of the worsening situation. That is why it is under judgment. Is history now overtaking religion? Are its sins, long indulged in, catching up with it and finding it out while the whole world looks on? Is it now reaping the fruitage of what it has sown for centuries? As we endeavor to answer all these vital questions we cannot escape

---

1. What question must we now answer? Why is it so serious?
2. Why is the world situation so unusual, and why must we investigate what religion has done for mankind?

7

investigating the question, What has religion done for mankind? We must be honest with ourselves and courageously face the facts. The truth may hurt but will be beneficial. The grand climax of testing is certain to come shortly, and only the truth will endure.

[3] This word "religion" has a broad meaning. There is much that is called by this name, and we want to know whether the truth, the pure, absolute truth, is associated with religion. So it becomes necessary for us at the start to set out the meaning of the term as here used, in order to understand what we are talking about and to come to right conclusions. In various languages this word has some equivalent. The word the Hebrews used for it literally meant "service". The Germans have long called it "Gottesdienst", which means "service of God". The Russian Communists, following the German Socialist Karl Marx, call it "the opium of the people". But the English, French, Spanish, Portuguese, and Italians, whose languages are drawn largely from the Latin of the Roman empire, use the term "religion". In Latin it is *religio*. This word, says the great Roman orator and author Cicero, is made up of two words *re* and *légere,* which, together, mean "to read over again", to reflect upon or to study the sacred books in which religion is delivered.[*] So he called it the "pious worship of God". But according to a later Latin author Lactantius it

---

[*] *De Divinatione,* Book 4, by Cicero.

---

3. From what comes the word "religion", and how has it been defined?

comes from *re-ligáre,* meaning "to bind back", because it reveals to us the obligation which binds us to a higher power.*

⁴ The word occurs in the Latin Vulgate Bible. There it is applied to the Jewish religion, to worship of angels, and to Christianity. Testifying before a Roman law court, the Christian apostle Paul tells of when he was a Jewish Pharisee and says: "According to the strictest sect of our religion I lived a Pharisee."† Writing to Christian believers at Colóssae, he warns them: "Let no man seduce you, willing in humility, and religion of angels."‡ Still earlier the book of The Wisdom of Solomon (14:18, 27) applied the word to the worship of idols. Now, although Paul calls by the name "religion" the cult of the Pharisees and the worship of angels, things which he considers to be wrong, his fellow writer James applies the name to true Christianity, saying: "If any man think himself to be religious, not bridling his tongue, but deceiving his own heart, this man's religion is vain. Religion clean and undefiled before God and the Father, is this: to visit the fatherless and widows in their tribulation: and to keep one's self unspotted from this world."‡

---

* *De Civitate Dei,* Book 10, chapter 3.
† The Bible, at Acts 26:4, 5, translated from the Latin by the Catholic Biblical Association of America, 1941.
‡ The Bible, at Colossians 2:18 and James 1:26, 27, according to the Douay Version, translated from the Latin Vulgate. In the original Greek text the word is *thrēskeía,* which is derived from the Hebrew word meaning to seek, search or inquire, that is to say, seek for God or a higher power.

---

4. How do the Christians Paul and James apply the word "religion"?

[5] Taken according to the way it is used, "religion" in its simplest definition means a system of worship, a form of worship, without regard to whether it is true or false worship. This agrees with the meaning of the Hebrew word for it, *'a·boh·dáh,* which literally means "service", regardless of to whom it is rendered. Adopting this plain meaning of the word, notice how the *New World Translation* of James' words above reads: "If any man seems to himself to be a formal worshiper and yet does not bridle his tongue, but goes on deceiving his own heart, this man's form of worship is futile. The form of worship that is clean and undefiled from the standpoint of our God and Father is this: to care for orphans and widows in their tribulation, and to keep oneself without spot from the world." It is in the sense of system or form of worship that we use the term "religion" in this book.

[6] Religion is universal. No matter how loudly they claim to be godless, religion is practiced even by the Red Fascists or Communists, as we shall show to their embarrassment. Despite this fact, the world of today is not bound together in one. More so than political beliefs, religion is a divisive force today. It itself is divided. There are many kinds of religion. Each conscientious devotee of a religion will insist that his own is the true one, which is why he sticks to it. But he finds in it something which keeps him from enjoying complete harmony with someone who holds some oth-

---

5. In what sense is the word used in this book? Why?
6. What kind of force is religion today, and why so?

er belief. For him to get along with the other person he must practice religious toleration. Intolerance has been a curse to mankind, but it is still rife today and threatens to do more damage than it has already wrought throughout the centuries. So divisive is religion that the Assembly of the United Nations, an organization which represented sixty different member nations in 1951, cannot open its sessions with united prayer to a common deity, through one religious spokesman. At most they can only rise and all have a minute of silent meditation. A chapel has been proposed for use of all in common, where anyone of any belief may go of his own accord and indulge in individual prayer to his own deity.

⁷ What, then, are we to do with religion in order to unify the world? Are we to say that all the many kinds stand for a sincere worship, and so, because of the sincerity of heart, they will all be accepted? Are we to encourage each and every one to be religious according to his own way, because the kind of religion does not matter, just so the person is religious and this makes him a better person? That may stand for toleration, but mere religious toleration will never unify this world. No more so than the provision for this in the Constitution of the United States of America has unified this country. What, then, are we to do? Try to synthesize all kinds and build up a fusion religion? Is that the way it will be able to survive in this perilous day? We see movements

---

7. Why will religious toleration not unify this world? And how is unification proceeding?

toward unification, especially among the Protestant sects and organizations, to protect themselves and to create internal strength. And the head of the mighty papal system at Vatican City is constantly pleading for the Protestant systems to return to the Roman Catholic fold. In fact, the pope designated the 1950 "Holy Year" as the "year of the great return". However, the cleavage between the great systems still continues. In some instances the rift widens.

[8] A movement toward a world fusion-religion was begun toward the close of the last century. In Chicago, Illinois, during the World's Columbian Exposition, what was called the World's Parliament of Religions was held in September of 1893. It was promoted mainly by the Protestant systems, but it extended the honors of opening and closing the parliament to clergymen of the Catholic church. Representatives of the great systems of belief and worship in all parts of the world were invited to attend and deliver speeches, explaining their creeds and their way.

[9] For seventeen days so-called Christian met with pagan, Jew with Gentile, Hindu with Presbyterian, Buddhist with Baptist, Confucian with Methodist, Christian Scientist with Lutheran, Monotheist with Polytheist, apparently to come to a better understanding of what the other believed and to find some common ground for blending with one another in belief and practice. It was to be a grand

---

8. What movement toward a world fusion-religion was begun in 1893?
9. How was this Parliament of Religions really a meeting of compromise?

meeting of compromise, with each one admitting he did not have "the whole truth and nothing but the truth". Those who most showed themselves willing to compromise on even their basic principles were the Protestants. No conviction of having the truth, but peace at any price! As one Protestant clergyman, of the Disciples church, expressed himself: "This first Parliament of Religions seems to be the harbinger of a still larger fraternity—a fraternity that will combine into one world-religion what is best, not in one alone, but in all of the great historic faiths. It may be that, under the guidance of this larger hope, we shall need to revise our phraseology and speak more of *Religious unity,* than of *Christian unity.* I rejoice that all the great cults are to be brought into touch with each other, and that Jesus will take his place in the companionship of Gautama, Confucius and Zoroaster."*

[10] Did that World's Parliament of Religions have heaven's blessing and work toward world peace and unity? Evidently not. Twenty years later the world entered into a period of disunity and turmoil such as it had never before known, with the outbreak of the first world war in 1914. The rupture of peace and harmony began, not in so-called "heathendom", but in Christendom where all are supposed to be Christian brothers who show that they follow Christ because they love one another and lay down their lives for one an-

---

* *The Battle of Armageddon,* published in 1897, page 183.

10. What shows whether the Parliament worked for world peace and unity?

other, not kill one another. Catholic and Protestant clergymen ignored the rule laid down by their professed Leader Jesus Christ, when he said: "I am giving you a new commandment, that you love one another; just as I have loved you, that you also love one another. By this all will know that you are my disciples, if you have love among yourselves."* Contrary to this, these sectarian leaders patriotically divided on the national and political issues of the time and prayed to this one and the same Christ to bless and prosper the death-dealing weapons of whichever side they were on. This same course was followed in World War II, and every indication is that it is to be the course followed in further international conflicts.

[11] For the duration of the conflict each great religion of Christendom becomes nationalized, while the clergy on top reap the benefit, win or lose their side militarily. No second World's Parliament of Religions is proposed, not even on the basis of the United Nations of many religions. To judge from the results of the first one, world unity would not be furthered by such a parliament with its efforts toward a fusion world-religion. Besides, conditions are even far more unfavorable toward one now than in 1893.

[12] Since hope does not rest in a synthesized re-

---

* The Bible, at John 13:34, 35, *New World Translation*.

---

11. Why does existence of the United Nations not favor a second such religious Parliament?
12. As respects religion, what is this crucial time the opportunity for?

ligion for all mankind, what then? Does it rest with any one kind? Back there, one of the leading promoters of the parliament of 1893, a Protestant clergyman, expressed it this way: "Some one has said that the time is now ripe for the best religion to come to the front. The time for a man to put on any airs of superiority about his particular religion is past."* The task of making certain which is the best religion in Christendom or in heathendom would be an endless one, a fruitless one, especially when even such "best" one is examined in the face of the question, What has religion done for mankind? Another thing, the task of getting all mankind to adopt such "best" one, even for the sake of world unity, would be humanly impossible. This is not the time of opportunity for what *men* may decide is the "best religion". This most crucial time in human history is the ripe time for the *true* religion to come to the front and unite all honest hearts that yearn for justice, truth, peace and brotherly love.

[13] No one can escape this issue. Since the radi-

The New York Times

Oct. 10, 1949

RELIGIOUS FAKES DECRIED

Dr. W. L. Pettingill Calls Much of Modern Teaching a 'Curse'

The weakness of the church today is largely the result of the absence of persecution and suffering, the Rev. Dr. William L. Pettingill, pastor of the First Baptist Church, Broadway and Seventyninth Street, said in a sermon yesterday morning.

"Religious teaching that is dished out now is a curse and not a blessing," he declared. "Most of it is false religion which ignores the teachings of Christ. These false beliefs called religion are our greatest enemies.

"Even right here in New York City there are many churches which do no more than parade under the name of God. Ninety-nine per cent of religion in this city should be scrapped because one cannot believe man and God at the same time. One must believe God."

---

* *The Battle of Armageddon,* page 182, ¶¶ 4, 5.

13. What shows whether any one worldly religion will unify all nations? Why cannot all religions be right simply because sincerely practiced?

cals who boast of their godless materialism have a form of worship which differs from other kinds only in the naming of things, even they have been forced by this day of judgment of the nations into choosing a religion. With this they hope to integrate the world under one political control allowing for only one allegiance. That they will not succeed, we propose to prove on reliable authority. But, then, what other religion of this world will succeed in unifying all nations, races, colors, and languages? Based on past performance, upon what they have already done for mankind, not one, not even the "best", if there be such, will prove able to do so. We owe it to our fellow man to respect his right to worship according to what mode or system he prefers. But because sentimental people view worship as sacred and beautiful when it is conscientious and sincere, this does not make all beliefs and forms of adoring some higher power right and leading to endless life, liberty and happiness. They cannot all be right and leading to the same happy end, for they all differ and disagree with one another and contradict one another.

[14] Though all other kinds disagree with it, there must be only one kind of worship, one religion, that is right. This is the one in harmony with the absolute truth. Since there is just the one that is true, set against so many hundreds of others that prove to be false, it follows that those who adopt and practice the true must necessarily be

---

14. Why must only one religion be right? Why is it shown intolerance by others?

in the minority. History proves that this has always been so. The contradiction of the minority by the majority does not prove they are in the wrong. While not tolerating falsehood for themselves, they exercise most genuine tolerance toward all others in the world in their privilege of choosing the gods whom they want to serve. Unjustly they are rewarded with the greatest intolerance in political, social, economic, legal and religious ways. But this will not crush them out of existence. The intolerant religionists who oppose them are the ones that are in fear for their form of belief and worship, both fear from the truth as well as fear from the violent radical classes who claim to be antigod.

[15] The truth has endured till now, and those who have it need not fear. The truth is eternal. It will last forever, after all error has been exposed and perishes. So those who worship with spirit and truth can afford to exercise true toleration toward all other religions as long as this old world of which such are a part lasts. But this toleration does not mean they are obliged to put the quietus on the proclamation of the truth by which men may be turned from darkness to light, from false worship to right worship. The fact is, they are under moral obligation to their fellow men to let them hear and examine it and then say, "It is the truth."

[16] It is with a sense of this obligation that this

---

15. Why may those with the truth be tolerant but not silence the truth?
16. In recognition of what right of the people is this book published?

book is published. Nothing is accomplished by saying that your religion is good enough for you, and his is good enough for him, and ours is good enough for us; so do not cause religious disturbance but let everything stay as it is. That which is false has come to its day of reckoning and will perish amid the great ruin which it is bringing upon itself. Those who hold to it, even in their ignorance, will perish with it, just as, when a blind guide falls into the ditch, the blind person he is guiding will tumble in with him. So those blinded with falsehood have a right to hear the truth and need to hear it to escape destruction.

[17] Truth is one and is for all who love it, the same way as proved science is for all. Being for all, it is the only thing that will bind all men together. By modern developments the whole earth is now one close neighborhood, and we are one human race, from one original human father, and on one earth, and faced with a world-wide trouble in common. The pure worship is the one thing that will unify the universe in a new world and lead to the fatherhood of God and the brotherhood of man. The rule is sure, By the fruitage of a tree you will know the tree for what it is. So with tolerance toward the rights of all, but in the interests of unity and salvation by the truth, we now proceed to examine the fruitage and see what religion has done for mankind. Indifference toward the true religion puts you in peril.

---

17. For whom is the truth, and so what universal condition can it bring about? How, then, do we proceed to our investigation?

CHAPTER II

The Standard for Judging Religion

WHAT is the measuring stick for all religions? What is it that distinguishes the true one as such? Is religion only what man develops naturally through his contact with the material creation? Or is there a revealed religion which has come to him by supernatural means? These are questions which persons of all creeds and beliefs must have answered according to reason and the facts before they can decide whether they have what is the true knowledge and worship or whether it is necessary for them to make a change, in the interest of their eternal welfare.

[2] In the world today there are a number of religions of great age and with large followings. For example, Hinduism, Buddhism, Taoism, Confucianism, Shinto, Judaism, Mohammedanism, and Christianity. These all have their sacred writings. Hindus have the Vedas, their four books of knowledge; Buddhists their scriptures called the "Three Baskets of Wisdom"; Taoists their holy book *Tao Te King;* Confucianists their classics such as "Spring and Autumn"; Shintoists their

---

1. What questions must be answered before we can decide whether we have true knowledge and worship?
2. What questions must be settled concerning the religions of great age and their sacred writings?

Kojiki or "Records"; orthodox Jews their Talmud; Mohammedans their Koran; Christians their Holy Scriptures or Bible. A number of these sacred writings are regarded by their devotees as being *revealed* religion, from a source higher than man. But recognizing that there are powers higher than man that are good and bad, we must ask, Did each such set of supposed "sacred" writings have its revelation from a good source or a bad source? Which one is the true revelation?

[3] There is every need for a supernatural revelation. We cannot depend upon what men call "natural religion". Men have the senses of seeing, hearing and feeling. They can observe the marvels of the natural world, the earth and the sun, moon and stars. They see, hear and feel the phenomena resulting from the operation of the laws that govern this natural world. By experiment they determine what is hurtful and what is beneficial. They have relations with one another in human society and so set up standards of what is proper conduct. They come in touch with many forces and phenomena that they cannot understand or explain and they attach some superstitious connection to these. Thus they build up a "natural religion", a system of rules of conduct and of worship toward what is visible or invisible.

[4] But honesty must compel us to admit that all men are imperfect and subject to mistake and error. In different parts of the earth, widely sep-

---

3. How is "natural religion" developed?
4. Why does "natural religion" differ in places and fall short of truth and righteousness?

arated, men have different experiences, different associations, different things to contend with and different sources of information. Hence the development of natural religion is bound to differ in various sections of the earth. Men are debased, too, and often prefer what is bad to what is good, because of the selfish satisfaction which they get out of this reversal of matters. They are also limited in knowledge. The result is that mere natural religion falls far short of truth and righteousness. In many cases it violates that which is pure, healthful, just and upbuilding. Hence there must be a revelation from a higher truthful source in order to correct the wrong tendencies of natural religion and in order to instruct the human conscience in the right way.

[5] Natural religion, even such as the higher critics and materialistic scientists are trying to develop today, could never be sufficient. It can never explain the mystery of life, how it got its start and what keeps it going. How did this wonderful natural world with all its variety in earth, sea and sky come into existence? Who is responsible for all this? What did we humans come from? Where did

5. In view of what questions could natural religion never be sufficient?

this thing called "sin" together with imperfection and error come from? Why is it that
the human organism, which shows every possi-
bility of being kept in operation for eternity,
dies? Is there a life after death? Or will there be
a return from death to life on this earth? Are
there invisible persons different in make-up from
man and higher than man? Do they serve man's
interests or does man need protection from them?
Will this stupendous material creation in heaven
and earth pass away and all human and animal
existence cease? If there are higher powers superior in intelligence and power to man, what are
our duties to them? Are they to be worshiped,
and how? What have they to do with the destiny
of mankind? Is there but one God over all things,
or are there many gods? To these questions many
others could be added. The answers to these natural religion could never work out of itself. Modern science also provides no satisfactory, unchangeable answer, but it too shows it is subject
to human disabilities and limitations.

⁶ All progressive nations are turning to modern
science in order to keep abreast of the rest of
the world, and, as they hope, for the sake of their
independence, survival and liberation from the
backwardness of the past. The more the scientists
study the universe the more they can see that
there is an intelligence behind it, and that the
master mind behind it is a great mathematician.
The famous Einstein, whose theory of relativity

---

6. What do progressive students and scientists see more
and more behind the universe?

played an important part toward the invention of the atomic bomb, had this to say:

> "It is enough for me to contemplate the mystery of conscious life perpetuating itself through all eternity; to reflect upon the marvelous structure of the universe, which we can dimly perceive, and to try humbly to comprehend even an infinitesimal part of the INTELLIGENCE MANIFEST IN NATURE."

[7] Then there is Dr. Robert A. Millikan who has been rated the dean of American scientists, being the first of them to study cosmic rays and winning the Nobel Prize for being the first to determine the charge and mass of the electron, an electrical particle of all matter. Addressing the meeting of the American Physical Society at Washington, D.C., on April 29, 1948, he expressed himself in the terms of a believer in the theory of the evolution of man and yet he said with conviction:

> "There's a Divinity that shapes our ends. . . . Just how we fit into the plans of the Great Architect and how much He has assigned us to do we do not know, but if we fail on our assignment it is pretty certain that part of the job will be left undone. But fit in we certainly do somehow, else we would not have a sense of our own responsibility. A PURELY MATERIALISTIC PHILOSOPHY IS TO ME THE HEIGHT OF UNINTELLIGENCE. Wise men in all the ages have always seen enough to at least make them reverent."

Then he quoted Einstein's notable words above and went on to speak of God as the "Great Architect" and of our responsibility to Him.—New York *Times,* April 30, 1948.

---

7. What did an American scientist say about a "purely materialistic philosophy", and why?

[8] However, wise persons do not need these modern scientists to prove to them that there is a living intelligence behind visible and invisible creation and that He is all-powerful, all-wise, supreme and just, and harmonizes all things. Nineteen centuries ago such a wise man showed that mankind are inexcusable for not recognizing that there is such a God. Why? "Because what may be known about God is manifest among them, for God made it manifest to them. For his invisible qualities are clearly seen from the world's creation onward, because they are understood by the things made, even his eternal power and Godship, so that they are inexcusable; because, although they knew God, they did not glorify him as God nor did they thank him, but they became empty-headed in their reasonings and their unintelligent heart became darkened."*

[9] From our own experience we know that intelligence is associated with mind. The mind which can understand some of the things about the universe is associated with a brain in a body of a definite shape and individuality. So this great intelligence, this great mind responsible for all creation must be the Supreme Being, the great Person who is God, with a definite body and individuality and powers, all this distinguishing him from all creation.

* Paul of Tarsus in the Bible, at Romans 1:19-21, *New World Translation*.

8. Why do really wise persons not need modern scientists to prove a living intelligence to be behind all creation?
9. How, then, do we reason that there must be a Supreme Being?

[10] Natural religion, resulting from man's own observations and investigations, cannot reveal to us who this God is and what his name is. Only a direct revelation from this Supreme Being himself can inform us of this. Only this revelation can give us the truth on how he made creation, what is the correct way to worship him, what his will is for us in the different periods of human history, what his purposes are, and why he has permitted sin, imperfection, selfishness and death to mar his creation and bring disunity into it. If mankind are to learn to worship in the proper, acceptable manner, there has to be a revealed religion; and to be in perfect agreement with truth and righteousness this religion must come from the living and true God, the Supreme Intelligence and Great Architect of all creation. Since we are his creation gifted with intelligence and entirely dependent upon him for true knowledge and guidance, it is only reasonable that he would give us a revelation of his will and purpose. Every loving parent imparts reliable information and instruction to his child for its protection, safety, welfare and understanding. How much more would the Creator, from whom we draw the quality of love, do so to his intelligent creatures! This he would do in order for us to know him, understand our relationship to him, see what are his requirements of us, and faithfully fulfill our responsibilities that we might harmonize our lives with him and gain his approval.

---

10. To inform us on what must there be a revelation from him, and why is it reasonable to expect it?

[11] What is reasonable and proper to expect He has done. He has given us a revelation of himself beyond what the so-called "book of nature" has to tell us. He has caused it to be written down and preserved that we might go to it and learn truth, righteousness and pure worship. But there are many writings which the various religions hold sacred and for which they claim higher inspiration. Which of all these is the true God's written revelation? To save time and space and to get at once to the point, we confidently reply, The Holy Scriptures or Bible, written originally in Hebrew, Aramaic and Greek, and upon which true Christianity is based.

[12] What! many will exclaim, That book upon which the hundreds of religious systems and sects of Christendom claim to rest but upon the teachings of which none of them agree, exercising the greatest intolerance toward one another, persecuting one another and even going to war with deadly weapons of violence over their doctrinal and other disagreements? Yes, we mean *that book,* The Holy Bible, but not the sectarian creeds which falsely claim to rest upon it. The reasons for accepting it as the divine revelation are not those of childish, blind credulity, but they spring from mature study of it, experience with it and sound facts of history.

---

11. Has he given us such a revelation, and, if so, where is it?
12. What will some exclaim in objection to this, but why is our acceptance of it not based on blind credulity?

[13] Let us dismiss from our minds what the jangling creeds of Christendom have to say about the teachings of the Bible and let us consider the Book itself. The only way to explain its existence and what it teaches and how and why it has survived till this perplexing day is that it is the divine revelation. There must be some providential reason why it has been translated into more than 1,125 languages and is the most widely published, circulated and read book on earth today. All this in spite of the fact that its publication has been most bitterly opposed, and those who have spread it have been most hotly persecuted, and it has been attacked and misrepresented by not only non-Christian religions and powers but also by those who possessed it and claimed to be its friends, and the most wicked and violent efforts have been made to destroy it from all existence. Only the Almighty God its Author could have preserved it till now to become the foremost book on earth.

[14] The Creator who is from everlasting to everlasting is the only One who could have inspired the Holy Bible. That is why it is the oldest book on earth, for the written document upon which its account of the creation of earth and its inhabitants rests goes back almost six thousand years, to near the time of the creating of man and woman. Today the Bible, composed of the ancient He-

---

13. How only can its existence and survival till now be explained, and its becoming the foremost book on earth?
14. For what special reason must the Creator who is from everlasting have been the Bible's Inspirer?

brew Scriptures and the Christian Greek Scriptures, is made up of 66 books, the last of these being written in the closing decade of the first century after Christ. Hence the entire book was about four thousand years in being written. Some thirty-five men took part in writing it, especially counting from the prophet Moses, who wrote the first book of the Bible and wove it together from eleven earlier written documents. Even if we begin its writing from Moses in the sixteenth century before Christ, the Bible was over sixteen centuries in being written. So the thirty-five writers lived at different periods of time, few of them were contemporaries, and the time gap between the first writer Moses and the last writer the apostle John is very great. Thus, though they were all Hebrews or Jews, few had direct communication with each other. Their occupations in life were quite varied, some being warriors, shepherds, kings, temple Levites, fishers, with a tax collector and a physician among them, and men of other ordinary professions.

[15] Their style is different, their writings include narratives, history, cosmogony, hygienic rules, governmental rules, laws, doctrine, poetry and proverbs. Some wrote in Hebrew, others in Aramaic, and others in the common Greek of the first century after Christ. Notwithstanding this, their writings are all in agreement from first to last, and they show the gradual revelation of the divine will and purpose. Only the great First

---

15. What is it that makes its harmony remarkable, and why does this argue for one author of it?

Cause, who has immortality, could have caused a book of such diversified contents and written over so long a time by such widely separated men to harmonize with itself from start to finish. He is the one Author of this most important book.

[16] Written by men, indeed! But this fact is no objection to the divine authorship of it. Had it been written by heavenly angels, it could have been no truer, for God would even have had to inspire them to do the writing the same as he did his earthly human writers. We are informed concerning the sacred secrets that these men of God were inspired to write into the Bible: "Into these very things angels are desiring to peer."* Men are an easier medium for us to receive divine revelations through than angels are, who on numbers of occasions were terrifying in their glorious appearance to men. We are plainly told that the Bible writers did not know or understand the meaning of many things they wrote, particularly the prophecies, and yet no confusion and disagreement resulted. Not their own mental ability, but the spirit or invisible active force of Almighty God was responsible for these releases of sacred Scripture. Some writers testify to this, and the apostle Peter builds up our faith in God's written Word, saying: "You know this first, that no prophecy of Scripture springs from any private release. For prophecy was at no time brought by man's will, but men spoke from God as they

---

* The Bible, at 1 Peter 1:12, *New World Translation*.

16. Why does its being written by men not deny its divine authorship?

were borne along by holy spirit." (2 Peter 1:20, 21, *NW;* 1 Peter 1:10-12) This makes the Most High God the one great Author of the Book, though it was written by men's hands.

¹⁷ Throughout the centuries men of this world, and particularly in these last few centuries the materialistic scientists as well as irreverent radical thinkers, have attacked the Bible as historically incorrect, unscientific, contradictory, ancient and not advanced enough for our day. But scientists have repeatedly had to correct themselves. The advances made by them and the search for ancient records found in writing and on the buried relics of former days have brought discoveries which have more and more confirmed the Bible as true rather than supported the arguments of its attackers. Compared with the so-called "creation tablets of Babylon" which are filled with senseless fables, the Bible account of creation is plain, simple, and fully supported by the findings of modern science. None but the Creator could have inspired that account.

¹⁸ The Bible solves the great mysteries that have baffled mankind. In this it displays that its great Author knew the end from the beginning of his works toward mankind. It tells how sin entered the universe and how it will be wiped out, and how all its sad effects upon mankind will be cleansed away. It tells how God would send a great Liberator for mankind and how he would

---

17. How and by whom has the Bible been attacked, and how has it received only further confirmation?
18. What baffling mysteries does the Bible solve, so proving God its Inspirer?

be identified and how he will finally bring full deliverance to the groaning creation, in the near future for us of this day. According to the law of probabilities, there would be an infinite number of chances against one that all these foretold marks of identification could be fulfilled in one Liberator. And yet well-established history and the testimony of eyewitnesses prove they were faithfully fulfilled, a fact which stamps the Bible as the truth and the all-wise God as its Author and Inspirer.

[19] This Book, too, explains how the demons came into existence and why the fear and worship of them is so prevalent throughout the earth. It tells how Babylon was founded and how all the great variety of languages and religions got started. It foretells how the Greater Babylon with all the religions that it includes within itself will be destroyed, and that at now no distant day. The Bible has always been ahead of the latest generation of men. It is no old-fashioned, static book, showing the ignorance of a former day, and giving only past history. It is far in advance of the latest thought of our time. Its prophecies foretold events centuries, yes, millenniums, in advance; and the unfolding events of history from the first century after Christ until now prove those prophecies true. They are finding a climax of fulfillment in the strange world events since World War I in 1914. Those prophecies do not halt with our momentous epoch, but carry on a thousand years into the

19. How is it in advance of the latest thought of our day, and what assures its complete fulfillment?

future. The faithful, accurate fulfillment of Bible prophecy thus far gives full assurance that those prophecies of that future glorious time will also be carried out to the letter, when all wickedness will be erased from the universe, death will be abolished from the earth, and paradise will be restored here for a perfect race of humans to enjoy forever with honor and praise to their worshipful Creator and to his Liberator for mankind.

[20] The Bible reveals the development and progress of the pure religion in contrast with all the false kinds and shows its early triumph over all error of belief and practice. It sets forth principles that are eternal and unchangeable. It is a Book of liberation from all the power and evil of the false religion. That is why it has been so fought against by the practicers of falsehood, who try to prevent men from getting free from the power of darkness and entering into the light and blessing of the pure knowledge and worship of the living and true God. Already in this day of world change the Bible stands vindicated as his Word of truth. There can be no question about it: The Holy Scriptures of the Bible are the standard by which to judge all religions. Follow this volume through its further chapters and prove it.

---

20. Why has it been so fought against by practicers of falsehood, and as whose word does it already stand vindicated?

CHAPTER III

When There Was One Religion

C AN you imagine our earth without a temple, a shrine, an altar, an image, a priest, or a sacred holiday? Well, that is the way it was on earth when there was but one religion throughout the universe. You are interested in how this could be, seeing that these things have become so associated with the various forms of worship. So let us examine the inspired Record of those days.

² The first book of the Bible is entitled "Genesis". This is a word drawn from the Greek language and meaning "beginning". It corresponds with the opening words of the book in the original Hebrew, "In the beginning," and which words the Hebrews use to designate that book. From the first verse of Genesis on we are taught that there is but the one God, the Creator: "In the beginning God created the heaven and the earth." (Genesis 1:1) Here the Hebrew word for "God" is *Elohim*. This Hebrew word *Elohim* is in the plural number, not to indicate that there are several persons in God, but to indicate the excellence

1. What present-day religious things was the earth without when there was but one religion?
2, 3. (a) Why is the Bible's first book appropriately named? (b) What does *Elohim*, meaning "God", indicate, and what is his unique name?

33

of God, just as when, in old English, the king of England used to be addressed in the plural number, "Your Majesty," not, "Thy Majesty." For this reason *Elohim,* when meaning "God" the Creator, is always used with an adjective and a verb in the singular number. Does God give himself a name? Yes. In Genesis, chapter 2, verse 4, it first occurs: "These are the histories of the heavens and the earth, when they were created, in the day that Jehovah Elohim made earth and heavens."—*Darby's* translation; see also *American Standard Version,* also *Young's.*

³ That is the name which He has exclusively given himself, and no creation of his may take it to himself. "I am Jehovah, that is my name; and my glory will I not give to another, neither my praise unto graven images." (Isaiah 42:8, *AS*) Testifying to God's exclusive possession of this unique name, the sacred song writer prays to Him against his enemies and says: "That they may know that thou alone, whose name is Jehovah, art the Most High over all the earth." (Psalm 83:18, *Da; AS*) His name is to be held sacred.

⁴ The materialistic scientists are led by their investigations and discoveries to appreciate only more and more the wisdom with which God created the heavens and the earth. The reverent psalmist long, long ago showed his appreciation of that when he said: "O Jehovah, how manifold are thy works! In wisdom hast thou made them all: the

---

4. Who were already in existence when God began creating the earth, and so who must have been his first creation?

earth is full of thy riches." "Jehovah by wisdom founded the earth; by understanding he established the heavens." (Psalms 104:24; 136:1, 2, 5, *AS;* Proverbs 3:19, *AS*) At the time that Jehovah began creating the earth there were heavenly spiritual creatures in existence. Men who cannot see spirit creatures could not know this, but Jehovah God himself informed us of this fact when he put questions to the faithful man Job on what he knew concerning the construction of the earth: "Where wast thou when I laid the foundations of the earth? . . . When the morning stars sang together, and all the sons of God shouted for joy [all the heavenly beings shouted for joy, *AT;* all the angels chanted in their joy, *Mo*]?" (Job 38:4, 7) Since these spiritual sons of God came ahead of man, one of these heavenly sons of God must have been Jehovah's first creation. Does the Bible bear that fact out? Yes, and it shows us who he was.

⁵ Like endless space, God has no beginning and no end. He is the source of all creation and of all life and intelligence. To show his everlastingness in the past and in the future he described himself as "I am that I am" and spoke of himself as the "I am". He used the name 6,823 times throughout the inspired Hebrew Scriptures, and that name "Jehovah" is understood to mean "He causes to be". Thus he declares himself to be the Creator of all things, the great First Cause. (Exodus 3:14, 15, *AS*) He gives life to all his sons, whether they

---

5. By what description did he show his everlastingness, and what does his name mean and also indicate?

are in heaven or on earth. He is their heavenly Father, and as such he precedes every one of his sons.

[6] There is one of his heavenly sons whom the Bible calls "his only-begotten Son". This was the one who became for a time a man on earth named Jesus Christ. In order to return to heaven this only-begotten Son of God died so as to sacrifice his human nature for mankind's restoration to everlasting life, and God raised him from death to heavenly life again as a spiritual Son more glorious than ever before. This glorified Jesus confessed to being the first creation of God. This he did when he gave a revelation to his apostle John and said: "These are the things the Amen says, the faithful and true witness, the beginning of the creation by God." (Revelation 3:14, *NW; RS; Ro*) So he was the chief one of God's creation. (*Yg; Mk*) Since God created him first, without the co-operation or agency of anyone else, because there were no other creatures then existing, he is rightly called God's "only-begotten Son". He is also called "the only-begotten god" in these inspired words: "No man has seen God at any time; the only-begotten god who is in the bosom position with the Father is the one that has explained him."—John 3:16; 1:18, *NW; Ro; Sp; Ly*.

[7] The eternal Jehovah filled his only-begotten Son with wisdom. He became the very symbol of

---

6. What did his "only-begotten Son" confess to being, and so how was he properly the "only-begotten" One?
7. Under what symbol was his creation described in Proverbs, and how was he used and what title was he given?

wisdom. In the proverbs of wisdom he speaks of himself as wisdom and calls attention to his being a creation of the eternal heavenly Father. He says: "The Eternal formed me first of his creation, first of all his works in days of old; I was fashioned in the earliest ages, from the very first, when earth began; I was born when there were no abysses, . . . when he laid foundations for the earth; I was with him then, his foster-child, I was his delight day after day, playing in his presence constantly, playing here and there over his world, finding my delight in humankind." (Proverbs 8:22-31, *Mo; AT; Ro*) This Son's wisdom must not lie idle. So God his Father gave him something to do. God used him as his agent or servant in creating all other things. Because this Son was his chief representative and was to be his spokesman to all other intelligent creatures, God gave his only-begotten Son the title "The Word". How this Son was used in making all other creations we read:

[8] "In the beginning the Word existed. The Word was with God, and the Word was divine [and the Word was a god, *NW*]. It was he that was with God in the beginning. Everything came into existence through him, and apart from him nothing came to be. It was by him that life came into existence, and that life was the light of mankind." (John 1:1-4, *AT; Mo; NW*) "He is the image of the invisible God, the firstborn of all creation, because by means of him all other things were created in the heavens and upon the earth, the

---

8. How is his making of all other creations stated?

things visible and the things invisible, no matter whether they are thrones or lordships or governments or authorities. All other things have been created through him and for him. Also he is before all other things and by means of him all other things were made to exist, and he is the head of the body, the congregation. He is the beginning, the firstborn from the dead, that he might become the one who is first in all things, because God saw good for all fullness to dwell in him." —Colossians 1:15-19, *NW*.

⁹ In harmony with this all-inclusive statement the only-begotten Son was used in creating the earth and man upon it. Although it is not said who it was, this must be the one to whom God spoke, when the account of creation tells us: "And God said, Let us make man in our image, after our likeness: and let them have dominion over the fish of the sea, and over the fowl of the air, and over the cattle, and over all the earth, and over every creeping thing that creepeth upon the earth. So God created man in his own image, in the image of God created he him; male and female created he them." (Genesis 1:26, 27; also 3:22; 11:7) The credit for man's creation was given to God, but the rest of the Bible testifies he used his wise Son. The way man has been made bears witness to the wisdom and understanding with which God made him. Man was a perfect piece of workmanship. It could not have been otherwise, for God was his Creator, and concern-

9. How is his association with God in creating mankind indicated, and in what condition did mankind start?

ing Jehovah God it is written: "His work is perfect; for all his ways are justice: a God of faithfulness and without iniquity, just and right is he." (Deuteronomy 32:3, 4, *AS*) Consequently, when he finished his earthly creation by making the perfect man and woman, he could approve of what he had made. He did so on the sixth and last day of such creative work. "And God saw every thing that he had made, and, behold, it was very good." Thus mankind started out perfect.—Genesis 1:31.

¹⁰ Did God place man on earth to stay just a while in human form and then to pass on and assume some other form and nature, that of a lower animal on the same earth or that of an angel in heaven? Was man made with a thing called a "soul" which was separate and distinct from the human body? And could this soul exist apart from the body and also go into other bodies, that of say a cow or an insect or a spiritual angel? You might not believe us if we answered for ourselves. So we let God's own inspired Record speak for itself, at Genesis 2:7, 8, quoting from a Roman Catholic translation: "And the Lord God formed man of the slime of the earth: and breathed into his face the breath of life, and man became a living soul. And the Lord God had planted a paradise of pleasure from the beginning: wherein he placed man whom he had formed." (*Dy;* also *Kx*) The Christian apostle Paul endorses that account of man's creation by quoting from it and saying: "The first man Adam was made into a living

---

10. What questions arise on the human soul, and how does the creation account indicate what it is?

soul." (1 Corinthians 15:45, *Dy*) There we have two inspired statements, fifteen centuries apart, that man *became* or *was made into* a living soul. God did not breathe into him an immaterial, invisible soul that could exist independently of the body and leave it and go somewhere else. A living soul was what the perfect man became and not what man had inside him. A living man has soul, that is to say, he has life or existence as a human soul, but he does not have an intelligent, separate something inside him which can abandon his body for a new existence elsewhere. Man and woman are human souls. But how the religions of this world, including those of Christendom, have twisted that fact and deceived mankind!

[11] Man was not the first material soul on earth.

11. Was man the first material soul on earth? How does the account show whether?

On the fifth and sixth days God created material souls ahead of man. They were the lower animal creatures. "And God said, Let the waters swarm with swarms of living souls, and let fowl fly above the earth in the expanse of the heavens. And God created the great sea monsters, and every living soul that moves with which the waters swarm, after their kind, and every winged fowl after its kind. . . . And there was evening, and there was morning—a fifth day. And God said, Let the earth bring forth living souls after their kind, cattle, and creeping thing, and beast of the earth, after their kind. And it was so." These animal souls were kept alive with food. God told man of the food provisions for him and said: "It shall be food for you; and to every animal of the earth, and to every fowl of the heavens, and to everything that creepeth on the earth, in which is a living soul, every green herb for food. And it was so."—Genesis 1:20-24, 29, 30, *Da; Ro.*

[12] Every animal soul was made after its kind. No such animal soul could transmigrate out of its body and go into the body of some different kind of animal. The first man did not receive a soul by transmigration from some heavenly angel or from some lower animal or insect. Those animal souls were not immortal and able to pass on after the animal or insect died. This is a fundamental fact of inspired Scripture, and the rest of the Bible does not contradict it. In the very last book of the Bible we read of these animal souls: "A third

12. Why could the first man not have a soul transmigrated from some other dead creature?

of the creatures that are in the sea which have souls died, . . . and every living soul died, yes, the things in the sea." (Revelation 8:9; 16:3, *NW;* *Ro*) Man's creation toward the end of the sixth creative day was separate absolutely from that of the lower earthly creatures. God breathed into the created human body the principle of life which is sustained by breathing and man became a living soul. Being God's perfect workmanship, with no parts lacking and with no useless, unnecessary parts, the first man was no product of a supposed law of human evolution. Human souls cannot mix with the lower animal souls. Not such animals, but man alone on earth was made in the image and likeness of God.

[13] The loving Creator gave man a perfect home. He put him in the paradise of pleasure or garden of Eden. That man might not be alone in Eden God created for him a human counterpart, in this way: "Jehovah God caused a deep sleep to fall upon the man, and he slept; and he took one of his ribs, and closed up the flesh instead thereof: and the rib, which Jehovah God had taken from the man, made he a woman, and brought her unto the man. And the man said, This is now bone of my bones, and flesh of my flesh: she shall be called Woman, because she was taken out of Man." (Genesis 2:21-23, *AS*) Jesus Christ, who in heaven had served as God's agent in creating man and woman, confirmed this account as true by quoting from it. He showed that it set out God's law

---

13. How did God give the first man a human counterpart?

governing the relationship of man and woman, husband and wife.—Matthew 19:4, 5.

[14] Did man in Eden's paradise have communication with God? Did God leave the perfect man to develop a natural religion by merely what he saw, felt and heard, or did God make a revelation to him for his perfect guidance? God made a revelation, and that evidently through his only-begotten Son, the Word, who acted as spokesman.

[15] In this way God assigned the man to his work and gave him the divine commandments. "And Jehovah God took the man, and put him into the garden of Eden to dress it and to keep it. And Jehovah God commanded the man, saying, Of every tree of the garden thou mayest freely eat: but of the tree of the knowledge of good and evil, thou shalt not eat of it: for in the day that thou eatest thereof thou shalt surely die." It was after God had presented man with a perfect wife that he revealed to them both the purpose of their being together on the earth. "And God blessed them: and God said unto them, Be fruitful, and multiply, and replenish the earth, and subdue it; and have dominion over the fish of the sea, and over the birds of the heavens, and over every living thing that moveth upon the earth. And God said, Behold, I have given you every herb yielding seed, which is upon the face of all the earth, and every tree, in which is the fruit of a tree yielding seed;

14. Was man left to develop natural religion or did he receive a revelation? How?
15. (a) For what disobedience was man told he would die? (b) What were man and woman told was the purpose of their being together?

to you it shall be for food." (Genesis 2:15-17; 1:28, 29, *AS*) However, the prohibition which God had expressed to Adam regarding the tree of the knowledge of good and evil still stood, until they passed the test which God had imposed upon them. Then they might eat of it with divine ap- proval, and also of another tree, "the tree of life also in the midst of the garden," as an indication of their God-given right to live forever in the paradise.—Genesis 2:9.

[16] There was just one religion on the earth, just one form of worship, and that was according to the truth of the divine revelation. But how was it carried out? Did not God command the man to build him a temple for the worship of his Creator there? Search the entire Record, and no such com- mand to Adam will be found. Surely God himself could not dwell in such a man-made building. Thousands of years later the wise King Solomon who was commanded to build a temple to Jehovah at the city of Jerusalem correctly sized up Jeho- vah when he said: "But will God in very deed dwell on the earth? behold, heaven and the heaven of heavens cannot contain thee; how much less this house that I have builded!" The holy of holies of Solomon's temple was only a small picture of the heavens where God actually dwells surrounded by his heavenly hosts, and where he in due time re- ceived his great High Priest with the sacrifice for the everlasting life of humankind in a righteous

---

16. What was there then in the way of religion, and why was no temple commanded to be built for it?

new world.—1 Kings 8:27, *AS;* Hebrews 9:23-26; 8:1-5.

[17] Because of the costly, imposing temples, basilicas, cathedrals and "churches" which the various sects and cults have built in Christendom, the uninformed persons are liable to draw wrong conclusions. God's Son Jesus never commanded his followers to waste their time, money and energy in rearing such proud structures and putting the poor people to the expense of maintaining them. Because of his life-giving work he is called "the last Adam", and he foretold a return to the simple worship such as the first Adam offered in Eden's paradise. He told the Samaritan woman near Mount Gerizim: "The hour is coming when neither in this mountain nor in Jerusalem will you people worship the Father. God is a Spirit, and those worshiping him must worship with spirit and truth." His faithful follower Stephen, just before suffering a violent martyrdom, said to the Jewish court at Jerusalem: "The Most High does not dwell in houses made with hands; just as the prophet says: 'The heaven is my throne, and the earth is my footstool. What kind of house will you build for me? Jehovah says. Or what is the place for my resting? My hand made all these things, did it not?' "

[18] Years afterward Saul of Tarsus, who was a witness of Stephen's death, stood in the Grecian city of Athens which was full of temples, altars

17. Did Jesus command the building of material temples, and what did he say regarding a return to simple worship?
18. How did Paul's and John's testimony agree with this?

and images for worship, and he said to the Athenian court: "The God that made the world and all the things in it, being, as this One is, Lord of heaven and earth, does not dwell in handmade temples, neither is he attended to by human hands as if he needed anything, because he himself gives to all persons life and breath and all things." (John 4:21, 24 and Acts 7:48-50; 17:24, 25, *NW*) True Christians who obey Jesus' example have not engaged in building temples. In describing his vision of the righteous new world that is near at hand the apostle John said: "I did not see a temple in it, for Jehovah God the Almighty is its temple, also the Lamb [Jesus Christ] is."—Revelation 21:22, *NW*.

[19] So in that righteous first world God acted in harmony with his own being and did not order Adam to construct a temple or even an altar. God dealt with the perfect man Adam without even a priest or a human mediator. Such things were not needed. No sacrifice was necessary to be offered, for Adam was perfect. Neither was he instructed to act as priest for his wife Eve, for she, too, was perfect. There was no need to appease an angry God. Adam in his innocence was "the son of God", a human son, and the relations between God and him were those of a father and a son. (Luke 3:38) His form of worship toward God was that of the obedience of a son toward his Father, according to God's revealed will. He could

19. So how did God deal with the perfect Adam, and how did Adam worship God?

worship him every day by such obedience and service.

20 God gave him no religious holiday to observe or celebrate. It is true the account of creation says: "On the seventh day God brought his work to an end on which he had been engaged, desisting on the seventh day from all his work in which he had been engaged. So God blessed the seventh day, and consecrated it, because on it he had desisted from all his work, in doing which God had brought about creation." (Genesis 2:2, 3, *AT*) This was merely a revelation to Adam of how God was proceeding, but it was no command to Adam in Eden to keep a weekly rest day or sabbath day of twenty-four hours.

21 That "seventh day" on which God desisted from work and which he consecrated was not a 24-hour day, but is of the length of the preceding six days. The Bible speaks of this "seventh day" as still continuing, because it is 7,000 years long. During it God has been desisting from earthly creation. Soon he will usher obedient men of good will into his great rest. (Hebrews 3:18 to 4:11; John 5:9-17) So there is no inspired record that the first man observed any religious holiday in his paradise of pleasure. He and his wife worshiped their Creator and Father as God with spirit and truth, in harmony with the divine revelation. So there was just the one religion on earth, the pure and undefiled kind.

20, 21. (a) Did Adam in Eden observe any religious holiday? (b) Why is not Genesis 2:2, 3 against this answer?

CHAPTER IV

How the False Kind Began

THE government in mankind's first paradise of pleasure was a theocracy. That is to say, it was a rule by God the Creator, the great Owner of the earth on which man lives. God did not draw his power to govern from the consent of mankind whom He governed. He was not subject to being guided by their wishes. It was not a people's rule or democracy. The great Creator is the Most High. He is the Sovereign over all the universe, of which our earth is but a tiny part. The teeming nations which have descended from the first man and woman are to the Creator as but a drop from a bucket and as the fine dust in the scalepan of a balance. Or, in fact, as nothing. (Isaiah 40:15-17) All human life is dependent on him. He is the only rightful Lawgiver and Universal Sovereign, for he has the absolute power to save and to destroy. Being almighty and perfect in wisdom, justice and love and supreme in position, he is the God worthy of worship. True worship he properly requires of his creatures, including his only-begotten Son, and such worship is rendered by loving service and obedience to God in harmony with his revealed purpose and com-

---

1. Why was the government in Eden theocratic, and man's worship also theocratic?

48

mandments. This is theocratic worship, and this is what Adam and Eve were required to render their Maker. It was a theocratic world in which they lived. It was their privilege to worship God and to acknowledge his universal sovereignty by unswerving obedience. That was true religion, and it bound the entire universe together, for it was rendered to the one God.

² How, then, was it possible for a false kind to get started? The answer now appears simple, By disobedience. But why would perfect creatures, living amid perfect conditions, want to disobey the living, true God, the supreme Benefactor upon whom all life depends? The Scriptural answer is, Because of selfishness or selfish d e s i r e. That means, Because of the creature's loving himself more than God the Creator. Selfishness would express itself in willfulness, that is, in rebellion against the theocratic government in a desire to be independent of it so as to shape one's own course in life. Hence we see that the all-important question of God's universal sovereignty is implicated here. True religion holds creatures to his universal sovereignty. The only thing that false religion can do is turn creatures away from acknowledging and worshiping Jehovah as universal sovereign. False religion springs from selfishness. The inspired account makes this clear.

³ Here cherubs come into the picture. The first spirit creatures whom Adam and Eve saw mani-

---

2. How did the false kind of religion get started, and in what direction does it turn creatures?
3. What spirit creatures now come into the picture, and what relationship were they shown to have to God?

fest themselves to human sight were cherubs, or
cherubim according to the Hebrew language. They
were stationed at the entrance to the paradise of
Eden after God drove Adam and Eve out. Concerning God's sovereignty we read: "Jehovah
reigneth; let the peoples tremble: he sitteth above
the cherubim; let the earth be moved." "Thou
that sittest above the cherubim, shine forth."
(Psalms 99:1 and 80:1, *AS*) The prophet Moses
was commanded to make images of them upon
the sacred chest that held God's written law. Later King Solomon made cherub images for the
interior of the temple. They were symbols of how
God is surrounded with cherubim. The people in
general were not permitted to see these images.
They were not to be worshiped. Trouble started in
the universe when a cherub in the garden of Eden
or paradise of pleasure schemed to gain worship.

⁴ Being spirit and hence invisible to Adam and
Eve, this glorious cherub was stationed over the
young human pair in Eden. Cherubs, when ap-
pearing in a supernatural vision to God's prophets,
are pictured with wings. So the one in Eden is
spoken of as a "covering cherub". He was then a
perfect son of God. Addressing him in symbolic
language through a later worshiper of him, the
king of Tyre, Ezekiel prophesied: "Thus saith the
Lord Jehovah: Thou, who sealest up the measure
of perfection, full of wisdom and perfect in beauty,
thou wast in Eden, the garden of God. . . . Thou
wast the anointed covering cherub, and I had set

---

4. What kind of cherub was this one in Eden called, and
who was he, according to Ezekiel's prophecy?

thee so: thou wast upon the holy mountain of God; thou didst walk up and down in the midst of stones of fire. Thou wast perfect in thy ways, from the day that thou wast created, till unrighteousness was found in thee."

⁵ But because of what did unrighteousness spring up inside him? The revealed facts show it was self-admiration and the desire for worship by creatures under him. So we read: "By the abundance of thy traffic they have filled the midst of thee with violence, and thou hast sinned; therefore have I cast thee as profane from the mountain of God, and have destroyed thee, O covering cherub, from the midst of the stones of fire. Thy heart was lifted up because of thy beauty; thou hast corrupted thy wisdom by reason of thy brightness: I have cast thee to the ground, I have laid thee before kings, that they may behold thee." —Ezekiel 28:11-17, *Da*.

⁶ How, now, did this covering cherub in Eden succeed in turning worship away from the living, true God and start false religion in the earth, yes, in the universe? His method is described for us in chapter three of Genesis. The Christian apostle Paul accepted this account and referred to it, saying to Christians in his day: "I am afraid that somehow, as the serpent seduced Eve by its craftiness, your minds might be corrupted away from the sincerity and the chastity that are due the

---

5. Due to what did unrighteousness spring up inside him?
6. By what methods did this cherub turn worship away from God, and how is this shown by the names Satan and Serpent given him after that?

Christ. . . . for Satan himself keeps transforming himself into an angel of light." (2 Corinthians 11:3, 14, *NW*) Betraying the unrighteousness that had now developed in his heart and ruined his perfection, the covering cherub in Eden began to work against clean worship and against God's universal sovereignty. In that way he became Satan, for the name *Satan* means opposer or antagonist. Misusing his spiritual powers, he obsessed or took control of a serpent in Eden. He used it to convey a lie to Eve while her husband Adam was away. He made sure to pose, not as her enemy, but as her benefactor, "an angel of light." In that way he became a deceiver, and a proper name for him would be also Serpent or Snake. Because this now unfaithful "covering cherub" was the first to practice deception and to establish false worship, the Bible calls him "the original serpent" or "that old serpent".

⁷ Glorifying the snake or serpent as a symbol of enlightenment, Satan the adversary spoke to the woman. "And it said to the woman, Is it even so, that God has said, Ye shall not eat of every tree of the garden? And the woman said to the serpent, We may eat of the fruit of the trees of the garden; but of the fruit of the tree that is in the midst of the garden, God has said, Ye shall not eat of it, and ye shall not touch it, lest ye die." Satan the Serpent now slandered God whose words the woman had just quoted. For he proceeded to contradict the truth of God's words. He made out that God was frightening the woman and prevent-

---

7. In what way did the Devil come into existence?

ing her and her husband from gaining wisdom and intelligence and becoming gods, independent of Jehovah God and not subject to his standards of right and wrong but able to determine for themselves what is good and what is evil. Was not the forbidden tree called the "tree of the knowledge of good and evil"? So by this the covering cherub made himself a devil, for the name *Devil* means a slanderer or defamer. "And the serpent said to the woman, Ye will not certainly die; but God knows that in the day ye eat of it, your eyes will be opened, and ye will be as God [or, as gods], knowing good and evil."—Genesis 3:1-5, *Da,* margin.

[8] This was the first pronouncement of false religion. It put light for darkness and darkness for light. It misrepresented Jehovah God as a false god against mankind's interests and not able to maintain his universal sovereignty. It presented the serpent, or the unfaithful covering cherub whom it symbolized, as the prophet of enlightenment. It made the woman, to whom this supposed enlightenment was first offered, the medium for passing on the enlightenment. She was to be the first one to take the fruit of the forbidden tree in defiance of Jehovah God and to gain the wisdom and intelligence and then lead her husband to it, so leading him to liberation. It denied that disobedience to Jehovah God would result in death but held out that life as independent gods would result to them. The woman was not to consult

---

8. How did that first pronouncement of false religion present matters, and what was its intent?

her husband first on the matter of eating, although
God had made him first and had used him to instruct the woman concerning the forbidden tree.
No, but she was to exercise woman's rights and
show him she had better judgment. Then she was
to tempt him and lead him into disobedience to
God. All this was the big lie. By putting it over
on the mother of mankind Satan hoped to put it
over on all mankind and get them all into false
religion. Jesus Christ later said respecting the
Devil: "That one was a manslayer when he began, and he did not stand fast in the truth, because
truth is not in him. When he speaks the lie, he
speaks according to his own disposition, because
he is a liar and the father of the lie."—John 8:44,
NW.

⁹ Listening to that first pronouncement of false
religion induced selfish desire in the woman.
Hence she was tempted into rebelling against
God's sovereignty over her and the rest of the
universe. "And the woman saw that the tree was
good for food, and that it was a pleasure for the
eyes, and the tree was to be desired to give intelligence; and she took of its fruit, and ate, and
gave also to her husband with her, and he ate."
(Genesis 3:6, Da) Did Adam eat because he was
deceived by the teaching of false religion? The
answer is not our own. Again showing that he accepted what the Bible says on this as the absolute truth, the apostle Paul said: "Adam was
formed first, then Eve. Also Adam was not de-

---

9. (a) How was Eve tempted, and what course did she
take? (b) Why did Adam join in her course?

ceived, but the woman was thoroughly deceived and came to be in transgression." (1 Timothy 2:13, 14, *NW*) Unlike Eve, Adam got his information, not from a snake, but from Jehovah God. If Adam was not deceived, why, then, did he accept forbidden fruit at her hand, knowing that to eat it meant death according to God's decree? Evidently because Adam feared to lose her in death. So now, in the choice between having this visible beauty Eve and having the invisible God, he preferred having his wife and sharing the same end as she did.

[10] So Adam chose to join up with the new religion. It was just as in many lands today where the religious clergy dominate politics and commerce. The men who see the double-talk and double-dealing of the clergy have no use for these religious hypocrites. But because their womenfolk hold to the religious system, the men make no disturbance about it just in order to keep their women and get along with them. And the religious clergy know the wily power of the women over their men, and so they craftily use the women.

[11] Some try to make the "tree of the knowledge of good and evil" to be just a symbol and argue that the sin which Adam and Eve here committed was their first act of sexual union. Such an argument is unreasonable. Sexual intercourse between man and wife is a natural thing. Only by this act could God's command to Adam and Eve be car-

---

10. How are many men today prevailed upon by religion for reasons like Adam's?
11. Why was our first parents' sin with the tree not an act of immorality between themselves?

ried out, when he blessed them and said: "Be fruitful and multiply, and fill the earth, and subdue it." (Genesis 1:28, *Da*) The purpose of their marriage was to bring children into the earth, children as perfect as themselves. With these they were to fill the entire earth, for that was the purpose of God's creating it: "He is the God—who formed the earth and made it—he established it —he did not create it a chaos, he formed it for a dwellingplace." (Isaiah 45:18, *AT*) In order to make all the earth a suitable place for perfect mankind to inhabit, it was necessary for them to obey God's command and subdue the earth outside of the paradise of pleasure and make the whole surface of the earth a garden of Eden. Then obedient mankind would dwell here forever.

[12] Do not take the word of some religious clergyman for it, but search the inspired written Record for yourself. See that God made no promise to Adam and Eve that if they continued obedient during all the period of their test God would end their existence on this earth and would take them to heaven. "The first man is out of the earth and made of dust." Man's natural and everlasting place of habitation is the earth, subdued into a paradise of pleasure. "The heavens are the heavens of Jehovah; but the earth hath he given to the children of men." (1 Corinthians 15:47, *NW;* Psalm 115:16, *AS*) Sexual intercourse between Adam and Eve would have been in obedience. Their sin

---

12. What shows whether Adam and Eve were to be taken to heaven if they proved obedient?

consisted in eating fruit of a literal tree in rebellion against God's universal sovereignty.

[13] Before Eve was created and hence before sexual intercourse was possible for the man, God had said to Adam: "In the day that thou eatest thereof thou shalt surely die." (Genesis 2:17) Adam was made a living soul. If he disobediently ate the forbidden fruit before or after Eve's creation, Adam would die as a human soul. God's law, stated thousands of years after this, is harmonious with this Edenic decree, for it declares: "Behold all souls are mine: as the soul of the father, so also the soul of the son is mine: the soul that sinneth, the same shall die." (Ezechiel 18:4, *Dy*) It follows that if the perfect Adam, "the son of God," never ate the fruit as long as it was forbidden and if he never sinned in rebellion against the Universal Sovereign, he would never die. So his life everlasting in Eden with perfect fruits to eat was conditioned on his everlasting obedience to his God. Clean religion in that original righteous world promised endless life for him as a human soul in the earthly paradise. False religion, as now introduced by Satan the original Serpent, promised new intelligence and a self-determining life as gods if they disobeyed Jehovah God. What did the adoption of the new religion do for mankind? This the following chapters will unfold.

---

13. On what was Adam's living everlastingly conditioned, how is this shown, and what did clean religion promise him?

CHAPTER V

Development of the False Before the Flood

FALSE religion got its start through selfishness, pride and rebellion against the universal sovereignty of Jehovah God and by means of deception and by contradiction of His word. Till this day all mankind are feeling the effects of it and yet the majority of them are engaged in practicing it. This is because our first human parents adopted it in the paradise of Eden by following the lead of the author of false religion and violating the law of God on a very simple thing.

[2] Adam and Eve did not die instantaneously after eating the forbidden fruit, but this does not prove God's warning false: "In the day that thou eatest thereof thou shalt surely die." Jehovah God now came for judgment in the garden of Eden. The guilty couple, even though no longer completely naked but with aprons of leaves which they had girded about their loins, hid themselves from him. Their consciences accused them and condemned them. But now how would their Maker and Judge condemn them? Would it be with an immediate execution of the sentence of death?

---

1. How did false religion get its start, and why have all of us felt its effects?
2. How did Adam and Eve show they felt self-condemned, and how did they try to justify themselves?

They tried not to testify against themselves, but Adam passed on the blame to Eve, and Eve passed it on to the serpent. As in the case of all false religion, there was an attempt at self-justification.

[3] God began at the root of the trouble. He showed he was the Supreme Judge, and not any one of his creatures. He also showed he was a Prophet, who sets before himself a great purpose and who knows its end from its beginning. He really spoke to the original Serpent, Satan the Devil, and pronounced condemnation upon the fallen "covering cherub" when He said: "Because you have done this, cursed are you among all animals, and among all beasts of the field; on your belly shall you crawl, dust shall you eat, all the days of your life. I will put enmity between you and the woman, between your seed and her seed; he shall crush your head, and you shall lie in wait for his heel."—Genesis 3:14, 15, CB.

[4] By this judgment the great Judge did not glorify the snake or serpent as a symbol of enlightenment, but made it a symbol of sin and of Satan the Devil. According to this the fallen "covering cherub", Satan the Devil, is cursed and declared to be degraded to the level of a snake. With lifeless dust as his food, the doing of his rebellious will cannot be life-sustaining food to him. No natural death awaits him; he is to be destroyed as when a snake has its head crushed. But who is

3. How did God show himself Judge and Prophet respecting the Serpent?
4. What did God's judgment signify for the Serpent, and why could the mother of the "seed" not be a human woman?

to do the crushing of his head? "Her seed," the seed of the woman. Who is this seed that does away with the instigator of false religion and its lies and deceptions? That was the sacred secret which God kept within his power to reveal in his own time. The "woman" whose seed this liberator was to be could not be a woman of the human race, a descendant of the now sinful Eve. God said he would put enmity or hostility between Satan the Serpent and the woman whom God meant, and this has not been true with women of the human race. The history of religion discloses that Satan the Serpent has used women most prominently in the system of false worship, even  exalting the female element above the male element in his religion. When, at his appointed time, God did uncover who the Promised Seed is, he at the same time revealed who the woman is who produces the Seed.

[5] What has the adoption of Satan's religion done for mankind? Examine it now as shown in the judgment God pronounced upon Eve and Adam: "To the woman he said: 'I will make great your distress in childbearing; in pain shall you bring forth children; for your husband shall be your longing, though he have dominion over you.' And to Adam he said, 'Because you have listened to your wife, and have eaten of the tree of which I commanded you not to eat: Cursed be the ground because of you; in toil shall you eat of it all the

---

5. What did God say in judgment upon Adam and Eve?

days of your life; thorns and thistles shall it bring forth to you, and you shall eat the plants of the field. In the sweat of your brow you shall eat bread, till you return to the ground, since out of it you were taken; for dust you are and unto dust you shall return.' "—Genesis 3:16-19, *CB*.

⁶ In these terms the great Judge pronounced the sentence of death upon Adam and Eve. From that very day they were as dead in God's sight, dead in trespasses and sins, as a later writer expressed it. Eve's bringing forth children showed she would live many years yet with her husband, who would have dominion over her. But this producing of children would be no fulfillment of the divine command given to them in their innocence, "Be fruitful and multiply, and fill the earth, and subdue it." It was no more a fulfillment of this than Adam's cultivating the soil outside of paradise was a fulfillment of that part of the same mandate which said, "Fill the earth, and subdue it." Against Adam's subduing of the earth God cursed the ground outside of the paradise of Eden, and sentenced Adam to life-long toil in working it. Instead of Adam's subduing it, the ground was one day to absorb Adam himself when he turned back to the dust from which he had been made. Adam lived long after that sentence of death, about 930 years, in fact; but notice that he did not live a full thousand years, nor a single one of his descendants. He lived less than a day accord-

---

6. How, then, did they die on the day they ate the forbidden fruit, and did they start filling the earth as commanded?

ing to God's great unit of time: "One day is with Jehovah as a thousand years and a thousand years as one day." "For a thousand years in thy sight are but as yesterday when it is past."—2 Peter 3:8, *NW;* Psalm 90:4.

⁷ Adam was no longer to look after Eden's paradise. There was a good reason, for God now disclosed that there was a "tree of life also in the midst of the garden", and Adam had not proved worthy of eating of this tree. Eating of that tree was a sign of the eater's right to live forever, and this would not fit in with God's sentence of destruction pronounced upon Adam and Eve. "And he said, 'Indeed! the man has become like one of us [Jehovah and his only-begotten Son, the Word], knowing good and evil! And now perhaps he will put forth his hand and take also from the tree of life and eat, and live forever!' Therefore the LORD* God put him out of the garden of Eden to till the ground from which he was taken. He drove out the man; and at the east of the garden of Eden he placed the Cherubim, and the flaming sword, which turned every way, to guard the way to the tree of life."—Genesis 3:22-24, *CB*.

⁸ God's words, "The man has become like one of us, knowing good and evil," may have been spoken sarcastically, but at any rate they indicate

---

* LORD is printed in all capital letters throughout the Scriptures to indicate that the Hebrew word in the original text is "Jehovah".

7. Why was Adam no longer to look after Eden's paradise?

8. How was Adam now "like one of us, knowing good and evil", and why could not his penalty have been eternal torment?

that man had moved himself out from under theocratic rule, the Theocracy. He had chosen to set up his own standards of what was good and evil, according to the religion he had adopted. But for this God did not sentence Adam and Eve to an eternity in a hell of fire and sulphur to be tormented endlessly, did he? How could that be possible, since God drove them out of paradise that they might not eat of the tree of life and live forever? To suffer eternal torment a creature has to live forever. The sentence was death for Adam and Eve, and death does not mean life after death. It was Satan the Serpent who said they would not die if they ate the forbidden fruit. God's Word states plainly: "The first man Adam was made into a living soul." "The soul that sinneth, the same shall die." (1 Corinthians 15:45 and Ezechiel 18:20, *Dy*) So when Adam died 930 years old the soul died. There was no intelligent, conscious, sentient soul that survived Adam's death to go anywhere. A religion that teaches otherwise is the Devil's religion.

[9] To prevent Adam's return to paradise the cherubim, together with a revolving flaming sword, were stationed at the entrance into the garden. All of us his descendants were born outside, all of us offspring of a sinner condemned to death. With what result to us all? Inborn sin, imperfection, disease, and death. How simple the true Bible explanation of the existence of evil in the earth for these past six thousand years!

___

9. How, then, does the Bible explain the spread of death to us all?

"Through one man sin entered into the world and death through sin, and thus death spread to all men because they had all sinned." (Romans 5:12, NW) The man Adam was the responsible one, because Eve of herself could not bring forth children and if Adam had not sinned and then had intercourse with her she could not have produced sinful, dying children. "Who can bring a clean thing out of an unclean? not one."—Job 14:4.

¹⁰ Eve's words at the birth of her first son showed she was not correctly applying Jehovah's Edenic prophecy concerning the seed of the woman. Under false religion Eve could not be a true prophetess and explain Scripture aright. "And the man knew Eve his wife; and she conceived, and bare Cain, and said, I have gotten a man with the help of Jehovah." (Genesis 4:1, AS; CB; Da) Instead of proving to be the promised seed of the woman, Cain turned out to be a religious persecutor and a murderer, a killer of worshipers of Jehovah. He proved himself a son of the Devil. "The children of God and the children of the Devil are evident by this fact: . . . We should have love for one another; not like Cain, who originated with the wicked one and slaughtered his brother. And for the sake of what did he slaughter him? Because his own works were wicked, but those of his brother were righteous." (1 John 3:10-12, NW) This is evidence that the fallen "covering cherub", Satan the Devil, was left in control of the fallen human race. For Adam's offspring it was now a

---

10. How is it shown that at Cain's birth Eve misinterpreted God's Edenic promise?

question of whether to serve the Devil through false religion or to serve Jehovah God the Universal Sovereign. Cain's younger brother, Abel, chose the latter service.

[11] Adam did not act as God's priest for his family. How could he? When he was about 129 years old, his sons Cain and Abel brought offerings to be presented to Jehovah God. Likely it was at Eden's entrance where the guardian cherubim were stationed. Cain as the firstborn evidently imagined he had the right to be the woman's seed and so was the one to be favored of the great Prophet Jehovah. He brought a farmer's produce as his offering. The shepherd Abel killed some firstlings of his flock and offered fatty pieces of them; they represented the sacrifice of life. It is reasonable that Abel built an altar. God indicated

----

11. How did Cain come to murder Abel, and with what penalty?

his acceptance of Abel's offering, no doubt by miraculous fire from heaven or from the revolving fiery sword at paradise's entrance. Cain burned with anger. God now for the first time mentioned sin to mankind and warned Cain that sin was lying at his door ready to devour him. Cain did not choose to do well and offer the right sacrifice with real faith in God. Like a serpent he lay in wait to dig his poisonous fangs into the heel of the one who might be the promised seed instead of himself. So he chose to serve Satan the Serpent. He did not humble himself to shed the blood of an animal, a lamb, in sacrifice, but chose to shed the blood of his own godly brother to whom God showed favor. Adam had plunged the whole human family into death, but God let him live on till 930 years of age. So God did not execute Cain or authorize Adam or any other human to put Cain to death, but sentenced him to a fugitive's life.—Genesis 4:3-15.

[12] Cain fled with one of his sisters as his wife, far from the entrance of paradise and its cherubim. He built the first city and named it, not in honor of Jehovah, but in honor of his son Enoch. His descendants developed the arts of tentmaking, herding, music and working in metals, brass and iron. Whether it was with a weapon of brass or iron that his great grandson Lamech killed a young man we are not told. As a son of the Devil Cain, together with his offspring, furthered the false religion.—Genesis 4:16-24.

---

12. Whom did Cain marry, and how did he and his offspring distinguish themselves?

[13] Shortly after Cain's murder of Abel, Eve had another son, whom she named Seth, to mark him as a substitute for Abel. Seth became the father of Enosh. In his days something worthy of Bible mention took place; in these words: "Then people began to call on the name of Jehovah." (Genesis 4:26, *Da; AS*) Or, to render the Hebrew text more literally: "It was then begun to call with or by means of the name of Jahveh."* This was evidently done in false worship, to bring reproach upon God's holy name, to degrade him in human eyes. Why is that the right understanding? For this reason:

[14] When Enosh was 387 years old, Enoch his great-grandson was born; and when Enosh was 821 years old his descendant Noah was born and after that he lived 84 years. And yet out of all those generations during Enosh's 905 years, the great chapter on faith, Hebrews 11, mentions only Enoch and Noah as outstanding men of faith: "By faith Enoch was transferred so as not to see death, and he was nowhere to be found because God had transferred him; for before his transference he had the witness that he had pleased God well. Moreover, without faith it is impossible to win his good pleasure, for he that approaches God must believe that he is and that he becomes the rewarder of those earnestly seeking him. By faith Noah, after being given divine warning of things

---

* F. Delitzsch's *New Commentary on Genesis*, Vol. I, page 203; also Rotherham's *The Emphasised Bible*.

---

13. What is mentioned as beginning in the days of Enosh, and was it sincere or not?
14. What proves this calling was done in false worship?

not yet beheld, showed godly fear and constructed an ark for the saving of his household, and through this faith he condemned the world, and he became an heir of the righteousness which is according to faith." Also more than 105 years before Enosh was born, Abel had begun to offer sacrifice to Jehovah with true faith in the invisible God and was accepted. So the calling with or by means of Jehovah's name which began in Enosh's time must have been without the true faith. It was false religion.—Hebrews 11:5-7, *NW*.

¹⁵ The correct worship back there was based upon faith in Jehovah's promise, his covenant in Eden to raise up the seed of his woman to bruise the Serpent's head. God's acceptance of Abel's sacrifice gave a further revelation of God's will on the proper manner of making offerings to him. The sacrifice of the firstlings of Abel's flock pictured the sacrifice of the promised Seed of God's woman, which sacrifice was hinted at in the heel wound that the Serpent lying in wait for the Seed would inflict. (Genesis 3:15) The correct worship also avoided the company of those who became part of that wicked world outside of Eden, for it is written concerning the men of genuine faith: "Enoch walked with God. . . . Noah walked with God."—Genesis 5:22, 24; 6:9.

¹⁶ To add to the revealed religion from God, Jehovah gave Enoch a vision of a coming judgment

15. On what was correct worship back there based, and what did such worship avoid?
16. To add to revealed religion, what did Jehovah reveal to Enoch and then to Noah?

day to warn those who were hypocritically using the name of Jehovah. We read: "Yes, the seventh man in line from Adam, Enoch, prophesied also regarding them, when he said: 'Look! Jehovah came with his holy myriads, to execute judgment against all and to convict all the ungodly concerning all their ungodly deeds that they did in an ungodly way and concerning all the shocking things that ungodly sinners spoke against him.'" (Jude 14, 15, *NW*) A remarkable further revelation of God's purpose was that made to Noah, that there would be a global flood to wipe out all the ungodly but some humans would survive it, that is, Noah's immediate family. Noah did not then know that such flood would be typical, a prophetic picture of the great trouble with which this present world will end, but with Jehovah's faithful servants surviving as Noah's family did into a righteous new world for our earth. Noah was a "preacher of righteousness". Such preaching was a part of clean religion.—2 Peter 2:5; 3:5, 6.

[17] What, then, did false religion do for that preflood world? It filled it with violence and led to its destruction. In Noah's day supernatural forces appeared on the scene to promote more religion of the false kind. Both the "sons of God" and Nephilim appeared. The Hebrew term *Nephilim* means "fellers", that is, those who cause others to fall by attacking them. The Scriptures indicate they were giantlike in size; in fact, some translations render the Hebrew word *Nephilim* as

---

17. In Noah's day what two new factors promoted false worship on the earth?

"giants", and *Moffatt's* translation says 'Nephilim giants'. (Genesis 6:4; Numbers 13:33) How did these come into existence in Noah's days? By marriage of these "sons of God" with the beautiful daughters of mankind. "The sons of God saw the daughters of men that they were fair; and they took them wives of all that they chose. And Jehovah said, My spirit shall not strive with man for ever, for that he also is flesh: yet shall his days [till the flood] be a hundred and twenty years. The Nephilim were in the earth in those days, and also after that, when the sons of God came in unto the daughters of men, and they bare children to them: the same were the mighty men that were of old, the men of renown."—Genesis 6:2-4, *AS.*

[18] Such marriage resulted in Nephilim or giant fellers because those "sons of God" were not men descended from the fallen Adam. Adam by sinning had ceased to be a "son of God". It was not till Jesus Christ came more than twenty-three centuries after the Flood that men received the opportunity to become the "sons of God" again. (Luke 3:38; John 1:12; 1 John 3:1) So those on earth in Noah's day must have been some of the angelic "sons of God" that had witnessed the creation of our earth and shouted for joy over it. (Job 38:7) In fact, the Alexandrine manuscript of the Greek *Septuagint* translation of Genesis says "angels" instead of "sons of God". It is doubtless for this reason that *Moffatt's* translation reads: "The angels noticed that the daughters of men

---

18. Who must those sons of God have been, and why so?

were beautiful, and they married any one of them that they chose. . . . (It was in these days that the Nephilim giants arose on earth, as well as afterwards whenever angels had intercourse with the daughters of men and had children born to them; these were the heroes who were famous in the days of old.)"—Genesis 6:2-4, *Mo.*

[19] This means that these angelic sons of God did not materialize human bodies and appear now and then to the daughters of men but that they kept their materialized bodies and took up residence on earth in order to be with their wives continually. This was improper for them, for the creatures of God's universe are meant to stay each to its own kind and realm. Even on earth, creatures must stay to their kind: "Not all flesh is the same flesh, . . . And there are heavenly bodies, and earthly bodies." So the marriage of these materialized angels with women was contrary to God's law and was a disobedience to him. The faithful materialized cherubim at Eden's entrance did not do such a thing, and so were not an improper example to such angels. Just as, long afterward, the men of Sodom desired sexual intercourse with the bodies of materialized angels at Lot's home, so here the materialized angels desired sex connections with the daughters of men. The inspired writer Jude shows this: "And the angels that did not keep their original position but forsook their own proper dwelling-place he has reserved with eternal bonds under dense dark-

---

19, 20. Why was their conduct improper and disobedient?

ness for the judgment of the great day. So, too, Sodom and Gomorrah and the cities about them, after they IN THE SAME MANNER AS THE FORE-GOING ONES had committed fornication excessively and gone out after flesh for unnatural use, are placed before us as a warning example by under-going the judicial punishment of everlasting fire." Jude warns us that there are hypocritical reli-gionists like that today who sneak in and try to defile the morals of Christian congregations. —Jude 6-10, *NW;* Genesis 19:1-11.

[20] The Christian apostle Peter also testifies that these "sons of God" were spirit creatures who had materialized in flesh for disobedient purposes. After telling that Jesus Christ was made alive from the dead as a spirit, Peter adds: "In this state also he went his way and preached to the spirits in prison [those eternal bonds under dense darkness], which had once been disobedient when the pa-tience of God was waiting in Noah's days, while the ark was being constructed, in which a few people, that is, eight souls, were carried safely through the water."—1 Peter 3:18-20, *NW*.

[21] Since these "sons of God" were incarnated spirits, that is, spirit persons clothed with flesh, they had superior life forces. The natural out-come was that their offspring by the daughters of men were extraordinary, unusual in size, freaks, unlawful hybrids. They could not repro-duce children. In Hebrew they were called *Gib-*

---

21. Why did their marriage with women produce Nephi-lim, and for what Grecian and Roman myths was the basis here laid?

borim, which means "mighty ones". Offspring of passion, they helped to fill the earth with violence, as is indicated by their other name Nephilim, fellers. For this they made a name for themselves, "men of renown," to the reproach of God. From this preflood intermarriage of angels and women and their having superhuman offspring there originated all the religious myths of the ancient Greeks and Romans about the love affairs their gods had with women on earth. In this way false religion again perverted the facts. Those fallen angels, together with the fallen "covering cherub" Satan the Devil, became demons and later influenced men to twist the truth.

²² Amid all this violence and debasement of the human race Noah walked with God, that is to say, in harmony with his will, and Jehovah made him a prophet. Among all the generations that grew up during Noah's six hundred years before the flood Noah was a clean and blameless man, not defiled by that ungodly ancient world. He brought up his three sons with faith in God. (Genesis 6:9, 10, AT) God determined to drown that violent, wicked world in a global flood, but to preserve Noah and his godly family through the world destruction. That way he would wipe out the false religion and its practice from the earth, and would preserve the pure, clean, truthful kind as far as it had then been revealed.

---

22. What kind of person was Noah in his generations, and what did God then determine to do?

CHAPTER VI

Apostasy After the Deluge, with Variety

FALSE teachings have been spread by the religious systems inside and outside of Christendom concerning what the end of this world means. Does it mean, as they say, the destruction of the earth, sun, moon and stars, that is, the dissolving of all material things that we see, hear, taste, smell and feel, and leaving only a spiritual realm in which only spirit persons can live? Such a thing is unreasonable in itself. Just think of the countless millenniums of time which the Universal Sovereign was in creating all these visible, material marvels. And then to think that he would destroy all his own creation because of the waywardness of men who have been on this tiny earth only about six thousand years! Such a teaching is not only unreasonable, giving rise to groundless fears, but also unbiblical. God will give a kingdom to the promised Seed of his woman, the Seed who is to crush the head of Satan the Serpent. God's sworn word shows this kingdom will be forever and that heaven, sun, moon and earth will be just as everlasting as that kingdom. Hear God say: "His seed shall endure for ever, and his

1. Why are false religion's teachings on the end of the world unreasonable and unbiblical?

74

throne as the sun before me. It shall be established
for ever as the moon, and as the faithful witness
in the sky." It is with point that the inspired wise
man says: "One generation passeth away, and
another generation cometh: but the earth abideth
for ever."—Ecclesiastes 1:4; Psalm 89:36, 37, *AS*.

² The end of the world of today does not mean
the end of the earth under our feet. This is proved
by the end of the old world in Noah's day. Men
scoff at the fact that this world will end. Peter
the apostle foretold this, and commented: "According to their wish, this fact escapes their notice, that there were heavens in ancient times and
an earth standing compactly out of water and in
the midst of water by the word of God, and by
those means the world of that time suffered destruction when it was deluged with water." (2 Peter 3:5, 6, *NW*) Mark: The "world of that time"
was destroyed, but we are living on the same
earthly globe and under the same sun, moon and
stars as those which existed before that world
was blotted out. From this it is clear that by the
end of the world the Bible does not mean the earth
created by God, and hence world and earth are
not the same. *World* means an organization or
arrangement of things dominating our earthly
globe. One such world can end and be succeeded
by another, and yet the earth abide forever.

³ The "world of that time" consisted of two

2. What illustrates that the world that is to end and
the literal earth are not the same?
3. Of what did the "world of that time" consist, and
how so?

parts to the organization, a heavenly or spiritual part and an earthly or human part. Aside from the fallen "covering cherub" whose influence was plainly evident in the false worship that was promoted in the earth, there were the fallen angels. These disobedient "sons of God" did not keep their original position but forsook their own proper dwelling place in the invisible heavens in order to marry like men and have beautiful wives and indulge in fleshly passion. The incarnated spirit creatures hastened the corruption of mankind and the filling of the earth with violence, especially through their monstrous offspring, the Nephilim. So Satan the Devil and those fallen angels constituted the higher or spiritual part of that antediluvian world. The people, whose thinking was never anything but evil and who hypocritically called upon Jehovah's name, made up the corrupt human or lower part of that ungodly world. That was the world which perished. Being no part of it, Noah and his family survived its end.

4 "And God said unto Noah, The end of all flesh [outside of your family] is come before me; for the earth is filled with violence through them; and, behold, I will destroy them with the earth." Even the literal earth had to bear the brunt of this destructive work because it had been desecrated by the corruption and violence of men and angels. For a year and ten days it sustained the waters of the global deluge, resulting in vast changes in the appearance of its surface after these waters

---

4. How did God then destroy "all flesh" together with the earth?

had drained off into the sea basins created for them.—Genesis 6:13; 7:11; 8:13.

⁵ An end of a world can be survived by people on this earth under God's protection, and that holds true for the end of this world. Eight persons, including Noah, survived the end of the old world. Since clean religion means obedience and service to God according to his revealed will, Noah and his family showed they had the true religion by obediently building the ark as God commanded and by preaching righteousness as witnesses of Jehovah. Then on notification from him, Noah and his family took specimens of the birds and animals into the ark and went in themselves. "And Jehovah shut him in." (Genesis 7:16, *AS*) Then suddenly, while everything was going on as usual outside, as people were eating, drinking, building, planting, taking and giving wives in marriage, the deluge broke on that ancient world. That it was a global flood permitting none but those in the ark to survive is proved by the physical evidences that are increasingly being noted in the surface of the earth and in the legends of a flood which are common to nations, tribes and settlements of people in all parts of the earth, no matter how widely separated and inaccessible to one another.

⁶ Jesus Christ, the Founder of Christianity, stamped the Flood as a historic occurrence and as

5. How did Noah and his family show they had the true religion, and what corroborates the fact that the Flood was global?
6. How did Jesus stamp the Flood as a historic fact, and what about it gives promise of survivors for this end of the world?

a part of true religious belief. Recall his prophecy regarding the end of this world: "Just as the
days of Noah were, so the presence of the Son of
man will be. For as people were in those days before the flood, eating and drinking, marrying and
giving in marriage, until the day that Noah entered into the ark; and they took no note until the
flood came and swept them all away, so the presence of the Son of man will be. . . . Keep on the
watch, therefore, because you do not know on
what day your Master is coming." (Matthew
24:37-42, NW) For these reasons we have interested ourselves in the events of Noah's days, both
before and immediately after the Flood. His family's survival of the end of that world gives promise that some will survive the end of this world.

⁷ When Noah and his family and the birds and
animals came out of the ark on a mountain of the
Ararat chain, what was the first thing Noah did?
He engaged in worshiping the God with whom he
walked. "And Noah builded an altar unto Jehovah, and took of every clean beast, and of every
clean bird, and offered burnt-offerings on the
altar." That was a right start, and Jehovah was
pleased. He tells us: "I have sworn that the waters of Noah shall no more go over the earth."
(Genesis 8:20 and Isaiah 54:9, AS) This sworn
promise is a part of the true religious faith and
is contained in the rainbow covenant that Jehovah established with Noah and his family as rep-

---

7. What did Noah do after leaving the ark, and what
command did God issue to him and his family? So what
may we expect?

resentatives of all the human family. With them God could give a righteous, though not perfect, new start to the human family. So to them he repeated what he had said to Adam and Eve in Eden: "And God blessed Noah and his sons, and said to them, Be fruitful and multiply, and fill the earth." As it was in those days of Noah, we may expect it to be in the early days after the end of this world. That is, the survivors of its end will receive a similar mandate to marry, multiply and spread their children over all the face of the globe.—Genesis 9:1, *Da*.

⁸ One important thing that false religion ignores today: Jehovah included in his rainbow covenant with those representatives of the human family the sanctity of human and animal blood. He said: "As for every moving thing that hath life yours shall it be for food,—like the green herb have I given you all things. Yet flesh with the soul thereof, the blood thereof, shall ye not eat; and surely your blood of your souls will I require, from the hand of every living creature will I require it, —and from the hand of man, from the hand of each one's brother, will I require the soul of man: he that sheddeth man's blood, by man shall his blood be shed,—for in the image of God made he man." (Genesis 9:3-6, *Ro*, margin) This was a change from Cain's case, for God authorized no man's hand to shed Cain's blood because he had murdered his godly brother Abel.

---

8. What important thing today generally overlooked did God include in the rainbow covenant?

⁹ But now man who would bear God's image, standing as His theocratic representative, would be authorized to exact the blood of a criminal for a murder. And, of course, every living creature that killed a man or woman would be required to pay for this with its life. About twenty-four centuries later the governing body of the Christian congregation recognized that this law of the sacredness of blood applied to Christ's followers also. Hence they wrote to Christians who before becoming believers had eaten or drunk blood from another creature: "Keep yourselves free from things sacrificed to idols and from blood and from things killed without draining their blood and from fornication. If you carefully keep yourselves from these things, you will prosper." (Acts 15:19-29; 21:25, *NW*) How few religionists in Christendom keep this rule today!

¹⁰ The rainbow should remind us of this rule, rather than of a so-called "pot of gold" at its end. The first rainbow that man ever saw was after the Flood when Jehovah made this covenant with humankind. He said: "The bow shall be in the cloud; and I will look upon it, that I may remember the everlasting covenant between God and every living soul of all flesh that is upon the earth. . . . This the sign of the covenant which I have established between me and all flesh that is upon the

---

9. Under this covenant how would man act "in the image of God", and how did the Christian congregation recognize this covenant?
10. So of what should the rainbow remind mankind, and what will be one of the reasons for the slaughter at Armageddon?

earth." (Genesis 9:12-17, *Da*) One of the reasons
for the universal war of Armageddon with which
the present world will end in the near future is
mankind's failure to observe this rainbow covenant which requires respect for the blood of living
creatures. For grossly ignoring it and for befoul-
ing the earth with creature blood unrighteously
spilled the covenant-keeping Jehovah will exact
the blood of mankind at that universal war of
Armageddon. That will be one of the things that
false religion does for mankind.—Revelation 16:4-
7; 6:9, 10; Numbers 35:33, 34.

[11] The eight flood-survivors took up life again
on *terra firma* with the clean worship of the living, true God and with a fresh covenant and revelations from him. There were no mighty Nephilim
in the earth. Those terrifying hybrids from the
union of incarnated "sons of God" with women
had been exterminated in the Flood. Neither were
there any incarnated angels to make improper
advances to the four women surviving the Flood.
Those disobedient spirits lost their human wives
in the Flood and were forced to quit their unnatural life with them in the flesh. They had to
dematerialize the human bodies and return to the
invisible spirit realm. They became the demons
who have played an invisible part in the course
of this world till now and who are responsible for
the practice of spiritualism. Satan became their
ruler and came to be called "Beelzebub, the ruler
of the demons". In Jesus' days on earth he ex-

---

11. As a result of the Flood what happened to the
Nephilim and to the incarnated "sons of God"?

pelled many demons from people possessed with them. (Matthew 12:24, *NW;* 9:34; Mark 1:32-34, 39) The "eternal bonds under dense darkness" with which God has reserved the demons for judgment day have placed bars upon their activities. Peter tells us: "God did not hold back from punishing the angels that sinned, but, by throwing them into Tartarus [or a humiliated position], delivered them to pits of dense darkness to be reserved for judgment; and he did not hold back from punishing an ancient world, but kept Noah, a preacher of righteousness, safe with seven others when he brought a deluge upon a world of ungodly people." (2 Peter 2:4, 5, *NW*) How, then, did false religion get started again after the Flood?

[12] It was by an apostasy, a falling away from the true faith and practice, as in the paradise of pleasure. Noah's three sons who survived the flood with their wives were Japheth, Shem and Ham. From these the three great branches of the human family today developed. It was when Ham had become the father of his fourth son, Canaan, that this apostasy began to shape up. Instead of honoring his father as a son should Ham shamed Noah. Expressing disapproval of what Ham, the father of Canaan, had done, Noah uttered a prophecy: "Cursed be Canaan; a servant of servants shall he be unto his brethren." "And he said, Blessed be Jehovah, the God of Shem; and let Canaan be his servant. God enlarge Japheth, and let him dwell in the tents of Shem; and let Canaan

---

12. How did false religion get started after the Flood, and through what branch of the human family?

be his servant." (Genesis 9:20-27, *AS*) God did not thus curse all of Ham's descendants, but only the Canaanites. This curse was especially fulfilled when Shem's descendants, the Israelites or Jews, were brought into the Promised Land, the land of Canaan, and Jehovah God ordered them to destroy the Canaanite inhabitants and their false religion. God's curse did not turn Canaan apostate, but his father Ham had set him a bad example. Ham's grandson Nimrod became outright apostate.

[13] The evidence is that Noah carried written documents with him into the ark and these gave a brief history of mankind from the beginning and an inspired account of the creation. One of these three documents or histories Noah himself had been inspired to write. "This is the history of Noah." (Genesis 2:4; 5:1; 6:9, *Da*) Thus the remembrance of Jehovah's Edenic covenant that the Seed of the woman was to bruise the head of the original Serpent Satan was carried through the Flood and Noah taught it to his sons and grandsons. Noah was not that promised seed. The fact that apostasy broke out in his own day in the time of his grandchildren proves he was not the seed, for the original Serpent was thus proved to be still alive and at work to foist the false religion upon mankind despite its righteous new start. To get ahead of the real Seed and block him, the Serpent Satan could tempt one of Noah's offspring, as he did Cain, with selfish ambitions

---

13. How was the Edenic promise carried through the Flood, and with what false ambition could someone be infected after the Flood?

to be that promised seed and set himself up as such to draw followers after himself. The original Serpent Satan is a sly deceiver and counterfeiter. Trace now his slimy, sinuous trail in the earth.

[14] Noah's words of blessing, "Blessed be Jehovah, the God of Shem," strongly hinted that the promised seed would come through Shem's line and that the true worship of Jehovah would be kept alive through his line. So Satan the Serpent got control of one of the descendants of the shameless Ham. Cush, whose name is understood to mean "chaos, confusion", is named first among Ham's sons. One of Cush's six sons came in for special mention: "And Cush begat Nimrod: he began to be a mighty one in the earth. He was a mighty hunter before Jehovah: wherefore it is said, Like Nimrod a mighty hunter before Jehovah. And the beginning of his kingdom was Babel, and Erech, and Accad, and Calneh, in the land of Shinar. Out of that land he went forth into Assyria, and builded Nineveh, and Rehoboth-Ir, and Calah, and Resen between Nineveh and Calah (the same is the great city)."—Genesis 10:6-12, *AS; Da.*

[15] How much respect for the rainbow covenant regarding the sacredness of blood did Nimrod the mighty hunter have? His description as a mighty hunter "before Jehovah" does not mean

14. Through which human branch was true worship to be carried forward, and how did one of Ham's grandsons come in for special mention?
15. In what sense was it "before Jehovah" that Nimrod was a mighty hunter?

he was "bold, too, by God's grace, at the hunt". (*Kx*) Here "before Jehovah" means "in defiance of Jehovah", as does the same expression at Genesis 6:11. The Jewish writer Josephus* and the Chaldee Targums† of the Jews so present the matter. The Chaldee paraphrase of 1 Chronicles 1:10 says: "Cush begat Nimrod, who began to prevail in wickedness, for he shed innocent blood, and rebelled against Jehovah." One modern translator has rendered Genesis 10:8-10 as follows: "And Cush begot Nimrod; he began to be a mighty tyrant in the land. He was a terrible subjugator, defiant before the face of Jehovah; wherefore it is said, Even as Nimrod, the giant hunter, presumptuous in the presence of Jehovah. And the original seats of his empire were Babel, and Erech, and Accad, and Calneh in the land of Shinar."‡ According to one interpretation his name "Nimrod" means "subduer of the leopard", which meaning is in keeping with his hunting prowess. "Merodach," another name applied to him as a god, means "the great rebel". This names him as a defier of Jehovah God.

[16] Have you ever wondered where man-made kings got their start? Not with Noah or Shem, whose God was Jehovah, but with Nimrod, the

---

* Josephus' *Antiquities of the Jews,* Book 1, chapter 4, paragraphs 2, 3.
† The Targum of Jonathan and the Jerusalem Targum in Chaldee.
‡ Dr. Alexander Marlowe's *The Book of Beginnings,* 1938, page 36, paragraph 1.

16. Hence how did man-made kings get their start, and what prime question was thus posed before all creation for settlement?

founder of a religion in defiance of Jehovah. He
is the first king named in human history. By his
hunting prowess he made a name for himself and
got the people to trust in him more than in Jehovah, the God of Noah and Shem. He became the
standard of comparison. Even today people call
huntsmen Nimrods. He put himself in power as
king or *mélech* (Hebrew), from which the names
of the false gods Molech, Milcom and Malcam are
drawn. He set up his own kingdom in rebellion
against the universal sovereignty of Jehovah the
Most High God. Thus again, as in Eden's paradise, the prime question for settlement was posed
before all creation, Is Jehovah God the rightful
Sovereign of all the universe, heaven and earth?
Nimrod's kingdom challenged Jehovah's sovereignty and reproached his holy name. The nucleus
or chief seat of his kingdom was Babylon. In the
Babylonian tongue that name (*Bab-ilu*) was interpreted to mean "Gate of God". By exalting himself as king and also posing as the people's savior
and the one to be worshiped, served and obeyed,
Nimrod united in himself religion and the political
state. As he was both god and king, his government was a mimic theocracy or god-rule. His
mimic theocracy operated for the oppression of
the people.

[17] While Noah was still alive Nimrod's city of
Babylon was built, not on a mountain, but in the
plains of Shinar. Nimrod's propaganda could
spread among all the people, because they all

---

17. Where was Babylon built, and with a tower to
whose honor?

spoke one language with one accent or the "same speech". When a migration of people reached those plains of Shinar they hit upon an idea like Cain's, that of building a city. This proved to be Babylon or Babel. Here Nimrod set up his mimic theocracy. We read: "And they said one to another, Come on, let us make bricks, and burn them thoroughly. And they had brick for stone, and they had asphalt for mortar. And they said, Come on, let us build ourselves a city and a tower, the top of which may reach to the heavens; and let us make ourselves a name, lest we be scattered over the face of the whole earth." (Genesis 11:1-4, *Da*) So the tower was not to be a tall monument honoring God's name, but to be one to honor man.

[18] Their proposed heaven-high tower showed lack of faith in God's sworn covenant that there would be no second global flood. Their proposing to make it reach to heaven may also mean that the tower would be surmounted with a temple, which would be a place for their god or gods to dwell. So its top level and its temple shrine would be azure blue, to represent the celestial ocean of the sky. The purpose of the city and tower was not in harmony with the divine command to Noah and his sons, "Be fruitful and multiply, and fill the earth," but was to hold the people to that locality in Shinar and prevent them from being "scattered over the face of the whole earth". It was to provide a world capital, and to hold the

18. Why was the tower meant to reach to heaven, and how was the city and tower against God's command to Noah and his sons?

people to it in a common political and religious allegiance, in a strong spirit of nationalism and patriotism, and to allow for the concentration of power in the hands of a dictator. It worked in well with Nimrod's scheme to be an absolute monarch, a religious, political dictator.

[19] These city-minded men had quickly forgotten that Jehovah God was the universal sovereign, as he had demonstrated by inundating the ancient world with destruction. Thus about 150 years after the Deluge, in the days of Peleg, whose name means "division", the time had again come for the Universal Sovereign to teach false worshipers on earth who is Supreme and who has absolute control over the earthly part of his universe. By means of powers greater than those of modern television he saw what these religious apostates were scheming in defiance of him. He visited them by turning his attention and irresistible power down toward them. "And Jehovah came down to see the city and the tower which the children of men built. And Jehovah said, Behold, the people is one, and have all one language; and this have they begun to do. And now will they be hindered in nothing that they meditate doing. Come, let us [Jehovah and his only-begotten Son the Word] go down, and there confound their language, that they may not understand one another's speech. And Jehovah scattered them thence over the face of the whole earth. And they left off building the city. Therefore was its name called Babel; be-

19. When and how did the city come to be called "Babel"?

cause Jehovah there confounded the language of the whole earth. And Jehovah scattered them thence over the face of the whole earth."—Genesis 10:25; 11:5-9, 16-19, *Da.*

[20] By this Jehovah showed his power to break up any world unification of mankind for a purpose against his will. The United Nations, which has its skyscraper capital in New York city and which glorifies man's assumed ability to make world peace, is no exception to this. By a means simple to him, that is, by affecting their brains and their lips, Almighty God wrecked their oneness of speech and their ability to understand one another. Suddenly he made it impossible for them to understand one another. He gifted none of them with the ability to translate or interpret. That was no Christian Pentecost for those apostates. The city became filled with strife and confusion. What they had schemed to prevent by building the city and monumental tower they now found it compulsory to do under the miraculous change of conditions. So scatter they did, over all the earth. Jehovah caused the city to be called, not Bab-ilu, meaning "Gate of God", but Babel or Babylon, meaning "confusion". This strange act of God was meant, not to convert those apostates, but to balk their united purpose. Wherever they scattered they carried their false religion with them, to be practiced under new terms in their new language and new location. Thus varieties began.

---

20. What was the purpose of this act of God, and how did varieties of false religion begin?

[21] In the Bible's very first book Babel or Babylon became a symbol of a mimic theocracy, or rebellion against the universal sovereignty of Jehovah, and of apostasy from the clean religion, and so a symbol of organized false religion. Since false religion has spread out from Babylon to the ends of the earth, she became the mother of false religion. As such, she was a good symbol of Satan the Devil's woman, for he is the father of all impure religion. The last book of the Bible uses her in the same style as symbolizing organized false religion which mothers all forms of apostasy unclean and disgusting to God. It says: "Upon her forehead was written a name, a mystery, 'Babylon the Great, the mother of the harlots and of the disgusting things of the earth.'" (Revelation 17:5, *NW*) In its infancy Jehovah showed his superior power over Babylon. Even when it reached the zenith of its earthly power seventeen centuries later, Jehovah again showed his superiority over it, in 539 B.C. In the last book of his inspired Word Jehovah foretells how he will make his greatest demonstration of power over the greater mysterious Babylon which has affected all nations and peoples for millenniums till this day. She plays a prominent role in all wrong religion. Do you see the many nations in difficulty today because of the language barriers? Then know that this is one of the things false religion has caused for mankind.

---

21. Of what did Babylon become a symbol, and how has God shown his superiority over it, and how will he again show it?

CHAPTER VII

Further Revelation on the Sacred Secret

INTEREST in the sacred secret given out in the garden of Eden was universal. The terms of it had been carried through the flood by Noah and he taught it to his sons and grandsons after that world catastrophe. Who was to be the seed of the woman whose heel the Serpent would lie in wait for to wound it mortally? How would he recover and turn around and crush the Serpent's head? Who would be the Serpent's seed with whom the woman's Seed would be at enmity? Noah's blessing upon his second son Shem indicated that the seed would come through the Shemitic branch of the human family. For none but a selfish reason apostate men tried to crack the secret and work out their own man-made answer to it. The Serpent, the archdeceiver, was out to pervert the true secret and to block its true unfolding. He had many ambitious men and women on earth to draw into his conspiracy and become his children, the visible seed of the Serpent. They would eagerly play or assume to play the role of the woman and her seed, the mother and child. In this role they could glorify themselves and extend superstitious power over duped mankind. These

1. In what secret was there universal interest, and how was Satan bent on perverting and blocking its true unfolding?

91

could be turned aside from the true Seed of the woman. For fooling the whole world on this, the original Serpent is spoken of in the last book of the Bible as "the one called Devil and Satan, who is misleading the entire inhabited earth".—Revelation 12:9, *NW*.

[2] The evidence is that Satan began twisting the application of the sacred secret with his first visible kingdom and his first organization of apostate religion at Babylon, the city ruled by the first human king, the mighty hunter Nimrod. He was Ham's great-grandson and hence not of the Shemitic branch whose God was Jehovah. But that did not matter to Nimrod or his backers. They would work out the secret their way and not wait on God's way. After getting the people to look to him for protection and salvation as the "mighty hunter before Jehovah" or "in defiance of Jehovah", Nimrod came to his end. Just how the Bible does not state. The agreement or similarity between the many legends and traditions that have been recorded by ancient pagan historians is that he met a violent death. Whether this was due to the power and influence of Noah acting in the "image of God", that is, as the executioner representing Jehovah God, we do not know for certain. But his death was violent. For this he was greatly bewailed by his followers. Every year they mourned for him on the day of his death under the figure of Tammuz. To give an instance of the religious apostasy of the Jews in his day, the

---

2. With whom did Satan begin the twisting of the application of the secret, and how did this one meet his end?

prophet Ezekiel gives us a peek into the desecrated temple and says: "Behold, there sat the women weeping for Tammuz." (Ezekiel 8:14, *AS*) Yearly, wailing was made for Tammuz the same as for the Grecian god Bacchus, whose name means the "Bewept One" and who is another figure for Nimrod. His death was looked on as a calamity, an injustice, and Noah or the persons responsible were considered wicked representatives of the Serpent; they were the seed of the Serpent.

COIN SHOWING
THE BRANCH BEARER

[3] Take note, now, of the deifying of the false seed and his mother. Nimrod's mother was named Semiramis. In Chaldean this name is "Z'emir-amit", and is made up from *Ze,* meaning "the" or "that", and *emir,* meaning "branch", and *amit,* meaning "bearer". So, when its parts are put together, the name means "The Branch Bearer". At the time that the flood waters subsided, the bird which Noah sent out from the ark and which returned bearing an olive branch was the dove. So the name Semiramis was applied to a wild pigeon. Nimrod's mother, who was said to have been turned into a pigeon,* was given the name in a mystical sense. She was held to be the mother of that human branch who is the woman's seed, the crusher of

---

* "Semiramis in columbam," Ovid's *Metamorphoses* IV.

3. What was the mystical meaning of the name of Nimrod's mother, and what was the intent of it?

the Serpent's head. This was nothing but a devilish trick to divert the attention away from the true Seed whom God's prophecy was later to declare to be the real Branch and whose name was to be called "Jehovah is our righteousness". (Isaiah 11:1; Jeremiah 23:5, 6, AS, margin; Zechariah 3:8; 6:12, 13; Revelation 22:16) This was a big step forward toward false worship, apostate religion, a falling away from the truth. With such views of mother and son it was simple to make a goddess and god out of them, to glorify falsehood.

[4] The evidence is that the first woman to be deified after the Flood was Semiramis, at Babylon. The name of the Babylonish goddess was "The Dove", or Branch Bearer, which is also the meaning of the name of the Roman goddess Juno, the Romans' "queen of heaven". In the sculptures which have been discovered at the ruins of ancient Nineveh the wings and tail of the dove in a triune emblem represent the *third* member of the idolatrous Assyrian trinity. This agrees with the fact that Semiramis, under the name of Astarte, was worshiped as an incarnation of the spirit of God, by which spirit the promised seed was to be born. So, too, the first man deified after the Flood was Semiramis' son, Nimrod, and this doubtless at the inspiration of his mother. She maintained that at his execution he had not died, but had been transported to the skies as a god. The constellation Orion stands for him deified, for that name is the

4. After the Flood who were the first woman and man to be deified, and under what mystic names, forms or figures?

one given to the giant and mighty hunter by the ancient Greek poet Homer.* The Hebrew word translated "Orion" in the Bible is $k^e sil$ and means "stupid fellow; fool"; that is, impudent, defiant, godless, adjectives which well befit Nimrod, the mighty hunter.—Job 9:9; 38:31; Amos 5:8.

[5] By thus deifying the dead Nimrod his mother Semiramis taught the immortality of the human soul in defiance of God's law, "The soul that sinneth, the same shall die." Under the name Ninus, meaning "male child or son", Nimrod was worshiped as the son of his wife.† From that comes the thought that Nimrod was the husband as well as the son of his wife; he was his own father and his own son. His real father Cush was put in the background, and Nimrod's mother was thus represented as being a virgin mother. In this way three forms of divinity took shape, the father, the mother, and the son, and they constituted a triad or trinity. The mother and son have always been given the prominence in all the similar forms of trinity worshiped among the pagan nations, even to this day. The father was always put in the background. It was a glorification of the false woman and her seed, to blind men's minds to the true Seed of God's woman. This is true also of the trinity

---

* Homer's *Odyssey*, Book 5, lines 120, 121.
† In Egypt the god Osiris, who corresponds with Nimrod, was the son and husband of the great goddess-queen of Egypt, Madonna Isis.

---

5. Why was the deification of Nimrod a falsehood, and how was he made part of a trinity?

taught by the clergy of Christendom, who push Jehovah God the Father into the background.

⁶ It was understood that the lying in wait for the Seed of God's woman and the bruising of his heel meant his death, from which he would be recovered. And so at his death Semiramis had Nimrod glorified and worshiped as the woman's promised seed, "Zero-ashta," or, more modernly spoken, "Zoroaster," meaning "the seed of the woman". Not only was a day set aside for bewailing his death, but a day was established for celebrating his birthday. This date was December 25, the very day which has been adopted by

THE ASSYRIAN TRIAD

the clergy of Christendom for their religious purposes, but without a single bit of support from the inspired Scriptures. The very name with which Christmas is sometimes called in Christendom, namely, Yule Day, proves its pagan or Babylonian origin and its association with Nimrod, the counterfeit seed of the woman. In Chaldee the name *Yule* means "infant" or "little child". The pagan Anglo-Saxons celebrated it as Yule Day or "Child's day" long before becoming Roman Catholics, and at that time they celebrated, not the birth of the sun deity, but the birth of the moon-god, for among them the sun was feminine but the moon was masculine. Likewise in India the moon is

6. Under what name was Nimrod worshiped as the woman's seed, and with what modern religious celebration does his birthday coincide?

masculine. The moon worshipers of Arabia also celebrated the birth of the Lord Moon at that time. Even today we speak of the "man" in the moon. It is evident, therefore, that the 25th day of the tenth month (*December* means "tenth month") was celebrated, not because of the winter solstice of the sun, but because it was from ancient time the accepted birth date of Nimrod, the false seed of the woman. The Holy Bible indicates a different season for Jesus' birth.

[7] The Yule log which was stripped of all its branches and which was dragged to the fireplace and burned the night of December 24 pictured the executed Nimrod, prone in death. The decorated and adorned tree that was seen standing on the morning of December 25 represented the slain Nimrod come to life again in a new incarnation, to triumph over his enemies and to bless mankind. In Rome this tree was a fir tree and was set up on December 25 as the day *Natalis invicti solis,* "the birthday of the unconquered sun." In Egypt the symbol of the reincarnated Nimrod was the palm tree, whose leaves were used to symbolize victory. It is quite significant that at Isaiah 14:4-20 (*AS*) Jehovah speaks of the fallen king of Babylon, the "day-star, son of the morning," as being a tree that has been chopped down to the earth. So Nimrod evidently was, and so, too, his distant successor, Belshazzar, was chopped down, when mighty Babylon was overthrown at Jehovah's appointed time.—Daniel 5:22-30.

---

7. At this celebration how have trees been used to symbolize Nimrod?

[8] While the great Deceiver, the Serpent, was thus developing false ideas and false worship respecting the seed of the woman, the great Father of the true Seed was proceeding with the unfolding of the mystery or sacred secret in his own way. In the very neighborhood where the mother system of religious falsehood was built up, God made a disclosure of further truth to a man of faith, Abram, at the city of Ur of the Chaldees in the plains of Shinar or Mesopotamia. Though Abram, who was later called Abraham, lived in the Chaldean city of Ur less than two hundred miles from Babylon, he was not a Hamite like Nimrod. He was a descendant of Shem whom Noah had blessed. He had come through the line of Eber. So Abraham was called a "Hebrew", a descendant of Eber, and his God was Jehovah, true to Noah's blessing upon Shem. Showing that Nimrod was a false messiah or seed, Jehovah appeared to Abraham at Ur and said:

[9] "Get thee out of thy country, and from thy kindred, and from thy father's house, unto a land that I will shew thee: and I will make of thee a great nation, and I will bless thee, and make thy name great; and thou shalt be a blessing: and I will bless them that bless thee, and curse him that curseth thee: and in thee shall all families of the earth be blessed."—Acts 7:2, 3; Genesis 12:1-3.

[10] This was plain notice that the promised Seed

8, 9. To whom did Jehovah now make a disclosure of further truth near Babylon, and with what promises?
10. What did this disclosure indicate about the Seed, and how was this substantiated shortly afterward?

was to come through the Hebrew Abraham. This was substantiated after he entered the land shown him and Jehovah said to him: "Unto thy *seed* will I give this land." In the light of this further revelation Abraham worshiped the true God: "And there he builded an altar unto Jehovah, and called upon the name of Jehovah."—Genesis 12:7, 8, *AS*.

[11] God's blessing continued with Abraham. An expression of this came when Abraham was returning after rescuing his nephew Lot from foreign invaders and plunderers. He came near to Salem, which became later the city of Jerusalem. The king of Salem worshiped Jehovah God. Besides being king, this ruler named Melchizedek was also a true priest of God. How he came by the priesthood we are not told, but God accepted him and used Melchizedek in a prophetic way.

[12] The inspired account tells us: "And Melchizedek king of Salem brought forth bread and wine: and he was priest of God Most High. And he blessed him, and said, Blessed be Abram of God Most High, possessor of heaven and earth: and blessed be God Most High, who hath delivered thine enemies into thy hand. And he gave him a tenth of all." (Genesis 14:18-20, *AS*) When Abraham gave him a tithe of all the spoils of victory it proved that he recognized Melchizedek as God's true priest.

[13] According to God's covenant with Abraham, Melchizedek was to be blessed for blessing Abraham. This he was, for God preserved the record

11, 12. What expression of divine blessing did Abraham receive, and through what servant of Jehovah?
13. How was Melchizedek blessed for blessing Abraham?

of him in the Bible and made him a prophetic picture of the Promised Seed in the capacity of a King-Priest of Jehovah. At Psalm 110:4-6 the writer King David was inspired to address the head-crushing Seed of God's woman and to say: "Jehovah hath sworn, and will not repent: Thou art a priest for ever after the manner of Melchizedek. The Lord [Jehovah] at thy right hand will strike through kings in the day of his wrath. He will judge among the nations, he will fill the places with dead bodies; he will strike through the head in many countries."–*AS,* margin; *Ro,* margin.

[14] During a temporary stay in Egypt on account of the famine in that land of Canaan Abraham's wife Sarah was put in danger of being defiled by the Egyptian ruler, Pharaoh. By divine interference she was preserved from defilement and was restored to her husband in whom all families of the earth were to be blessed. Sarah grew to seventy-five years of age without a child. Her bearing a child to continue the line leading up to the Promised Seed seemed hopeless. So she turned over her Egyptian servant girl to Abraham to bring forth a child by him and which she, Sarah, might adopt. Ishmael was born to this Egyptian or Hamitic girl Hagar. But God showed that He, and not man, was working out the line of the Promised Seed. He rejected Ishmael and promised Abraham a son by his Shemite wife Sarah, to be named Isaac. When Isaac was weaned, Jehovah

---

14. How did Abraham come to have a son by both a servant girl and his wife, and which son was the divine choice?

declared his will definitely to Abraham, saying: "What will be called 'your seed' will be through Isaac." (Hebrews 11:18; Genesis 21:12; Romans 9:7, *NW*) So the Seed must come through Isaac.

15 When Isaac had grown to be a lad, Jehovah God seemed to work against his own purpose and his covenant with Abraham. He commanded Abraham to go and sacrifice his only son by Sarah on Mount Moriah near Salem. This command was to put Abraham's faith and true worship to the test. But Abraham was not led into temptation by this and enticed by selfishness into disobeying his God in order to spare his only son for the sake of the Promised Seed. Without delay he traveled with Isaac to Mount Moriah, built an altar and prepared to offer Isaac as a human sacrifice to Jehovah. The evidence was now plain that Abraham had the clean and undefiled religion. So Jehovah's angel stepped in and held back Abraham from killing Isaac and said: "Now I know that thou fearest God, seeing thou hast not withheld thy son, thine only son, from me." Jehovah miraculously provided a ram to be sacrificed as a burnt offering instead of Isaac, and hence "Abraham called the name of that place Jehovah-jireh [meaning, Jehovah will see, or, provide]: as it is said to this day, In the mount of Jehovah it shall be provided".—Genesis 22:12, 14, *AS*.

16 What was the point, then, in having Abraham

---

15. How did Jehovah test and prove Abraham in connection with Isaac as respects true religion?
16. What was the point in having Abraham go through this dramatic performance, and whom did the actors picture?

go through this dramatic performance? Not merely to prove Abraham's faith in Jehovah to be unwavering, but also to give a preview of how the coming Seed of God's woman would be actually sacrificed but how Almighty God would resurrect him from the dead to triumph over the Serpent and his seed and to bless all the families of the earth. This is not our own private interpretation. It is the inspired one written down for us at Hebrews 11:17-19 (*NW*), where we read: "By faith Abraham, when he was tested, as good as offered up Isaac, and the man that had gladly received the promises attempted to offer up his only-begotten son, although it had been said to him: 'What will be called "your seed" will be through Isaac.' But he reckoned that God was able to raise him up even from the dead; and from there he did receive him also in an illustrative way." In this prophetic drama Abraham pictured Jehovah God the Father, whereas Isaac pictured his only-begotten Son the Word. The aged wife Sarah who had been barren till ninety years of age before she bore this only son of hers pictured God's "woman" who produces the Seed. Did Jehovah, then, know his works in connection with his purpose, from the beginning of them to the end? From this further revelation it is clear that he did.—Isaiah 46:9, 10; 14:24-27; Acts 15:17, 18.

[17] Now to strengthen not only Abraham's faith but also that of us who trust in the Promised Seed, God gave his oath on his own supreme

---

17. What did Jehovah, swearing by his own supremacy, promise Abraham to do?

name to his declaration of purpose. "And the angel of Jehovah called unto Abraham a second time out of heaven, and said, By myself have I sworn, saith Jehovah, because thou hast done this thing, and hast not withheld thy son, thine only son, that in blessing I will bless thee, and in multiplying I will multiply thy seed as the stars of the heavens, and as the sand which is upon the seashore; and thy seed shall possess the gate of his enemies; and in thy seed shall all the nations of the earth be blessed; because thou hast obeyed my voice."—Genesis 22:15-18, *AS*.

[18] This promise corresponded with Abraham's name, meaning "father of a multitude". Because God did not give away the secret then of how many members would be included in the seed, Abraham's seed was left numberless like the stars and the sands of the seashore. But, for all that, Jehovah did disclose by this that his only-begotten Son was to have quite a number of brothers, children of the Greater Abraham, Jehovah God, to be associated with him in blessing all nations. That the promised seed was first to possess the gate of his enemies meant there would be a conflict with the Serpent and his wicked seed. But Jehovah's Seed by his "woman" would gain the victory over the enemy organization and its gates.

[19] When Isaac was forty years old, Abraham sent and procured Rebekah as a wife for him

---

18. What is indicated in that Abraham's seed was to be like the stars and sands and his seed would possess the enemy gates?

19. By whom did Isaac have children, and through whom was the favored line from him to run?

from his own Shemitic relationship. He did not take a wife for Isaac from the Canaanites who then occupied the Promised Land. The Canaanites were descendants of Ham and were under the curse which Noah had pronounced upon Ham's son Canaan and were to be servants to the Shemites like Isaac. First, twenty years later, Rebekah bore children to Isaac, the twins Esau and Jacob. Through which was the favored line leading up to the Promised Seed to be carried, through Esau the firstborn or through Jacob? According to man's rule concerning the firstborn it should have been Esau, but Jehovah indicated not so before the twins were born. Paul the apostle points to the case of Ishmael as against Isaac and says: "Yet not that case alone, but also when Rebekah conceived twins from the one man, Isaac our forefather: for when they had not yet been born nor had practiced anything good or vile, in order that the purpose of God respecting the choosing might continue dependent, not upon works, but upon the One who calls, it was said to her: 'The older shall be the slave of the younger.' Just as it is written: 'I loved Jacob, but I hated Esau.' "—Romans 9:10-13, *NW*.

[20] This shows where false religion has made its mistake and has deceived the majority of mankind. Men, acquainted with Jehovah's Edenic covenant concerning the woman's seed, might selfishly wish and presume to be that promised seed

---

20. How does this show that false religion has made a mistake in the matter of the choice for the promised seed?

and might do a lot of running like Nimrod in order to attain to that privilege. And as wished by Semiramis, false religion might be developed and it might name the one worshiped in that religion as the promised seed. Ishmael may have thought he was the favored one in line for the seed because he was Isaac's senior by fifteen years. But Jehovah rejected him. Esau thought himself rightfully in line for the seed but he turned hunter like Nimrod and was willing to sell what he considered his birthright for a savory red stew for his belly. Later he ran in chase of game in order to cheer his father Isaac into passing on the blessing to him, ignoring the previous sale of his birthright. But by the inspiration of Almighty God the blessing went to Jehovah's choice, Jacob. (Genesis 25:27-34; 27:1-30) The apostle Paul says Esau was a man "not appreciating sacred things", and God did not change his mind concerning Esau, neither did Isaac do so. It follows, then, that we must accept Jehovah's choice respecting who is to be the seed, and not man or woman's choice nor that of false religion in Oriental lands or Western lands. The divine rule stands unchangeable: "So, then, it depends, not upon the one wishing nor upon the one running, but upon God, who has mercy." (Romans 9:16 and Hebrews 12:16, 17, NW) For this reason we continue tracing the line of the true seed in the book of true religion, His Bible.

CHAPTER VIII

Egyptian Cult Menaces the True Worship

IN THE days of Abraham's grandson Jacob Egypt was already the first world power in Bible history. It came to be a symbol of the whole world after the Flood, so that even Jesus Christ was said to have been hanged on a stake there till dead. Revelation 11:8 speaks of the world as "Egypt, where their Lord was also impaled". (*NW*) From that early date till now the land of the Nile river has always played an interesting part in human history, but mainly in favor of false religion and in opposition to Jehovah God and the Seed of his "woman". At its beginning the people and government of Egypt were Hamitic the same as Nimrod's Babylon. It was called the "land of Ham", it being settled by a son of Ham named Mizraim, an uncle of Nimrod and a brother of Canaan. In fact, the land of Egypt was called Mizraim, which means "the embanker of the sea", referring to the embanking of the water so as to create a channel for the Nile river, especially in lower Egypt. It is suggested that Mizraim, Noah's grandson, was the first king of Egypt's dynasties. Her rulers were called by the common title *Pharaoh*. (Psalm 105:23, 27; 106:22; Genesis 10:6, 13,

---

1. How did Egypt come to be the first world power, and of what was it used as a symbol?

106

14, *Mo*) Egypt followed the example of Babylon and became a mighty seat of apostate religion. Her course fits well the description of apostasy given us by Paul as follows:

[2] "Although they knew God, they did not glorify him as God nor did they thank him, but they became empty-headed in their reasonings and their unintelligent heart became darkened. Although asserting they were wise, they became foolish and turned the glory of the incorruptible God into something like the image of corruptible man and of birds and four-footed creatures and creeping things. Therefore God in keeping with the desires of their hearts gave them up to uncleanness, that their bodies might be dishonored among them, even those who exchanged the truth of God for the lie and venerated and rendered sacred service to the creation rather than the One who created, who is blessed forever. Amen. That is why God gave them up to disgraceful sexual appetites, for both their females changed the natural use of themselves into one contrary to nature, and likewise even the males left the natural use of the female and became violently inflamed in their lust toward one another, males with males, working what is obscene and receiving in themselves the full recompense which was due for their error. And just as they did not approve of holding God in accurate knowledge, God gave them up to a disapproved mental state, to do the things not fitting."—Romans 1:21-28, *NW*.

---

2. How does Paul's description fit Egypt as a seat of apostate religion?

THE CELESTIAL COW

[3] Image-making and the worshiping of birds and quadrupeds and creeping animals ran riot in ancient Egypt. The sky was conceived of as a cow and was worshiped as the celestial cow, and as 'the queen of the heavens'. (Jeremiah 44:17-19; 7:18) The favorite Egyptian deity, Osiris, was pictured under the form of a young bull or calf called *Apis*, which means "the hidden one", the same as Saturn does. In the Nile delta the lioness was worshiped; at Bubastis the cat; at Hermopolis the baboon. The ram was sacred at various places, also the hippopotamus, the jackal, the ichneumon and the ichneumon fly. The crocodile was greatly feared and was kept well-fed and appeased. The smaller reptile, the serpent, was encouraged in houses, likely because of their driving away rats, which carried plague.

Among the birds the sharp-sighted vulture was sacred and the falcon was supposed to represent the soul of the king Pharaoh. These animal gods were unified with the Egyptian human gods, who were then represented with the heads of such animals or birds.

A FORM OF OSIRIS

3. How did image-making and worship of lower animals run riot in ancient Egypt?

[4] There were triads or trinities of deities in that land of demonized religion. There was even a triple trinity or "ennead". One of the divinities of the Egyptian hall of the gods was the Osiris group, namely, the god Osiris, the goddess Isis, and her sister Nephthys. Osiris was the son of Nephthys but was adopted by Isis as her own son. As a result, the favorite triad came to be the two mothers and the son. Correspondingly, at one time in Babylon the triad was the two goddesses Hera and Rhea and the god Zeus. At Rome the like triad was the two goddesses Juno and Minerva and the god Jupiter. Generally the triad was formed by assigning to the chief god a wife and son. In the Egyptian trinity Osiris corresponded with Nimrod, and his

THE OSIRIS GROUP

name *Osiris* literally means "the seed". His mother's name *Isis* means "the woman". She was held to be both his mother and his wife, so that one of the titles of Osiris was "Husband of the Mother", or *Kamut;* and the melody which was sung to him actually ran the musical *gamut* or scale. The worship of Isis was carried to Rome and was freely practiced there when Christianity was brought in.

---

4. What combinations of deities were developed in Egypt, and with whom were Isis and Osiris made to correspond?

⁵ To such degradation did worship of human and animal gods lead that it was nothing for women to couple up with male animals, a practice Jehovah's law condemns. (Leviticus 18:23; 20:16) The ancient historian Herodotus tells of a case between a woman and a goat that took place while he was in Egypt. One of the things that contributed to the degradation was phallic worship. On the Egyptian sculptures and paintings we see with great frequency their sacred symbol, what is called the *crux ansata*. This looked like the letter T with an oval handle on top. Actually this represented the male and female

CRUX ANSATA WITH ADAPTATIONS FOR PALLIUM

organs of reproduction combined, and so was the "sign of life". It was borne by Osiris and all the Egyptian gods. Thus there existed cross worship in Egypt long before it was adopted in Christendom. Roman Catholic archbishops wear this phallic symbol, the pallium, over their chasuble at mass, the neckhole of it corresponding to the handle of the crux ansata.

⁶ To illustrate how Jehovah will demonstrate to the entire world of today that he is the Supreme God and Universal Sovereign, it became necessary for him to show ancient Egypt and her Pharaoh

5. To what moral degradation did such false worship lead, and how was cross worship practiced there long before in Christendom?
6. How did Jacob come to be the father of twelve sons away from his father Isaac?

that her gods were false demon gods and that Jehovah only is the Most High God. It came about in this way. To avoid the murderous designs of his twin brother Esau Jacob left home for his relatives in Paddan-aram or Upper Mesopotamia. On the way there God sent him a dream one night, in which at the top of a ladder reaching from heaven to earth stood Jehovah God, not to condemn Jacob as a thief of a brother's birthright, but to bless him. He said to Jacob: "Thy seed shall be as the dust of the earth, . . . and in thee and in thy seed shall all the families of the earth be blessed." (Genesis 28:1-14) This assured Jacob that the Promised Seed would come through his descendants. Jacob procured his wives, Leah and Rachel and their servant girls, from his Shemite relative, and by these women he at length became the father of twelve sons.

⁷ On his way back to the Promised Land after twenty years of work among his relatives, Jacob was one night visited by a materialized angel of God. Jacob wrestled with him till daybreak for him to express the divine blessing. The angel then told him: "Thy name shall be called no more Jacob, but Israel: for thou hast striven with God and with men, and hast prevailed." His new name *Israel* means "He who strives with God". From then on his descendants were known as "Israelites". (Genesis 32:24-29; 35:9-15, *AS*) Thus we see that the line through which the Promised Seed was to come was the line that got the revelations

---

7. To what was Jacob's name changed and how did this occur?

from God, and properly by it His true worship was carried forward in the earth.

8 By God's strange leadings Jacob's beloved son Joseph became the prime minister of the Pharaoh of Egypt to save Egypt from the disastrous effects of a seven-year–long famine in that part of the earth. In this prophetic drama Joseph was a picture of the Seed of God's "woman" who saves Jehovah's favored people from the death-dealing effect of the great spiritual famine in all the earth today. At Beer-sheba in Palestine Jehovah spoke to Joseph's aged father Jacob and said: "I am God, the God of thy father: fear not to go down into Egypt; for I will there make of thee a great nation: I will go down with thee into Egypt; and I will also surely bring thee up again: and Joseph shall put his hand upon thine eyes." (Genesis 46:1-4, *AS*) So Jacob or Israel moved down into Egypt with all his family and they were settled in the land of Goshen, alongside the Nile delta. Israel's house then numbered seventy souls. How many were they to become during the two hundred and fifteen years of their sojourn in Egypt? And would they be able to hold to the true religion amid all that idolatrous influence of Egypt? The great Serpent and his seed were determined that they should not do so, in order to block the coming of the Seed through them.

9 The Israelites in Egypt multiplied and became welded together as one people of twelve tribes

---

8. How did Jacob together with his family come to locate in Egypt?
9. How was it first indicated through which one of the twelve tribes of Israel the promised seed was to come?

from Jacob's twelve sons. Now a feature of the
sacred secret had to be cleared up: Through which
of these twelve tribes was the Promised Seed to
come? This was cleared up as Jacob or Israel lay
upon his deathbed. He gave all his sons a farewell
blessing, but it was to his fourth son Judah, whose
name means "Praise", that he said: "Judah, thee
shall thy brethren praise: thy hand shall be on
the neck of thine enemies; thy father's sons shall
bow down before thee. Judah is a lion's whelp;
. . . The sceptre shall not depart from Judah, nor
the ruler's staff from between his feet, until Shiloh
come; and unto him shall the obedience of the
peoples be." (Genesis 49:8-10, AS) This made
Judah's the royal tribe, and it looked forward to
the time when the Promised Seed would be called
"the Lion that is of the tribe of Judah", the lion
being rated as the king of beasts. (Revelation 5:5,
AS) Israelites or Hebrews who from then on gathered around the tribe of Judah as the royal tribe
from which the woman's Seed would come were
called Judeans or Jews.—2 Kings 16:6; 25:25.

[10] In time a Pharaoh rose in Egypt who ignored
the saving benefit that Joseph had once brought
to Egypt. He took up persecuting the Israelites,
on the excuse that they were foreigners and were
becoming more numerous than the Egyptians and
hence a potential wartime internal-security danger to Egypt. Finally, acting as one of the seed of
the Serpent, he ordered all Hebrew male babies to
be killed right after birth. Without new male He-

10. In time how was an Egyptian attempt made to prevent the seed from being born?

brews growing up, the Hebrew nation or Israelites would die out. The devilish intent was to prevent the Promised Seed from being born, and thus
let the false worship of the counterfeit seed and
its mother go on.

[11] True religion was apparently in danger. Later
testimony shows the Israelites were being contaminated by the impure worship of Egypt. Look
at how they once took up the worship of the gold-
en calf after they finally got out of Egypt. (Ezekiel 20:4-9; Exodus 32:1-26) Then Moses was
born in the tribe of Levi to Amram and Jochebed.
Out of faith in Jehovah they spared this pretty
boy from death. They finally set him afloat on the
Nile waters in such a way that Pharaoh's daughter found him, adopted him, called his name
Moses, but arranged for his own parents to bring
him up. Thus Moses was brought up in the faith
of Jehovah God and not in the false cults of Egypt.
Only after this fundamental education he became
"instructed in all the wisdom of the Egyptians".
At forty years of age a powerful decision had to
be made by him: Become a working part of this
first world power and its false religion and sinful
pleasures, or take his stand with his oppressed
people the Israelites and suffer with them? He
chose the course of faith in the God of the enslaved Israelites. The apostle Paul tells us of it:

[12] "By faith Moses, when grown up, refused to
be called the son of the daughter of Pharaoh,

11, 12. How did Moses come to be a member of Egypt's
royal house, but what choice of future association did
he make?

choosing to be ill-treated with the people of God rather than to have the temporary enjoyment of sin, because he esteemed the reproach of the Christ as riches greater than the treasures of Egypt, for he looked intently toward the payment of the reward."—Hebrews 11:23-26, *NW*.

[13] So Moses made an inspection of the affairs of his people with a view to delivering them. After killing an Egyptian slave driver in defense of his Hebrew brother, Moses felt obliged to get out of Egypt to escape Pharaoh's vengeance. He took refuge in the land of Midian where descendants of Abraham by Midian lived. There he married priest Reuel's daughter, became father to two sons, and served as a shepherd. Forty years passed. While he was pasturing his father-in-law's flock at Mount Horeb in the Sinai Peninsula, Jehovah's angel appeared to him in a bush that burned with fire and yet was not consumed. There Jehovah, by his angel, announced that he was sending Moses back to Egypt to lead the Israelites out and to bring them to this mountain to serve the God of their forefathers Abraham, Isaac and Jacob. "And God said unto Moses, I AM THAT I AM: and he said, Thus shalt thou say unto the children of Israel, I AM [Hebrew, *Ehyeh*] hath sent me unto you. And God said moreover unto Moses, Thus shalt thou say unto the children of Israel, Jehovah, the God of your fathers, the God of Abraham, the God of Isaac, and the God of Jacob, hath sent me unto you: this is my name for ever, and this

13. Why was Moses obliged to leave Egypt, and how and why was he sent back?

is my memorial unto all generations." (Exodus 3:14, 15, *AS*) So now God chose Moses to bear witness to Egypt concerning God's memorial name Jehovah and to lead the Israelites into the free worship of God.

[14] Moses, with his brother Aaron as his spokesman, appeared before the Pharaoh of that day and said: "Thus saith Jehovah, the God of Israel, Let my people go, that they may hold a feast unto me in the wilderness." If this was the name of the God of the enslaved Israelites, then Pharaoh disdained and defied him. "And Pharaoh said, Who is Jehovah, that I should hearken unto his voice to let Israel go? I know not Jehovah, and moreover I will not let Israel go." Moses and Aaron replied: "The God of the Hebrews hath met with us: let us go, we pray thee, three days' journey into the wilderness, and sacrifice unto Jehovah our God, lest he fall upon us with pestilence, or with the sword." (Exodus 5:1-3, *AS*) Pharaoh's answer to these witnesses of Jehovah was to increase the hardships of the enslaved Israelites. His policy was one of genocide.

[15] It now became a contest between the false gods of Egypt and the God of the Israelites. True religion in the earth was now at stake. The outcome of the contest is of interest to all the world today, for ancient Egypt the enslaver of Jehovah's chosen people was a type of the world of today which

---

14. What request did Moses and Aaron make of Pharaoh, but what was the response?
15. Between whom did it thus become a contest, and who were to be made to know that Jehovah is God and how?

is guilty of the same crimes and false worship. The outcome of the great controversy today will be the same as that in ancient Egypt. "And Jehovah said unto Moses, Now shalt thou see what I will do to Pharaoh: . . . I will redeem you with an outstretched arm, and with great judgments: and I will take you to me for a people, and I will be to you a God; and ye shall know that I am Jehovah your God, who bringeth you out from under the burdens of the Egyptians. . . . And the Egyptians shall know that I am Jehovah, when I stretch forth my hand upon Egypt, and bring out the children of Israel from among them." Both the chosen people and the hostile Egyptians were to know by forceful proofs that Jehovah truly is God.—Exodus 6:1-7; 7:1-5, *AS*.

[16] Pharaoh had surrounded himself with wise men, sorcerers and magicians. To offset the miracles performed by Moses with his shepherd's rod these false religionists by their enchantments or secret arts turned their staffs into serpents, turned water into blood, and made frogs come up on the land. But when the test came to turn Egypt's dust into lice or mosquitoes, they were stumped, and had to admit that such a miracle "is the finger of God". They could no longer duplicate on a tiny scale the tormenting plagues that were striking all of Egypt in the name of Jehovah, the God of Israel.

---

16. How did Pharaoh try to offset the miracles of Jehovah through Moses, but how were his agents finally stumped?

[17] By each of the plagues the demon gods of Egypt were put to humiliation and disgrace before Jehovah whom Pharaoh defied: first, their river god the Nile, by the turning of it and all waters in Egypt into blood; then the frog-goddess *Heqt;* then *Watchit* the god of the ichneumon fly; then by the deadly pest upon Egypt's livestock the cow-goddess *Hathor** and her corresponding divinity *Apis* the bull; then by the plague of boils and blisters *Imhotep* the god of medicine; next by the plague of hail *Reshpu* and *Qetesh* the gods of storm and of battle; next by the plague of locusts the deities of providence responsible for Egypt's fertility and harvests; next by the three-day plague of darkness *Thoth* the counselor of Osiris and god of the moon as well as systematizer of sun, moon and stars; also *Amon-Ra* the god of the sun; and by the tenth and last plague the god *Ra,* who occasionally appeared as a male sheep and to whom all the firstborn were sacred, being dedicated to him from birth.

[18] During the seven last plagues the Israelites were spared, to demonstrate that Jehovah could protect them whereas the gods of Egypt could not protect the Egyptians, call on their gods as hard as they might. Each time that Jehovah relieved Egypt of a plague at Pharaoh's entreaty, this servant of

---

* Or, *Athor*, the name meaning "the Habitation of God". She corresponds with the Babylonian "queen of heaven".—Jeremiah 44:17-19, 25.

---

17. How were Egypt's demon gods humiliated by the ten plagues?
18. How did Jehovah show he could protect his people, and why was he so long-suffering toward Pharaoh?

Satan the Serpent would harden his heart against Jehovah's people. Why was Almighty God so long-suffering toward this seed of the Serpent? Before sending the seventh plague, that of terrific hail, Jehovah said to Pharaoh: "By now I could have stretched out my hand and struck you and your people with pestilence, so that you would have been effaced from the earth; but this is why I have spared you: to show you my power, and to have my fame [or, name] recounted throughout all the earth." (Exodus 9:15, 16, *AT; Mo; AS*) These words addressed to the visible seed of the Serpent explain why God Almighty has let Satan the Devil live on in wickedness till now. It is to demonstrate the superiority of God's power over Satan and all his associate demon gods and also to make all men of this world, the modern Egyptians, know that he is the only living, true God, whose name is Jehovah.

[19] And while Jehovah exercises this long-suffering toward this world, his witnesses have the opportunity to declare His name in all the earth. Ancient Pharaoh by stubbornly sticking to false religion and opposing Jehovah caused ruin to Egypt, the first world power. Today the stubborn practice of false religion is bringing ruin upon this world and will cause it to be destroyed at the coming universal war of Armageddon. Poor mankind!

---

19. What did Pharaoh's course bring upon Egypt, and what in our time corresponds with that?

CHAPTER IX

Establishing a National Worship Under Theocracy

ALL the nations of this world carry on forms of worship. The nations of Christendom today claim to worship and sacrifice to God. But the proof will show they are no exception to what the apostle Paul said: "The things which the nations sacrifice they sacrifice to demons, and not to God." (1 Corinthians 10:20, *NW; AS*) Ancient Egypt with its many gods, a prototype of this world, worshiped and sacrificed to demon gods. When the true God Jehovah sent Moses back to Egypt and made himself known to the suffering Israelites and also to the Egyptians, the Israelites renewed their worship of him as the God of their forefathers Abraham, Isaac and Jacob, to whom the promises concerning the Seed had been made. Not only that, but at the demonstration of Jehovah's power over the demon gods of Egypt, many Egyptians showed honesty, turned to the God of Israel and associated themselves with the Israelites. They formed a "mixed multitude", a great crowd of many strangers. (Exodus

---

1. (a) As typified by Egypt, to whom do this world of nations sacrifice? (b) What now bound the Israelites together, and others to them?

12:38, *AS; AT; Fn*) The twelve tribes of Israel were bound together by descent from common forefathers. But what furnished the main power to hold them together as a nation was the common worship of God according to the same faith shared by them as a result of His revelations. This is the only thing that can hold people of all nations, races, colors and tongues together.

² The divine purpose in liberating the Israelites from Egypt was that they might be free to worship him and that he might bring them into the land which he had promised to their forefathers. He must fulfill his covenant which he had made with Abraham concerning the land four hundred and thirty years previous. Nine ruinous plagues on Egypt had failed to soften Pharaoh into letting Israel take some holidays from slave labor in order to worship their God in the wilderness. Pharaoh, enraged, threatened to kill Moses if he tried to show his face to him again. So as Moses left, Jehovah inspired him to tell Pharaoh He would send one more plague upon Egypt, after which the Egyptians would beg them to leave the country. In this plague all the firstborn of Egypt's people and livestock would die, but again the Israelites would be spared.

³ Jehovah now set up among his chosen people an observance which was to mean much in the

---

2. What was Jehovah's purpose in liberating Israel from Egypt, why was a tenth plague necessary, and what was it to be?

3. What observance did Jehovah now set up among the Israelites, and how was this an affront to the demon-god Ra?

clean, undefiled religion. It was the passover celebration, so called because, for faithfully observing it, the angel of death would pass over the homes of the Israelites and spare their firstborn. There must be a sacrifice to take the place of the Israelite firstborn children. The prophet Moses could not become that sacrifice, for he too was an imperfect descendant of Adam and his life must be preserved for him to lead his people out of the land of slavery. So on the tenth of the month Nisan every Israelite household was to select an unblemished male sheep, one year old, and on the fourteenth day, after sundown, they were to kill it. Its blood they were to splash with a bunch of hyssop against the doorposts and lintels of their houses. They were then to retire indoors for the night and celebrate a special supper with this lamb, roasted with not a bone of its body broken. With it they were to eat unleavened bread, with bitter herbs, while they stood at the table, with their staffs in hand, their feet shod, all ready to leave Egypt. In doing this they defied the sungod of Egypt, Ra, who was said to visit the Egyptians occasionally under the form of a male sheep. Why, horrors, the sprinkling of the blood of the passover lamb upon the doorposts was an act of blasphemy against Ra! If Ra had the power, he would not spare the firstborn of the blasphemous Israelites but would protect the Egyptian firstborn who were dedicated as sacred to him. But who would prove superior in this matter, Jehovah or Ra?—Exodus 12:1-14.

[4] The Israelite day of twenty-four hours began at sunset, or at six p.m. At midnight of this Nisan 14 the demon god Ra proved impotent to save his dear firstborn. With the speed of light Jehovah's angel of death flew through Egypt and struck dead every firstborn of Egypt, from Pharaoh's son on down to the firstborn of captives in the dungeon and firstborn of animals: "there was not a house where there was not one dead." Truly the Most High God had carried out his word: "Against all the gods of Egypt I will execute judgments: I am Jehovah." All the demon gods had to bow before Him. But all the Israelite firstborn were delivered.—Exodus 12:12, 30, *AS*.

[5] Amid the wailing of all Egypt broken-down Pharaoh sent word to Moses to leave Egypt instanter with all his people and to do so without cursing him. In fact, the Israelites were all ready to go. "On the morrow after the passover the children of Israel went out with a high hand in the sight of all the Egyptians, while the Egyptians were burying all their first-born, whom Jehovah had smitten among them: upon their gods also Jehovah executed judgments." Exactly four hundred and thirty years after God made his covenant with Abraham concerning the Seed the Israelites marched out of Egypt. But not without companions, for a mixed multitude of many strangers marched out in company with them. They were now believers in Jehovah as God, for as at

---

4. How did the tenth plague affect Egypt and her gods?
5. How did the Israelites march out of Egypt, and accompanied by whom, and why?

the flood in Noah's day Jehovah God had proved his universal sovereignty in the sight of the Devil's first world power of Egypt. He had exalted himself as the great Liberator of his people, at the expense of the oppressive enemies. As he later said to them: "I am Jehovah thy God, the Holy One of Israel, thy Saviour; I have given Egypt as thy ransom, Ethiopia and Seba in thy stead. Since thou hast been precious in my sight, and honorable, and I have loved thee; therefore will I give men in thy stead, and peoples instead of thy life." So let all opposers of Jehovah's people in this world today beware. What he executed upon ancient Egypt foreshadowed what he will do now to all religious opposers.—Exodus 12:29-41, *LXX;* Numbers 33:3, 4, *AS;* Isaiah 43:3, 4, *AS.*

[6] God commanded the Israelites to celebrate a memorial of the passover every year afterward on the same date. This was because of what the passover symbolized. Egypt pictured this world filled with demon religion and which enslaves all mankind and tries to keep sincere worshipers from obeying and serving Jehovah God. Pharaoh of Egypt pictured Satan the Devil, who Jesus Christ said was the "ruler of this world". (Revelation 11:8; John 12:31, *NW;* 14:30) Pharaoh was worshiped as god by the Egyptians, and the apostle Paul says that Satan the Devil is the "god of this system of things" and is the "spirit that now operates in the sons of disobedience". (2 Corinthians 4:4 and Ephesians 2:2, *NW*) As for Moses, this

6. Whom did the actors in that ancient passover drama picture?

prophet represented Jehovah's only-begotten Son, the One who is primarily the Seed of God's woman. God said to Moses: "I will raise them up a prophet from among their brethren, LIKE UNTO THEE; and I will put my words in his mouth, and he shall speak unto them all that I shall command him." This Greater Prophet is the great Liberator who will crush the head of the Pharaoh of this world, Satan the Serpent. (Deuteronomy 18:15-18, *AS;* Acts 3:19-23) The sacrifice of the passover lamb pictured that this Seed of God's woman must die as a sacrifice to make mankind free from slavery to sin, death, and Devil. In due time this Son of God was pointed out as "the Lamb of God that takes away the sin of the world".—John 1:29, *NW*.

[7] Sprinkling the lamb's blood on the doorposts pictures that we believe and publicly confess this Son of God's life to be the price for our liberation from this world. Moses' leading the Israelites out of Egypt after the passover pictured how the Seed of God's woman, resurrected from the dead and so recovered from the heel wound, leads the worshipers of Jehovah out of bondage to this world.

[8] By a miraculous pillar of cloud by day and a pillar of fire by night Jehovah's angel led the Israelites under Moses to the shores of the Red sea. Pharaoh had now regretted letting his slave labor go free. So to restore the prestige of his humiliated gods he mustered his war chariots and

---

7. What did sprinkling the lamb's blood and Moses' leading the Israelites out of Egypt picture?
8, 9. (a) How did the progress of events lead to a climax at the Red sea? (b) What did Jehovah there make for himself?

military forces and pursued the Israelites to drag them back to slavery. Jehovah's angel in the cloud moved to their rear and prevented the Egyptians from overtaking them. Then divine power miraculously parted the waters of the Red sea and let the Israelites pass through on dry land.

⁹ When the cloud pillar lifted, the Egyptian hosts saw their prey escaping through the sea corridor. In they sped after them. But as the last of the escapees climbed out on the other side, on Sinai Peninsula, Jehovah God let go and the dammed-up sea waters roared together over the chariots and horsemen of Pharaoh and drowned them all. Their frantic cries to the gods of Egypt for rescue proved vain. Moses and the Israelites jubilantly sang: "I will sing unto Jehovah, for he is highly exalted: the horse and his rider hath he thrown into the sea. My strength and song is Jah, and he is become my salvation: this is my God, and I will glorify him; my father's God, and I will extol him. Who is like unto thee, Jehovah, among the gods?" (Exodus 15:1, 2, 11, *Da*) There Jehovah made a name for himself; as King David later said: "Who is like thy people, like Israel, the one nation in the earth that God went to redeem to be a people to himself, and to make himself a name, . . . before thy people, which thou redeemedst to thyself from Egypt, from the nations and their gods?"—2 Samuel 7: 23, *Da*.

¹⁰ The Israelite nation now definitely belonged

10, 11. (a) What government did Jehovah now rightly establish over Israel? (b) By his acts before them what had he made the Israelites?

to the Most High God. By his sovereign power he had delivered them from perishing as slave laborers under Egypt's genocide policy. He was established as their Supreme Ruler, their King. So Moses rightly sang: "Jehovah shall reign for ever and ever." The last book of the Bible shows that a like song is sung today by His delivered people: "And they are singing the song of Moses the slave of God and the song of the Lamb, saying: 'Great and wonderful are your works, Jehovah God, the Almighty. Righteous and true are your ways, King of eternity. Who will not really fear you, Jehovah, and glorify your name, because you alone are one of loving-kindness? For all the nations will come and worship before you, because your righteous decrees have been made manifest.'" (Exodus 15:18, *AS;* Revelation 15:3, 4, *NW*) Since God was the divine Ruler of his delivered people Israel, the government which he set up over them was a theocracy. It was a prophetic picture of the real Theocracy which he will establish in the hands of the Seed of his woman over all mankind. He was within his right in commanding that they worship him as a nation. He made them witnesses to the fact that he is the true, almighty God: "I, even I, am Jehovah; and besides me there is no saviour. I have declared, and I have saved, and I have showed; and there was no strange god among you: therefore ye are my witnesses, saith Jehovah, and I am God."—Isaiah 43:3, 10-12, *AS*.

[11] It was therefore in harmony with the truth to worship him alone. It was true religion to serve

him. So Jehovah led them to Mount Horeb or Sinai to teach them right worship.

¹² En route God the Creator established the weekly sabbath day among them. This was at the time that he sent them miraculous manna from heaven in order to supply them bread in the wilderness. The sixth day of the week they gathered twice as much manna to carry them over the seventh day of rest. "And Moses said, Eat that to-day; for to-day is a sabbath unto Jehovah: to-day ye shall not find it in the field. Six days ye shall gather it; but on the seventh day is the sabbath, in it there shall be none."—Exodus 16:25, 26, *AS*.

¹³ Back in Egypt they had never celebrated a weekly sabbath day. As slaves to pagan Egyptians for more than eighty years it was out of the question for them to do so. The command to celebrate a sabbath rest on the seventh day of the week was not given to their forefathers. (Deuteronomy 5:2-15) Sabbath observance began with the Israelites, and there in the wilderness of Sinai. It was a sign of covenant relationship between Jehovah and those natural Israelites, and no others. "Six days shall work be done; but on the seventh day is a sabbath of solemn rest, holy to Jehovah: whosoever doeth any work on the sabbath day, he shall surely be put to death. Wherefore the children of Israel shall keep the sabbath, to observe the sabbath throughout their generations,

12. What weekly holiday did God now establish for them, and how?
13. (a) What shows whether the weekly sabbath was restricted to the Israelites? (b) Of what was the sabbath a prophecy?

for a perpetual covenant. It is a sign between me and the children of Israel for ever: for in six days Jehovah made heaven and earth, and on the seventh day he rested, and was refreshed." (Exodus 31:15-17, *AS*) The Israelite sabbath was a prophecy, foretelling the great sabbath of rest from the rule of sin and of Satan the Serpent under God's established kingdom. Then anyone that does not obey the Kingdom's rule will be put to death. God's only-begotten Son, the Seed of God's woman, is the Lord of that sabbath period. —Matthew 12:8.

[14] Sustained by the manna, the Israelites came to the mountain of God, Mount Horeb or Sinai, in the third Jewish month, which is the month Sivan. While they were there encamped Jehovah God proposed a national covenant or agreement with them, and he used his prophet Moses as the mediator in drawing up the agreement. Jehovah's angel came down on the top of Mount Sinai. "And Moses went up unto God, and Jehovah called unto him out of the mountain, saying, Thus shalt thou say to the house of Jacob, and tell the children of Israel: Ye have seen what I did unto the Egyptians, and how I bare you on eagles' wings, and brought you unto myself. Now therefore, if ye will obey my voice indeed, and keep my covenant, then ye shall be mine own possession from among all peoples: for all the earth is mine: and ye shall be unto me a kingdom of priests, and a holy na-

---

14. At Sinai what agreement did Jehovah propose with Israel?

tion. These are the words which thou shalt speak unto the children of Israel."—Exodus 19:1-6, *AS.*

[15] By stating, "All the earth is mine," the Most High God asserted his universal sovereignty. Without injustice to anybody he can give any part of the earth to anyone he wants to, and he had promised to give the land of Canaan to the descendants of Abraham, Isaac and Jacob, namely, to these Israelites. The Canaanites who were occupying that land were under the curse God inspired Noah to put upon his grandson Canaan. Hence Canaan's descendants were destined to become the servants of these Shemites, the Israelites. (Genesis 9:24-26) The land of Canaan was therefore the land which he had reserved for giving it to the Israelites. By keeping his agreement or covenant their days would be long upon that land.

[16] The Israelites agreed to the terms of the covenant to be set forth by the great theocratic Ruler, their King and God. On the third day after that Jehovah, by his angel, caused a marvelous display of the forces of nature atop Mount Sinai; yes, the whole mountain quaked, so that the people stood far off in fear. Then they heard the voice of God's angelic spokesman delivering to them the fundamental laws of the covenant. The way those laws were stated showed they applied

15. By stating, "All the earth is mine," what did Jehovah assert, and what did this mean for the land of Canaan in view of his promise?

16. What fundamental laws did God then give them from Mount Sinai, and to whom did these laws show them their obligations?

to those natural Israelites, and not to the Egyptians and other non-Israelite peoples. The first four commandments showed the Israelites their supreme obligations to God. The remaining six showed their obligations, no, not to Caesar, but to their fellow Israelites. Caesar was not their ruler, and the law stated by Jesus Christ was not then proper: "Pay back, therefore, Caesar's things to Caesar, but God's things to God." There was no Caesar in control of Palestine until more than fourteen centuries after this. (Matthew 22:21, *NW*) This was a theocracy which Jehovah God was establishing over Israel. There were no outsiders like Pharaoh or any others ruling over them, and so there was no obligation at all owed to untheocratic rulers outside.

[17] Remembering the demon gods of Egypt and their grotesque images, part human part animal, and also Pharaoh's defiance of the divine name, we can appreciate the fitness of the first three commandments, which set out Jehovah's right worship as the most important thing. We read: "And God spake all these words, saying, [1] I am Jehovah thy God, who brought thee out of the land of Egypt, out of the house of bondage. Thou shalt have no other gods before me. [2] Thou shalt not make unto thee a graven image, nor any likeness of any thing that is in heaven above, or that is in the earth beneath, or that is in the water under the earth: thou shalt not bow down thyself unto them, nor serve them; for I Jehovah

---

17. What did the first three of the Ten Commandments set out as the most important thing, and why fittingly so?

thy God am a jealous God, visiting the iniquity of the fathers upon the children, upon the third and upon the fourth generation of them that hate me, and showing lovingkindness unto thousands of them that love me and keep my commandments. [3] Thou shalt not take the name of Jehovah thy God in vain; for Jehovah will not hold him guiltless that taketh his name in vain." The Fourth commandment was a statement of the sabbath law for each seventh day.—Exodus 20:1-11, *AS*.

[18] As Jehovah thus spoke his fundamental law of his covenant with the Israelites, they saw no shape or form of God. It is impossible for human eyes to see the glorious God and still live. Our minds cannot conceive what he is like. He is without equal. So to the Israelites it was commanded: "Take ye therefore good heed unto yourselves; for ye saw no manner of form on the day that Jehovah spake unto you in Horeb out of the midst of the fire; lest ye corrupt yourselves, and make you a graven image in the form of any figure, the likeness of male or female, the likeness of any beast that is on the earth, the likeness of any winged bird that flieth in the heavens, the likeness of anything that creepeth on the ground, the likeness of any fish that is in the water under the earth; and lest thou lift up thine eyes unto heaven, and when thou seest the sun and the moon and the stars, even all the host of heaven, thou be drawn away and worship them, and serve them." (Exodus 33:20; Deuteronomy 4:15-19, *AS;*

18. Why were the Israelites not to make an image to stand for God and then worship it, or worship any idols?

John 5:37) Since God would not let his people make an image supposed to be like him and worship it, he certainly would not let them worship any of God's creations or make images of these creations and worship these. To do so would be false demonistic religion, as in Egypt, which they had left.

[19] The Fifth commandment of this Decalogue said: "Honor thy father and thy mother, that thy days may be long in the land which Jehovah thy God giveth thee." (Exodus 20:12, AS) Honoring their natural parents did not include worshiping these earthly parents. Only Jehovah God the Creator was to be worshiped. Honoring the parents could therefore not allow for setting up ancestor worship, either by deifying them or by setting up little memorials of them and paying special reverence to such memorials. If we are not entitled to worship our parents while they are alive, then surely we are also forbidden to worship them after they are dead. They have not become gods by death. They are dead, powerless, unconscious, out of existence, and quickly fade from memory, and so they are unable to receive and enjoy any worship. "The soul that sinneth, it shall die." "For all have sinned and fall short of the glory of God." (Ezekiel 18:4, 20; Romans 3:23, NW) It is the demons who encourage false worship. In reality they receive such worship intended for dead ancestors. Instead of violating God's law

19. Why did the honor commanded to be given to living parents not include worship, and what bearing has this upon ancestor worship?

by worshiping the dead, we should comfort ourselves with the hope of the resurrection of them from the dead when God's kingdom by his Seed governs men.

[20] The remaining five of the Ten Commandments designate it as sin to murder, to commit adultery, to steal, to lie, and to covet or selfishly desire the property of one's fellow man. (Exodus 20:13-17) If the Israelites observed these commandments respecting their obligations toward one another, it would operate toward their doing of justice toward their fellow Israelites. It would make for a happy nation, in which the citizens got along with one another, and it would exalt them, not debase them. "Righteousness exalteth a nation: but sin is a reproach to any people." (Proverbs 14:34) The person contributing chiefly to their happiness would be the God whom they worshiped. He would bless them with the prosperity which he promised. "Happy is the people that is in such a case; yea, happy is the people whose God is Jehovah." (Psalm 144:15, *AS*) This illustrates that anyone who makes Jehovah his God and worships him according to his revealed religion is bound to be happy. "Happy is he that hath the God of Jacob for his help, whose hope is in Jehovah his God." (Psalm 146:5, *AS*) Hence Jehovah's Theocracy by his Promised Seed is the only government under which the peoples of all mankind can be blessed and happy forever.

20. What would observance of the last five of the Ten Commandments result in, and who contributed chiefly to Israel's happiness?

CHAPTER X

Prophetic Patterns

THE theocratic laws which Jehovah gave the Israelites together with the fundamental Ten Commandments were not only righteous in themselves but were also small-scale patterns of larger, grander righteous things to come. We have already (on page 129) pointed out that the sabbath law was prophetic, a foreshadowing of mankind's rest from the domination of sin and Devil through the liberating power of God's kingdom. Other features of God's law to Israel were also prophetic patterns. So on Mount Sinai when God by his angel gave Moses a vision of how he was to make the tent of worship and other matters, he was also showing Moses a miniature pattern of more important things to come. That is what we read at Hebrews 8:4, 5 (*NW*): "There being men who offer the gifts according to the Law, but which men are rendering sacred service in a typical representation and a shadow of the heavenly things; just as Moses, when about to make the complete tent, was given the divine command: For says he, 'See that you make all things according to the pattern [or, type] that was shown you in the mountain.'" Also: "The Law has a shadow of

---

1. Why does God's Law covenant with Israel hold a twofold interest for us?

135

the good things to come." (Hebrews 10:1, *NW*) It is therefore with twofold interest that we look into the things of the Law covenant of God with Israel, an interest in the working out of that covenant in the past and an interest in the future things it foreshadowed, things which have to do with us today.

² The Israelites agreed to God's terms stated in the Law covenant. So now the covenant was inaugurated toward them at Mount Sinai. "And Moses wrote all the words of Jehovah, and rose up early in the morning, and builded an altar under the mount, and twelve pillars, according to the twelve tribes of Israel. And he sent young men of the children of Israel, who offered burnt-offerings, and sacrificed peace-offerings of oxen unto Jehovah. And Moses took half of the blood, and put it in basins; and half of the blood he sprinkled on the altar. And he took the book of the covenant, and read in the audience of the people: and they said, All that Jehovah hath spoken will we do, and be obedient. And Moses took the blood, and sprinkled it on the people, and said, Behold the blood of the covenant, which Jehovah hath made with you concerning all these words." (Exodus 24:4-8, *AS*) The apostle Paul tells us that Moses also sprinkled the blood on the written book of the Law, to represent God's acceptance of the sacrifice over which the Law covenant was put into force. Paul also tells us that the inaugurating of that old Law covenant was a foreshadowing of

---

2. Where and how was the Law covenant inaugurated, and what did this foreshadow?

how a new and better covenant would be inaugurated over a better sacrifice, the sacrifice of the Seed of God's woman.—Hebrews 9:15-28.

³ From all this it is evident that the Law covenant with the Israelites was meant to last only till its shadows reached the solid realities which they foreshadowed. In this respect it is correctly said as a proverb: "Coming events cast their shadows before them." Or, more definitely said, the Law covenant was to last till the coming of the Promised Seed who was to inaugurate the new covenant. So the Law covenant did not do away with the promise which Jehovah made to Abraham concerning the Seed for blessing all the nations and families of the earth with life. The Law covenant was therefore not inaugurated as a means for the Israelites to gain everlasting life. For them to prove worthy of the gift of everlasting life under the Law covenant they would have to develop their own righteousness by the works of the Law and that Law would have to pronounce them righteous in God's sight by virtue of their own works. But instead of pronouncing them righteous in themselves and self-deserving of eternal life, that Law was meant to make them conscious of sin and to condemn them as sinners needing help from the Seed covenanted to Abraham years previous.

⁴ We read: "As to the covenant previously vali-

---

3. How long was that Law covenant meant to last, and was it meant to justify them or pronounce them sinners?
4, 5. How does Paul corroborate this at Galatians 3:17-19, and how did the Law make sin a living reality and condemn all the world?

dated by God, the Law that has come into being four hundred and thirty years later does not invalidate it, so as to abolish the promise. For if the inheritance is due to law, it is no longer due to promise; whereas God has kindly given it to Abraham through a promise. Why, then, the Law? It was added to make transgressions manifest, until the seed should arrive to whom the promise had been made, and it was transmitted through angels by the hand of a mediator." (Galatians 3:17-19, *NW*) Illustrating how the Law covenant and its Ten Commandments made him painfully aware of being a sinner needing salvation, the apostle Paul wrote further: "What, then, shall we say? Is the Law sin? Never may that become so! Really I would not have come to know sin if it had not been for the Law, and, for example, I would not have known covetousness if the Law had not said, 'You must not covet.' [The Tenth commandment] But sin, receiving an inducement through the commandment, worked out in me covetousness of every kind, for apart from law sin was dead."—Romans 7:7, 8, *NW*.

⁵ That is to say, the Law made sin a living reality by naming what sin was. Since the Law proved the Israelites also to be sinners, it condemned all mankind to be sinners. "Now we know," says Paul, "that all the things the Law says it addresses to those under the Law, so that every mouth may be stopped and all the world may become liable to God for punishment. Therefore by works of law no flesh will be declared righteous before him, for

by law is the accurate knowledge of sin."—Romans 3:19, 20, *NW*.

[6] To emphasize still more that the Israelites as well as all the rest of mankind were sinners and needed saving from the deadly effects of sin Jehovah established a priesthood for the Israelites. That was why he had Moses build that sacred tent for which he gave him the pattern in Mount Sinai. Moses belonged to the tribe of Levi, and Jehovah made the tribe of Levi the official servants of the sacred tent or tabernacle. Out of this tribe Jehovah made Moses' brother Aaron the high priest and Aaron's sons his underpriests. The priesthood was to remain in the family of Aaron the Levite as long as the Law covenant lasted. On the first day of the second year after the Israelites had been rescued from Egypt the sacred tent was completed and was set up in the midst of its court. "Then," as Moses tells us, "the cloud covered the tent of meeting, and the glory of Jehovah filled the tabernacle. And Moses was not able to enter into the tent of meeting, because the cloud abode thereon, and the glory of Jehovah filled the tabernacle." (Exodus 40:17, 34, 35, *AS*) That stamped the tent as divinely approved.

[7] It was after this divine acceptance of the tent that Aaron was installed as high priest and his sons as underpriests with the proper sacrifices and ceremonies. Remember that Hebrews 8:5 (*NW*)

---

6. With whom did Jehovah establish a priesthood in Israel, and why?
7. When was the priesthood installed, and whom did they picture?

has told us those men were "rendering sacred service in a typical representation and a shadow of the heavenly things". So Aaron foreshadowed Jehovah's great High Priest who would offer the real sacrifice that actually takes away the world's sin, namely, the Promised Seed of God's woman. Aaron's sons as his priestly assistants pictured those people who would be the first to be liberated by that Seed and who would be associated with him in blessing all the families of the earth with liberation from sin and Devil. All together, this priestly class make up the seed of Abraham which God back there had left unnumbered like the stars of heaven and the sands of the seashore. —Genesis 22:17, 18.

⁸ The entire nation of Israel was taken into the Law covenant through the mediator Moses. All the Israelites proving to be sinners, the entire nation became guilty of violating God's holy law. Foreknowing this, God arranged in the Law covenant for the nation to have a day of atonement each year. This national atonement day was fixed on the tenth day of their seventh month, or Tizri 10. (Leviticus 23:27, 28) It was a day of propitiation or day of sin-covering. The Hebrew word for making atonement (*káphár*) simply means "to cover". Our English word "atonement" is derived from the expression "at one" and has the Bible meaning. It does not mean the state where man is "at one" with God, a so-called "at-

---

8. When was their day of atonement to be held, and what does the word "atonement" Scripturally mean and show?

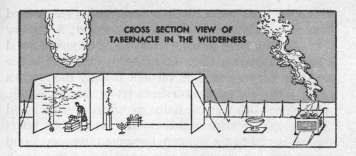

CROSS SECTION VIEW OF
TABERNACLE IN THE WILDERNESS

one-ment" with God, but it means a covering of sins. The thing which makes satisfaction for something that is lost or forfeited is what must be "at one" with that other thing. It must cover, coincide with and be exactly equivalent to it. Hence this shows what is required in the offering for sin: it must correspond perfectly, without overlapping or without coming short, with the thing for which it atones or makes a just satisfaction. Only by atonement through such a sin-offering could God's favor be restored to men who are under a natural disability before Him. That is why the animals which Israel's high priest offered for sin could not really take away human sins, because animals or beasts are so far below mankind.

[9] There must be a perfect human sacrifice to cover human sins. The perfect one who serves as the victim is the propitiatory sacrifice. That is to say, he is the sacrifice which makes God favorable again toward mankind who have been under

9. What must the real atonement sacrifice be, and in what way is it propitiary?

disability and under God's wrath and condemnation due to their birth from sinner Adam.

¹⁰ On this very point we read: "For since the Law has a shadow of the good things to come, but not the very substance of the things, men can never with the same sacrifices from year to year which they offer continually make those who approach perfect. Otherwise, would the sacrifices not have stopped being offered, because those rendering sacred service who had been cleansed once for all time would have no consciousness of sins any more? To the contrary, by these sacrifices there is a reminding of sins from year to year, for it is not possible for the blood of bulls and of goats to take sins away."—Hebrews 10:1-4, NW.

¹¹ On the yearly day of atonement (or sin-covering) Israel's high priest offered up first a young bullock for the sins of the tribe of Levi, which included the priestly family. Before going into the sacred tent with the bullock's blood, he went into its inner compartment or Most Holy and there burned fragrant incense before the sacred ark of the covenant. This gilded ark had two cherubim of gold mounted on its golden lid, and between these Jehovah's presence was symbolized as dwelling by the appearance there of a miraculous light called the Shekinah light. This lid was called "the mercy seat". (Exodus 25:17-22) Into this Most Holy now fragrant with the incense the high priest then brought the blood of the bullock.

---

10. So why was it necessary for the animal sacrifices of Israel to be offered from year to year?
11. For which tribe did Israel's high priest make atonement first, and what did this typify?

Some of it he sprinkled with his finger on the east side of the mercy seat and then seven times in front of it. This foreshadowed how the Seed of God's woman would be bruised and would be raised from the dead and would enter as High Priest into God's presence in heaven itself. There he would offer the value of his sacrifice first in behalf of his faithful followers, his fellow members of the "seed of Abraham" through whom all the families of the earth are to be blessed.—Leviticus 16:1-14.

¹² After sprinkling the bullock's blood in the Most Holy Israel's high priest then sacrificed a goat selected to be the goat for Jehovah. Its blood he sprinkled in the incense-filled Most Holy for the benefit of all the rest of the tribes of Israel. This did not picture another sacrifice by the Seed of God's woman. It merely showed how, after he had applied the merit of his sacrifice in heaven for the benefit of his spiritual followers, he would apply the merit of that same sacrifice of his for the benefit of mankind in general, to as many as believe and obey him when he reigns in God's kingdom for blessing all mankind.—Leviticus 16:15-19.

¹³ To install Aaron the high priest in office Aaron's brother, God's prophet Moses, anointed him with specially prepared holy anointing oil. By this anointing the high priest was sanctified for his sacrificial service. He was therefore called

12. How did the high priest then make atonement for the rest of the nation, and what did this typify?
13. By being anointed what did Moses' brother Aaron become, and so what did his sin-atoning work picture?

"the anointed of Jehovah" or the "Messiah of Jehovah". *Messiah* means "Anointed", or one sanctified by anointing. When the Hebrew Scriptures were translated into Greek during the first three centuries before Christ, the Greek word that was used for Messiah was "Christ", as it, too, means "Anointed One". (Exodus 30:30; Leviticus 4:3, 5, 16; 6:22, *LXX;* Numbers 35:25) This pictures that the Seed of God's woman who becomes Jehovah's High Priest to offer sacrifice for the sins of mankind must also be anointed; he, too, must be Jehovah's Anointed One or Christ. Concerning his sin-covering work for us the apostle Paul writes: "For Christ entered, not into a holy place made with hands which is a copy of the reality, but into heaven itself, now to appear before the person of God for us. Neither is it in order that he should offer himself often, as indeed the [Jewish] high priest enters into the holy place from year to year with blood not his own. Otherwise, he would have to suffer often from the world's foundation. But now he has manifested himself once for all time at the consummation of the systems of things to put sin away through the sacrifice of himself." (Hebrews 9:24-26, *NW*) So the Seed of God's woman must be the Messiah, the Christ.

[14] That the Seed would be bruised at the heel by the Serpent Satan the Devil and would die in outward disgrace was illustrated on the atone-

---

14. On atonement day how was it shown that the Seed of God's woman would die as a sin bearer in outward disgrace?

ment day. How? By the treatment of the scape-
goat or "goat for Azázel". The high priest confessed all the sins of the nation of Israel over its
head. It was then sent outside their camp and into
the wilderness never to return. (Leviticus 16:8-10,
20-22, *AS*) But there was another dramatic picture
that was enacted in Israel which prefigured how
the Anointed Seed would die outwardly in disgrace, but actually as a sin bearer who suffers a
curse for others that they may be relieved of their
sins and the penalty.

[15] Toward the end of forty years of traveling about in the wilderness the Israelites were
passing by the land of Edom toward the south-
east of the Salt Sea, now called the Dead Sea.
Quite some dissatisfaction arose over the miraculous manna they had been eating all those years,
and, besides, here there were no natural water
supplies. So disloyal talk broke out against God
and his prophet Moses. Such conduct certainly
merits death. "Then Jehovah sent fiery serpents
[or, stinging serpents] among the people, which
bit the people; and much people of Israel died. And the
people came to Moses and said,

BRONZE SERPENT FORESHADOWS CHRIST

15. How was this
same thing pic-
tured in the wil-
d e r n e s s when
murmuring over
w a t e r supplies
broke out?

We have sinned, in that we have spoken against Jehovah, and against thee: pray to Jehovah that he take away the serpents from us. And Moses prayed for the people." How, now, was the salvation of the people from the deadly serpents effected? "And Jehovah said to Moses, Make thee a fiery serpent, and set it upon a pole; and it shall come to pass, that every one that is bitten, and looketh upon it, shall live. And Moses made a serpent of brass, and put it upon a pole; and it came to pass, if a serpent had bitten any man, and he beheld the serpent of brass, he lived."—Numbers 21:4-9, *Da*.

¹⁶ The inspired apostle Paul plainly states that this event in Israel's journey to the Promised Land was typical and for a warning to us today. His words are: "Now these things became our examples, for us not to be persons desiring injurious things, even as they desired them. Neither let us put Jehovah to the test, as some of them put him to the test, only to perish by the serpents. Now these things went on befalling them as examples and they were written for a warning to us upon whom the accomplished ends of the systems of things have arrived." (1 Corinthians 10:6, 9, 11, *NW*) For the accurate interpretation of the prophetic meaning of this event we have none other than Jesus Christ himself. To the Jewish ruler Nicodemus he said: "No man has ascended into heaven but he that descended from heaven, the Son of man. And just as Moses lifted up the serpent in the wilderness, so the Son of

---

16. What did Paul say this event was, and how did Jesus interpret its meaning for us?

man must be lifted up, that everyone believing in him may have everlasting life. For God loved the world so much that he gave his only-begotten Son, in order that everyone exercising faith in him might not be destroyed but have everlasting life." —John 3:13-16, *NW*.

[17] That serpent of bronze which Moses suspended upon the pole pictured the only-begotten Son of God, who descended and was known on earth as "the Son of man". This meant that he, too, was to be impaled or fastened on a stake, to all outward appearance an evildoer, a low, groveling sinner, like a snake. He would die like one who is in league with the Devil, Satan the Serpent, whom Jehovah God cursed in the garden of Eden. That his hanging on a stake symbolized his being in the position of one cursed, God's own law stated in this way: "If any man has committed a sin deserving death, and if he is put to death by being impaled upon a stake, his corpse must not remain all night upon the stake; you must be sure to bury him the same day, for an impaled man is under God's curse, and you must not pollute the land which the Eternal your God gives you for your own."—Deuteronomy 21:22, 23, *Mo; AT*.

[18] But how could the Seed of God's woman die impaled on a stake like a cursed sinner and yet die as a perfect sacrifice for mankind? Inspired writers of Scripture answer: "He himself by im-

---

17. What experience did the suspending of the snake foretell for Jesus?
18. How could Jesus die thus and yet be a perfect sacrifice for mankind, and whom does he therefore draw to him?

putation bore our sins in his own body upon the
stake, in order that we might be done with sins
and live to righteousness. And 'by his stripes you
were healed'." "Christ by purchase released us
from the curse of the Law by becoming a curse
instead of us, because it is written: 'Accursed is
every man hanged upon a stake.' " (1 Peter 2:24
and Galatians 3:13, NW) It was only by having
the Anointed Seed die in this manner that the
Jews could be relieved of the curse for having
violated Jehovah's Law covenant with them, even
to rejecting the Son of God whom that Law identified as the Promised Seed, the Christ. The curse
means death as by a serpent's sting. Relief from
it can come only by our looking up to him who
was impaled on the stake and acknowledging him
as dying, not for any sins of his own, but for the
curse on the Jews and the condemnation of sin
on all mankind. We must be drawn to him as our
Sin Bearer. As he himself said a few days before
his death on the stake: "And yet I, if I am lifted
up from the earth, will draw men of all kinds to
me." John who heard him say this says: "This he
was really saying to signify what sort of death
he was about to die." (John 12:32, 33, NW)
Though he died a reproachful death, Jehovah vindicated him by resurrecting him from death to
heavenly life.

[19] All this meant that there would be need of a
new covenant. If the Israelites had followed the
leadings of the Law covenant, they might have

---

19. For what covenant did all this show the need, and
how did Jehovah foretell it through Jeremiah?

become, as God stated at Mount Sinai, "a kingdom of priests, and an holy nation." Himself a natural Jew once under the Law, the apostle Paul said: "Consequently, the Law has become our tutor leading to Christ, that we might be declared righteous due to faith." (Galatians 3:24, NW) With Christ the High Priest they could have become a kingdom of priests. But because of inborn sin and for lack of faith they broke the covenant and came under the curse it pronounced upon covenant breakers. Foreseeing their failure, Jehovah God over six hundred years in advance foretold the making of a new covenant that would really produce a people for his name. "Behold, the days come, saith Jehovah, that I will make a new covenant with the house of Israel, and with the house of Judah: not according to the covenant that I made with their fathers in the day that I took them by the hand to bring them out of the land of Egypt; which my covenant they brake, although I was a husband unto them, saith Jehovah." —Jeremiah 31:31, 32, AS.

[20] Men long wondered who the woman would be who would produce the Seed promised in Jehovah's Edenic covenant. His words here regarding the new covenant help us toward solving this secret. God likened his relationship with the nation of Israel to that of a man with a wife. Jehovah was the husband to the theocratic organization of Israel. This visible organization was as a wife to him. In an appeal to her to be faithful

20. To what did Jehovah liken the Israelite organization, and so as what did he finally reject it?

to him he said: "Return, O backsliding children, saith Jehovah; for I am a husband unto you: . . . Surely as a wife treacherously departeth from her husband, so have ye dealt treacherously with me, O house of Israel, saith Jehovah." (Jeremiah 3:14, 20, *AS*) But the natural house of Israel did not do so, and Jehovah points out that that was what false religion, with which she compromised, did for the house of Israel. So he rejected her as his woman for her unfaithfulness.

[21] But how does this help us identify God's woman who produces the Seed that is to crush the Serpent's head? In this way. Jehovah spoke of the once theocratic organization of Israel as a woman to whom he was a husband. Just so, too, the real "woman" who brings forth the Promised Seed is also a theocratic organization. The earthly organization of natural Israel is not the one that brings forth the Seed of the sacred secret. The Seed is the only-begotten Son of God who comes down from heaven. He comes from the heavenly organization, and it is this which produces him. This heavenly organization is made up of God's spirit sons who have stayed loyal and obedient to him with theocratic submissiveness. Because this holy spiritual organization is unbreakably attached to him in spite of the rebellion of the "covering cherub", and because it remains subject to God as its theocratic Head and furnishes him servants for his different purposes, it is likened to a wife and he is its husband. Jehovah owns her,

---

21. So how does this help us identify the woman who produces the Promised Seed, and who therefore is she?

for she is his creation, and so he is her Lord and Master.

[22] This is the organization which, after the sacred secret had lain unsolved for millenniums, finally brought forth the only-begotten Son to be the Seed, this causing great joy. As it is written: "Sing, O barren, thou that didst not bear; break forth into singing, and cry aloud, thou that didst not travail with child: . . . For thy Maker is thy husband; Jehovah of hosts is his name." (Isaiah 54:1-5, *AS*) The apostle Paul quotes this prophecy, but, before doing so, he shows that the earthly organization of Israel was not the "woman", and then says: "The Jerusalem above is free, and she is our mother. . . . Now we, brothers, are children belonging to the promise the same as Isaac was." (Galatians 4:26-28, *NW*) So Sarah the mother of Isaac was a prophetic picture of God's theocratic heavenly organization which produces the Anointed Seed. This is the "woman" of God's Edenic covenant. It is between her and the original Serpent that God puts enmity as well as between her seed and the Serpent's seed. There can be no compromise between the two sides.

---

22. What name do the Scriptures give her, and between her and what does Jehovah place enmity?

CHAPTER XI

Compromise with Demonism a Snare

A POSTATE religion has always resulted from a compromise with false religion. It has always worked out disastrously and has never had divine approval and blessing. Why does Christendom today stand at the brink of disaster? It is because she is dominated by apostate religion. Had she heeded the warning example furnished by the apostate organization of natural Israel, it would have been otherwise.

[2] Because the Israelites lacked faith in the God who had freed them from bondage in Egypt, they were condemned to wander forty years in the wilderness before being permitted to enter into the promised "land flowing with milk and honey". When the twelve spies were sent ahead to investigate the land, ten of them returned with a bad report. They thought that the giants they saw among the Canaanite inhabitants were the offspring of fresh unions between materialized angels and the daughters of Canaan. So these faithless spies frightened most of the Israelites, saying:

---

1. For failing to heed what warning example does Christendom stand at the brink of disaster today?
2. Why were the Israelites compelled to wander forty years in the wilderness, and what conflicting reports did spies give them?

"All the people we saw there were men of huge size. We saw the Nephilim there (the giant clans belong to the Nephilim); they made us feel like grasshoppers, and grasshoppers we were to them." These supposed Nephilim, however, were simply Anakim or sons of Anak, the "long-necked". (Numbers 13:28, 32, 33, *Mo; AT; AS*) Two spies, Joshua and Caleb, brought back an inviting report and expressed faith in Jehovah's power to brush aside the barriers and give them the land promised.

[3] For this, Joshua and Caleb were the ones that were at last permitted to enter the Promised Land. There they engaged in battle with those supposed Nephilim and proved them to be only mortal human giants and destroyed them. (Joshua 11:21, 22; 15:13, 14) As for the people who believed the bad report and wanted to go back to Egypt, God sentenced them to die in the wilderness, and not enter the Promised Land. "Wherefore," says Jehovah, "I sware in my wrath, that they should not enter into my rest." (Numbers 14:28-35; Psalm 95:10, 11, *AS*) Thus, more than twenty-five hundred years after he created man and woman, Jehovah showed that he was still enjoying his sabbath rest, the great seventh day in which he desists from earthly creation. The faithless Israelites were not to enjoy rest with him in the land of milk and honey. Without faith in him it is impossible to enter into his rest. (Hebrews 3:7 to

---

3. Who was and who was not permitted to enter into God's rest in the Promised Land, and what does His resting till then show?

4:11) It takes faith not to compromise with the enemy.

⁴ At the end of the forty years the Israelites that had survived encamped on the plains of Moab across the Jordan river from the land of Canaan. They had been taught the theocratic worship of the true God, but now they were to come in contact with the accursed Canaanites who worshiped false gods, demons, and idolized images of such gods. With these demon worshipers and their religion Jehovah's chosen people were not to compromise. They must keep the first and second of the Ten Commandments. So now, before bringing them across the Jordan, Jehovah brought the Israelites into another covenant, by which they solemnly agreed to be faithful to him in the Promised Land. It prohibited all compromise with demonism.—Deuteronomy 29:1-18.

⁵ Jehovah named the Canaanite nations and said to his people: "When Jehovah thy God shall deliver them up before thee, and thou shalt smite them; then thou shalt utterly destroy them: thou shalt make no covenant with them, nor show mercy unto them; neither shalt thou make marriages with them; thy daughter thou shalt not give unto his son, nor his daughter shalt thou take unto thy son. For he will turn away thy son from following me, that they may serve other gods: so will the anger of Jehovah be kindled

---

4. Just before bringing them across the Jordan, into what covenant did Jehovah bring the Israelites, and why?
5. What did he instruct them to do to the things of idol worship?

against you, and he will destroy thee quickly.
But thus shall ye deal with them: ye shall break
down their altars, and dash in pieces their pillars,
and hew down their Asherim [sacred poles], and
burn their graven images with fire."—Deuteronomy 7:1-5, *AS; AT; Mo.*

⁶ But was this not the rankest kind of religious
intolerance as well as genocide? Is this not the
kind of intolerance that is practiced in lands today
under totalitarian and dictatorial rule? Not at all!
This was the divine command and it was in favor
of keeping the pure religion alive in the land God
gave. The pure and the false could not exist side
by side without hurt to his people and danger to
their opportunity for eternal life in the new world.
They had agreed to worship only Jehovah as God,
and he was giving them the Promised Land to
possess. Hence he had the sovereign right to determine what should be done to demon religion in
the land. It was for their protection. He told them
why he gave them these strict orders: "For thou
art a holy people unto Jehovah thy God: Jehovah
thy God hath chosen thee to be a people for his
own possession, above all peoples that are upon
the face of the earth. And thou shalt consume all
the peoples that Jehovah thy God shall deliver
unto thee; thine eye shall not pity them: neither
shalt thou serve their gods; for that will be a
snare unto thee. The graven images of their gods
shall ye burn with fire: thou shalt not covet the
silver or the gold that is on them, nor take it unto

6. Why was this course not rank religious intolerance
and genocide?

GROVE FOR
PHALLIC WORSHIP

thee, lest thou be snared therein; for it is an abomination to Jehovah thy God. And thou shalt not bring an abomination into thy house, and become a devoted [or, doomed] thing like unto it: thou shalt utterly detest it, and thou shalt utterly abhor it; for it is a devoted [doomed] thing."—Deuteronomy 7:6, 16, 25, 26, *AS*.

[7] False religion is a trap of Satan the Serpent, and his seed practice it. By not compromising with it we save ourselves from the snare. It is for the protection of our eternal interests that we uncompromisingly worship the only true God Jehovah according to his commandments, for he is the one Source of life and preservation. False religion leads to death, as it did Adam and Eve, for it is disobedience. What it does to a nation and people it showed with the Canaanites whom it degraded to the lowest immoral level. For instance, God said: "Thou shalt not give any of thy seed to make them pass through the fire to Molech; neither shalt thou profane the name of thy God: I am Jehovah. Thou shalt not lie with mankind, as with womankind: it is abomination. And thou shalt not lie with any beast to defile thyself therewith; neither shall any woman stand before a beast, to lie down thereto: it is confusion. Defile not ye yourselves in any of these things: for

7. Why did the Israelites not dare compromise with false religion in the Promised Land?

in all these the nations are defiled which I cast out from before you; and the land is defiled: therefore I do visit the iniquity thereof upon it, and the land vomiteth out her inhabitants." (Leviticus 18:21-28, *AS*) To avoid themselves being vomited out of the land for defiling it the Israelites must not compromise with demonism.

[8] Hence the extermination of the demon worshipers in the Promised Land was no case of religious intolerance. It was not an authorizing of them to go outside the God-given land and invade the outside worldly nations and destroy their idols and wipe out their false religion and all those who practiced it. Neither is this any Scriptural basis for the Roman Catholic religion to torture and kill so-called "heretics" in lands where it dominates and to forbid other religious sects to carry on there. In doing so Catholics are not copying the Israelites' example. History shows that in the lands they have invaded they have not obeyed God's commands to the Israelites to smash the idolatrous images there and to destroy the demon worshipers. To the contrary, they have let these remain and have compromised with the practicers of demonism, so that the natives can still carry on with the things of demonism just so they are Roman Catholics in name. This accounts for it today that, for example, a native in Haiti can be

8. Why in its practice of religious intolerance in lands where it dominates is Roman Catholicism not copying God's law to Israel?

a Roman Catholic and at the same time practice Voodooism. The ones whom the Vatican's clergy try to exterminate by means of boycott, inquisition, torture, mob violence, persecution and the "sword of the state" are, not these demon worshipers, but those who profess to be Christians and who differ with the Hierarchy on the teachings of the Bible.

[9] Furthermore, in exterminating the degraded demon worshipers in the Promised Land, the Israelites were acting as executioners for Jehovah God. They were carrying on theocratic warfare against the accursed Canaanites, for they were fighting at God's command. He backed them up in it by working miracles to help them against superior foes, so that it was rightly said concerning the subjugating of the Canaanites: "And all these kings and their land did Joshua take at one time, because Jehovah, the God of Israel, fought for Israel." He had promised: "Jehovah your God who goeth before you, he will fight for you, according to all that he did for you in Egypt before your eyes, and in the wilderness." (Joshua 10:14, 42 and Deuteronomy 1:30, 31, AS) But neither Roman or Greek Catholics nor Protestants of Christendom are natural Jews under the Law covenant and neither are they being given a Promised Land in this world and so commanded to take such action against religious organizations of this world. In carrying on crusades, religious wars, etc., with death-dealing weapons and physical vio-

---

9. How in exterminating the pagans were the Israelites acting, but not so the religious systems of Christendom?

lence, they are not carrying on theocratic warfare, even if their clergy do bless the weapons and the fighters and call it a "holy war".

[10] When Christ, whom they claim to follow, sent out his missionaries, he did not tell them to go armed with sword and incendiary torch and compel people to abandon false religion. He told them: "All authority has been given me in heaven and on the earth. Go therefore and make disciples of people of all the nations, baptizing them in the name of the Father and of the Son and of the holy spirit, teaching them to observe all the things I have commanded you." (Matthew 28:18-20, NW) His apostle Paul said: "Though we walk in the flesh, we do not wage warfare according to what we are in the flesh. For the weapons of our warfare are not fleshly, but powerful by God for overturning strongly entrenched things. For we are overturning reasonings and every lofty thing raised up against the knowledge of God, and we are bringing every thought into captivity to make it obedient to the Christ." But, speaking against all compromise with devil religion, he said: "Put on the complete suit of armor from God that you may be able to stand firm against the machinations of the Devil; because we have a fight, not against blood and flesh, but against the [spiritual] governments, against the authorities, against the world-rulers of this darkness, against the wicked spirit forces [the demons] in the heavenly places."

10. How did Christ instruct his disciples to proceed against false religion for people's liberation, and how do they fight?

—Ephesians 6:11, 12 and 2 Corinthians 10:3-5, *NW*.

[11] We today can profit not only from the principle set forth in God's command but also from the warning example of the Israelites. After he had miraculously brought them through the Jordan river into Canaan land, they pushed a campaign of ridding the land of its accursed inhabitants and their demonism, and after six years of this the land was apportioned out among the tribes and the component families. Joshua had succeeded Moses, and during all his days and the days of the spiritually mature men who were joined with him the Israelites faithfully served and worshiped the Most High God. In his final address to the tribes Joshua showed them the right decision to make for their happiness and blessing. "Now therefore," said he, "fear Jehovah, and serve him in sincerity and in truth; and put away the gods which your fathers served beyond the River [Euphrates], and in Egypt; and serve ye Jehovah. And if it seem evil unto you to serve Jehovah, choose you this day whom ye will serve; whether the gods which your fathers served that were beyond the River [where Babylon was located], or the gods of the Amorites, in whose land ye dwell: but as for me and my house, we will serve Jehovah."—Joshua 24:14, 15, *AS*.

[12] The Israelites bore witness against themselves

11. What uncompromising stand did Joshua declare before the Israelites, and whom did they worship during his days?
12. For later compromising, what situation did God let remain with them, and what test does this picture to which we are subjected?

that they would do as Joshua encouraged them to do. In the course of time they weakened in their resolution, became tolerant toward demonized worshipers and compromised with them and became trapped. They did not keep their covenant. Then Jehovah, by his angel, told them they would have to suffer the consequences: "I have brought you up out of Egypt, and have brought you into the land which I promised on oath to your fathers, when I said, 'I will never break my covenant with you, but you on your part must make no covenant with the inhabitants of this land; you must tear down their altars.' But you have not heeded my injunction: what a way for you to behave! So now I add, 'I will not drive them out of your way; but they shall become your adversaries, and their gods shall become a trap for you.'" (Judges 2:1-3, AT) So ever after that they had these demon worshipers to contend with. Frequently they were brought into subjection to them for abandoning the pure revealed worship of God. When they realized the cause of their defeat and turned with repentant hearts to Him for deliverance, he raised up judges for their deliverance. Jehovah God was with the judges and fought miraculously for their victory. Therefore we cannot belittle the pure religion: it has to do with our real liberty and happiness. As with the Israelites, so with us: our being in touch with false religions in this world tests the integrity of our hearts toward Jehovah God.

[13] After a period of judges until Samuel the

---

13. How did they later make a serious compromise as to form of government?

prophet the Israelites made a serious compromise on the matter of form of government. Till then they had no visible human king. At the end of the book of Judges we read: "In those days there was no king in Israel: every man did that which was right in his own eyes." (Judges 21:25) Why did they need any? In his Law covenant Jehovah made no provision for a human king, in imitation of the Babylonish practice set up by Nimrod. Jehovah was their invisible King. Their God was their Ruler and Lawgiver. It was a theocracy over them, and all the tribal officials and the priesthood enforced the laws of his covenant. Yet all the nations and peoples around Israel had their human kings in addition to their idol gods whom they called Molech, Milcom, and Malcam, meaning "king", or Baal, meaning "lord; master". It was now about the year 1117 B.C., hundreds of years before Rome was founded. The elderly representatives of Israel came to Samuel and surprised him with asking: "Make us a king to judge us like all the nations." Theocratic Samuel felt hurt and prayed to God about it; he was not going to shove Jehovah aside as King just to please them. What was the will of Israel's invisible King Jehovah?

[14] "And Jehovah said unto Samuel, Hearken unto the voice of the people in all that they say unto thee; for they have not rejected thee, but they have rejected me, that I should not be king over them." (1 Samuel 8:1-7; 12:12, *AS*) Jehovah had

---

14. What did Jehovah do with their request, and what instructions had he already given with respect to a king over them?

foreseen such a move. Over 350 years before this he had said through Moses: "When thou art come unto the land which Jehovah thy God giveth thee, and shalt possess it, and shalt dwell therein, and shalt say, I will set a king over me, like all the nations that are round about me; thou shalt surely set him king over thee, whom Jehovah thy God shall choose: one from among thy brethren shalt thou set king over thee; thou mayest not put a foreigner over thee, who is not thy brother." Among other things this king must do, he must have a personal copy of the inspired Holy Scriptures and must carefully study it and follow it. So Israel's king was to be no foreigner, no usurper of the throne, no selectee of the people by democratic process, but was to be God's choice.—Deuteronomy 17:14-20, AS.

[15] The people were made to realize they had done wrong in this matter. So they asked Samuel: "Pray for thy servants unto Jehovah thy God, that we die not; for we have added unto all our sins this evil, to ask us a king." Samuel assured them of his prayers, but warned them: "If ye shall still do wickedly, ye shall be consumed, both ye and your king." (1 Samuel 12:19-25, AS) A human king was a danger. If he turned to false religion, he could enforce it upon the nation and swing the whole nation into demonism. How often their future history was to prove this!

---

15. In asking a king were they right or wrong, and how was a human king a possible danger to them?

CHAPTER XII

Kingship and Priesthood— Why Separate

IN THIS world few men can be trusted with a concentration of power in their hands. If, in addition to political power, they have religious power and control in their hands, the possibilities become doubly dangerous for the people under such a political, religious ruler. Remember Nimrod, Babylon's first king.

² In the kingdom which was set up in Israel the priestly office was kept separate from the king's throne. When the Israelites came asking God's prophet Samuel to set a king over them, they did not ask for a king like Melchizedek, for that ancient king of Salem was a priest upon his throne. The Israelites already had a priesthood which God had fixed in the household of Aaron, Moses' brother. So the Israelites asked for a king like those of the demon-worshiping nations round about. Samuel reminded them of the unfitness of their request, saying: "Ye said unto me, Nay, but a king shall reign over us; when Jehovah your God was your king." Samuel sensed the danger in this. He knew

1. What are the possibilities where religious control is put in a ruler's hands?
2. How were these possibilities guarded against in Israel, and what warning had Moses given against following an unfaithful king?

164

a human visible king would not in himself be able to save the nation from its foes, nor from internal evils and the consequences. He doubtless had in mind Moses' warning against following an apostate, covenant-breaking king: "Jehovah will bring thee, and thy king whom thou shalt set over thee, unto a nation that thou hast not known, thou nor thy fathers; and there shalt thou serve other gods, wood and stone." This was a long-range prophecy pointing ahead to their exile in Babylon seventy years.—1 Samuel 12:12 and Deuteronomy 28:36, AS.

[3] Whom, now, would God choose for their first human king? Back in Egypt he had inspired their forefather Jacob (Israel) to prophesy that the scepter would never depart from the tribe of Judah; and when it came to which tribe should go up first in the assault on the Canaanites in the Promised Land after Joshua's death, God said: "Judah shall go up: behold, I have delivered the land into his hand." (Genesis 49:10; Judges 1:1, 2) But God did not select Israel's first king from the tribe of Judah. The tribe of Benjamin must first be given the privilege of providing a ruling dynasty for Israel, because Benjamin, although Israel's youngest son, was the son of Israel's favorite wife Rachel, and so the full brother of Joseph. Due to these grounds for priority over Judah, God instructed Samuel to anoint a promising mature man of the tribe of Benjamin, Saul the son of Kish. From then on he was spoken

---

3. Whom did God choose for Israel's first king and why a man of that tribe, and how was he designated to office?

of as Jehovah's "Anointed". But he did not prove
to be a royal figure prophetic of the Christ, the
Seed of God's "woman", for Saul turned apostate.
—1 Samuel 12:3, 5; 24:6, 10, *AS;* 1 Chronicles
5:1, 2.

⁴ In the second year of his reign Saul showed
a lack of faith. He acted impulsively and took upon himself the sacrificial duties of the Levite
Samuel, something totally out of order for a Ben-
jamite, even though a king. In disapproval Samuel
said to Saul: "Now thy kingdom shall not continue: Jehovah hath sought him a man after his
own heart, and Jehovah hath appointed him to
be prince over his people, because thou hast not
kept that which Jehovah commanded thee." This
meant that Saul's godly son Jonathan would not
become king to succeed Saul. The man after God's
own heart who was to succeed Saul on the throne
of all Israel was not yet born. He was born after
Saul had reigned ten years. (1 Samuel 13:11-14,
AS) And now again Saul showed himself disobedient because of fear and selfishness. He did not
carry out fully his duties as Jehovah's executioner
against Israel's long-time enemy, the Amalekites.
He spared King Agag alive, and for fear of what
his warriors would think, he let them spare the
fine livestock of the Amalekites, contrary to God's
orders. To explain away his weakness in this, Saul
told Samuel: "The people took of the spoil, sheep
and oxen, the choicest of the devoted things, to
sacrifice to Jehovah thy God in Gilgal."

---

4. How did Saul early and later show a lack of faith
and obedience?

⁵ Samuel was not like the religious clergy of Christendom. He did not let Saul commit a crime and then think that by offering to God some of the material wealth gained by the crime he could bribe God into overlooking his crime. No; but Samuel fearlessly said to disobedient Saul: "Has Jehovah delight in burnt-offerings and sacrifices, as in hearkening to the voice of Jehovah? Behold, obedience is better than sacrifice, attention than the fat of rams. For rebellion is as the sin of divination, and selfwill is as iniquity and idolatry. Because thou hast rejected the word of Jehovah, he hath also rejected thee from being king." When Saul grabbed Samuel's garment as he was indignantly leaving and it tore, Samuel said: "Jehovah has rent the kingdom of Israel from thee to-day, and has given it to thy neighbour, who is better than thou." (1 Samuel 15:20-29, *Da*) By this Samuel vindicated Jehovah God as clean from all bribery; but Saul, although having a form of godly devotion, was denying its power and was really guilty of demonism and idolatry.

⁶ Because of rebelling against his heavenly Commander's orders of execution Saul was committing the sin of divination by deciding by spiritistic help what was better than Jehovah's will. By selfwill he was guilty of worshiping himself and so was chargeable with iniquity and idolatry. This agrees with the apostle's statement that covetousness is idolatry and a greedy person is an idolater.

---

5. How did Samuel here vindicate Jehovah as clean from all bribery?
6. How was Saul guilty of divination and idolatry?

(Colossians 3:5; Ephesians 5:5) A ruler guilty of such things could not be rewarded with having a line of kings run in his family.

[7] Saul's self-worshiping rebelliousness and greediness led him finally to resorting directly to witchcraft. In this act he was trying to counteract Samuel's refusal to see him any more: "So Samuel saw Saul no more until the day of his death, for Samuel grieved over Saul." Before Saul finished his reign of forty years, Samuel died. (1 Samuel 15:35; 25:1; 28:3, *AT*) As battle with the superior forces of the Philistines at Mount Gilboa impended, Saul faced his end. "His heart greatly trembled. And Saul inquired of Jehovah; but Jehovah did not answer him, either by dreams, or by Urim [the sacred lot], or by prophets." Here Saul turned straight to demonism with his request: "Seek me a woman that has a spirit of Python, that I may go to her and inquire of her." In defiance of God's law that a witch must be stoned to death in Israel and that any Israelite

defiling himself by consulting a witch must be cut off, Saul went by night to the witch located at Endor. (Leviticus 19:31; 20:6, 27) S a u l asked her to bring up Samuel from the dead.

7. How did Saul resort finally to demonism directly, and why?

⁸ Now the demons practiced a fraud upon Saul. The witch said she saw a god [or, gods] coming out of the earth. By the description she gave of this "god", Saul saw a resemblance of it to Samuel's appearance when alive. Then by the witch the "god" predicted dire calamity for Saul and his army and said, "To-morrow shalt thou and thy sons be with me." Spiritualists use this to argue that the human soul survives after death and that the dead may be communicated with and can tell us of the future, because they know more now than when they were alive. But instead of proving the immortality of the human soul, it proves demonism. Witches condemned to death by God cannot bring up the dead; only God Almighty can raise the dead. Samuel was dead and was buried in *Sheol* or mankind's grave. Concerning him as well as all the dead, Ecclesiastes 9:5, 10 says: "The dead know not anything, . . . Whatever thy hand findeth to do, do with thy might; for there is no work, nor device, nor knowledge, nor wisdom, in Sheol [hell, or, grave], whither thou goest."—*Da; AS; Dy.*

⁹ If Samuel refused to see Saul while he was alive, he would not let a condemned witch force

8. How did Saul now have a fraud practiced upon him, and why does this not prove the immortality of the human soul?

9. Why was Samuel not actually brought up but a trick performed?

him to come to see Saul after he was dead. If Jehovah refused to communicate a further message to Saul while Samuel was alive, would Jehovah let a witch, one of the seed of the Serpent, force Almighty God to communicate a message by Samuel after he was dead, and use the witch as a medium? Is a witch stronger than Almighty God? So this was all a trick of demonism. It was a demon that impersonated the dead Samuel and made a prediction in the face of the trend of developments and on the basis of what the demon knew of Saul's dealings with Samuel.

[10] Contrary to the demon's prediction, Saul's son Ishbosheth survived him, proving that the demon had not told the truth. Today it is no unusual thing for worried politicians to consult demons through spirit mediums for information on the future, just as unfaithful King Saul did. That is what false religion with its doctrine of human immortality does for mankind!—1 Samuel 28:4-19, *Da;* 2 Samuel 2:8; 1 Chronicles 8:33; see also Acts 16:16, *NW*.

[11] Now at last Jehovah God turned to the tribe of Judah for a king. Shortly after Samuel pronounced Jehovah's final rejection of King Saul, Jehovah sent him to Bethlehem-judah to anoint the shepherd lad David, the son of Jesse, to be the future king of Israel. He proved to be the man agreeable to God's own heart. Because of the popularity which David gained by killing the

---

10. What proved the demon prediction false, and yet who today similarly consult demons?
11. Whom did Jehovah have anointed to replace Saul, and how did Saul conduct himself toward that one?

Philistine giant Goliath with a stone from his shepherd's sling and winning other victories over the Philistines, Saul grew jealous of David, especially as he recognized in him God's favored one and the future king of Israel. Satan the Serpent, lying in wait for the seed of God's woman, goaded Saul on to outlaw David and hunt him down like an animal of chase. But in keeping with David's anointing, Jehovah preserved him from Saul's murderous hands. Finally Saul committed suicide, falling on his own sword at Mount Gilboa.

[12] The tribesmen of Judah now anointed David king over them at Hebron, in Judah's territory. Later, after opposition from the partisans of Saul's house was overcome, all of Israel's tribes anointed David as king over the whole nation. (2 Samuel 2:1-4; 5:1-3) David was thus anointed three times. He came to be called "Jehovah's anointed", or "Jehovah's Christ". As such, David became a prototype of the Seed of God's woman, Christ the King, the Messiah. He especially portrayed Christ ruling in the midst of his enemies during the "time of the end" of this world, our present time. (2 Samuel 19:21, AS; LXX; 23:1, 2) By his name "David", which means "beloved; dear", he pictured that Christ would be the beloved only-begotten Son of God; and by his birth at Bethlehem-judah he pictured that the Son of God would be born there as a man. In fact, the prophecies speak of the Messiah or Christ as "my servant David". (Ezekiel 34:23, 24; Matthew 3:17) David,

---

12. How did David now become king of all Israel, and whom did he picture in various aspects?

by his theocratic warfare, subdued all the enemies of his people in the Promised Land and extended their God-given inheritance to the boundaries which God had mentioned to Abraham. (Genesis 15:18-21) In this way David completed the subjugation of the land. Though the foes raged against his rule, he dashed them to pieces as with a rod of iron.

[13] After reigning at Hebron for seven and a half years, David captured the last resisting stronghold or citadel in Jerusalem and then made the entire city the national capital. Being such a man of faith in Jehovah God, David was fully devoted to his worship and endeavored to strengthen true religion in Israel.

[14] Owing to past interference by the Philistines the sacred ark of the covenant surmounted by its golden cherubim was not resting in the Most Holy of  the tent at Gibeon but was kept in custody at the home of a Levite. So King David had it brought up to Jerusalem and put in a tent he pitched for it on Mount Zion. As the ark was

13. What city did David make his capital?
14. How was Jehovah now represented as taking up residence on Mount Zion and reigning there?

being carried by the Levites to its resting place on Mount Zion, the Levites sang a song of King David's composition and said: "The world also is established that it cannot be moved. Let the heavens be glad, and let the earth rejoice; and let them say among the nations, Jehovah reigneth." (1 Chronicles 16:1-39, AS; Da) Thus Jehovah was symbolically represented as taking up his residence on Mount Zion and reigning there as King over Israel.

[15] Mount Zion or Jerusalem became by this a symbol of Jehovah's capital organization over the universe, namely, his theocratic kingdom in the hands of his anointed Seed of the woman, Christ. This is a heavenly organization, and Jerusalem or Mount Zion on earth was merely its visible symbol. It was called the "city of the great King". King David and his successors merely ruled there as representatives for the invisible Supreme King, and so they were said to sit upon the "throne of Jehovah". We remember that King Melchizedek, "priest of the most high God," had ruled at that city when it was known just as Salem.—Psalm 48:1; Matthew 5:35; 1 Chronicles 29:23, AS; Genesis 14:18; Psalm 76:1, 2.

[16] While David lived in a palace on Mount Zion he was dissatisfied to have Jehovah's ark of the testimony under a lowly tent. So he disclosed to the prophet Nathan his desire to build a worthy temple for it. But God said: "Thou shalt not build

15. What did Mount Zion thus come to symbolize, and on what did the kings there sit?
16. How did Jehovah now come to make a covenant with David, and for what was it?

a house unto my name, for thou art a man of war, and hast shed blood." (1 Chronicles 28:3, *Da*) It was then that Jehovah God made a covenant with David for a kingdom. By this the kingdom was to be established in David's family and he was to have a line of rulers sit on the throne until one of his descendants would come who was to rule forever.

[17] David's son was to build a material temple there at Jerusalem. But in this building work he was only a foreshadowing of the coming permanent Heir of the covenant who was to build a grander temple, a spiritual one. Jehovah said: "He shall build me an house, and I will stablish his throne for ever. I will be his father, and he shall be my son: and I will not take my mercy away from him, as I took it from him [Saul] that was before thee: but I will settle him in mine house and in my kingdom for ever: and his throne shall be established for evermore."—1 Chronicles 17:3-14.

[18] This fixes it unchangeably that the Christ, the Seed of God's woman, was to be an earthly descendant of King David. As a natural heir of his he was to receive the fulfillment of this covenant for the everlasting kingdom. In Psalm 89 Jehovah God said: "I also will make him my firstborn, the highest of the kings of the earth. My lovingkindness will I keep for him for evermore;

---

17. According to this, who was to build the temple and whom did he therefore foreshadow?
18. Whose descendant was the Seed of God's woman therefore to be, and so what would he be called, and how long would he rule?

and my covenant shall stand fast with him. My covenant will I not break, nor alter the thing that is gone out of my lips. Once have I sworn by my holiness: I will not lie unto David: His seed shall endure for ever, and his throne as the sun before me. It shall be established for ever as the moon, and as the faithful witness in the sky." (Psalm 89:27, 28, 34-37, *AS*) This heavenly kingdom of the Seed of God's woman or organization will rule over our earth for time and all eternity. It is the means by which the head of the Serpent will be crushed and the death-infected people be given a life-giving government of righteousness. Because of his descent from David this Seed on earth would be called "the son of David".—Matthew 1:1.

[19] According to the covenant for the everlasting kingdom this "Son of David" was to be infinitely higher than his forefather David. King David himself was led to recognize this unusual fact, and so he spoke prophetically of him as "my Lord (or Master)". He was inspired to sing: "Jehovah saith unto my Lord, Sit thou at my right hand, until I make thine enemies thy footstool. Jehovah will send forth the rod of thy strength out of Zion: Rule thou in the midst of thine enemies. Jehovah hath sworn, and will not repent: Thou art a priest for ever after the order of Melchizedek." (Psalm 110:1, 2, 4, *AS*) The Son of David was to be David's Lord or Superior because he was to sit enthroned at God's right hand in the heavens, not on an earthly Mount Zion but on the heavenly

---

19. How was he to be higher than David and where and for how long, and how was this foretold?

height symbolized by Mount Zion. Also David was only a king, and that for forty years, whereas his Son and Lord was to be both priest and king, just as Melchizedek of old had been. Also, he was to be such a royal priest forever, and was to be made such by Jehovah's sworn oath.

[20] Kingship and priesthood were to be united in this Son of David. Concerning him a later prophecy said: "Behold, the man whose name is the Branch: and he shall grow up out of his place; and he shall build the temple of Jehovah; even he shall build the temple of Jehovah; and he shall bear the glory, and shall sit and rule upon his throne; and he shall be a priest upon his throne." (Zechariah 6:12, 13, *AS*) In David's case the kingship had been separate from the priesthood, even as the priesthood in Israel had existed hundreds of years before the Davidic line of kings. This separation of kingship and priesthood in Israel allowed for the Aaronic priesthood to keep on functioning at Jerusalem even after there was an interruption in the rule of David's line and until the Messianic Son of David came. This royal Seed would be chiefly interested in clean religion and would build Jehovah's great temple.

---

20. What were to be united in him, but what did their separateness in Israel allow for?

CHAPTER XIII

Fall to Idolatry and Recovery

OWING to demon religion, the world today is filled with idolatry. This is just as true of Christendom as of that part of humanity which she calls "heathendom". This is leading on to world disaster, just as it led to disaster in the case of the nation of Israel. It was for solemn reasons that John, the last of Christ's twelve apostles, ended his letter with the words: "Little children, guard yourselves from idols."—1 John 5:21, *NW*.

² The second of the Ten Commandments forbade idolatry in Israel. When the glorious temple was built at Jerusalem by David's son Solomon, no image was made to represent Jehovah nor any set up in the Most Holy to be worshiped. The ark of the covenant was put into the Most Holy, and Jehovah was said to dwell between the two golden cherubim which surmounted the golden lid of the ark. Israel's high priest did not worship these golden cherubim, but from between them Jehovah by his invisible angel communicated messages at times to the high priest, the only one allowed to

1. Due to demon religion what is the world filled with now, and with what outcome of matters in view?
2. How was there no idolatry at the temple, even in connection with the golden cherubim, and to what extent did God dwell there?

enter the Most Holy. Jehovah did not actually dwell in that temple, but it was at most a footstool for him. The temple was, as David spoke of it, "a house of rest for the ark of the covenant of Jehovah and for the footstool of our God." "Thus saith Jehovah: The heavens are my throne, and the earth is my footstool."—1 Chronicles 28:2 and Isaiah 66:1, *Da; AS;* 2 Chronicles 5:2-10.

³ In harmony with the covenant which Jehovah made with David for the everlasting kingdom his son Solomon, whose name means "peaceful", built the temple in seven and a half years' time. "And Solomon began to build the house of Jehovah at Jerusalem on mount Moriah, where he appeared to David his father, in the place that David had prepared in the threshingfloor of Ornan the Jebusite. And he began to build on the second of the second month, in the fourth year of his reign." (1 Kings 6:37, 38; 2 Chronicles 3:1, 2, *Da*) Israel's kings counted the years of their reign from Nisan, the first month of the year, in the spring. Consequently, if Solomon began reigning in the fall of the previous year to fill out the remainder of that year for his father David, it was really about three and a half years after Solomon began reigning that he came to the temple work.

⁴ When the priests had carried the ark of the covenant into the Most Holy and deposited it there and came out, the account tells us, "the cloud

---

3. Who built the temple, when did he come to the temple work, and how long was it in building?
4. What occurred at the temple's dedication after installing the ark, and what request did Solomon make in prayer to God?

filled the house of Jehovah, so that the priests could not stand to minister by reason of the cloud; for the glory of Jehovah filled the house of Jehovah." Then Solomon prayed worshipfully and said: "But will God in very deed dwell on the earth? behold, heaven and the heaven of heavens cannot contain thee; how much less this house that I have builded!" So Solomon asked that Jehovah would nevertheless respect and hear prayer that was made at this temple. He asked that even a non-Israelite foreigner who turned with faith and good will to Jehovah as God and prayed there might be heard; "Hear thou in heaven thy dwelling-place, and do according to all that the foreigner calleth to thee for; that all the peoples of the earth may know thy name, to fear thee, as doth thy people Israel, and that they may know that this house which I have built is called by thy name." (1 Kings 8:3-43, *AS*) This request of Solomon gives hearty assurance today to people of good will who turn to Jehovah and worship and pray to him as the living, true God. Said Jehovah, and Jesus Christ centuries afterward quoted his words: "My house shall be called a house of prayer for all peoples." —Isaiah 56:7, *AS;* Mark 11:17.

[5] Visible evidence was given that the Most High God had sanctified this house to his service and that its altar was an acceptable place to offer sacrifice. For, when Solomon had ended praying, "the fire came down from the heavens and con-

---

5. What evidence from heaven was given of the acceptableness of the temple altar, and how many temples and altars are authorized?

sumed the burnt-offering and the sacrifices; and
the glory of Jehovah filled the house. And the
priests could not enter into the house of Jehovah,
because the glory of Jehovah filled Jehovah's
house." The Most High God put his name upon
this house. He did not authorize many such temples to be built either at Jerusalem or also in other cities nor many altars to be made, to correspond
with the hundreds of churches, for instance, in
Rome, with their hundreds of altars for the celebration of the sacrifice of the mass. The true God
had only one temple and one altar, at the holy
city where he had put his name. So, too, now he
has only one spiritual temple and one altar where
the one acceptable sacrifice has been made by his
Christ. It was at this one temple in Jerusalem
that the Israelites were commanded to assemble
three times a year for the feasts, and at this altar
alone the day of a t o n e m e n t was celebrated.
—2 Chronicles 7:1, 2, *Da*.

⁶ How g l o r i o u s the beginning of Solomon's
reign, but how sad its end! For not sticking strictly to the divine instructions respecting kings of
Israel Solomon in his old age was turned to idol
worship, to please his wives. According to the
promises in the Kingdom covenant with David,
the royal line was not cut off but ten tribes were
cut off from the rule of David's line. This split
occurred early in the reign of Solomon's son Reho-
boam. A northern kingdom of the ten seceding

---

6. (a) How did Solomon's reign end and with what consequences? (b) When did ruin come on the northern
kingdom of Israel, and why?

tribes of Israel was set up with its own king and capital; and only the tribes of Judah and Benjamin, together with the Levites, remained loyal to David's line. Not themselves taking to heart the cause of this national calamity, apostate religion, the northern kingdom of Israel turned to idolatry to hold its people away from Jehovah's worship at the foreign capital Jerusalem. National ruin may have been 257 years in coming, but that was because of the merciful interest and patience of Jehovah God. Just the same, it came unavoidably, and the northern kingdom of Israel fell before the Assyrians, the royal capital Samaria was destroyed, and the surviving Israelites were deported and transplanted in provinces of Assyria. Read 2 Kings 17:1-23 and learn the ruinous cause —apostate religion!

[7] Because the national organization was married to Jehovah like a wife to a husband, this forsaking of his worship and turning to idols and demon gods was spiritual adultery. So Jehovah divorced the northern kingdom of Israel and let her be taken captive by Assyria in 740 B.C. But, then, what about the kingdom of Judah with her kings of David's line and her temple of Jehovah? Would she, too, deserve to be divorced for spiritual adultery and turned over to her foes whose gods she preferred to Jehovah? Or would she profit from the warning lesson furnished by her sister kingdom of Israel and remain faithful to the clean

7. How did Jehovah divorce the northern kingdom of Israel, and what shows whether Judah heeded her warning example?

religion in harmony with Jehovah's revelation? Solomon had caused irreparable damage to the national interests by his lapse into demon worship. After him came nineteen kings of the line of David, with a continual battle to keep that kingdom of Judah from being overwhelmed by devil religion. Despite the temporary recovery to Jehovah's worship in the days of good King Josiah, Jehovah gave notice that Judah's national bent toward apostasy had leaned over far enough and that its existence as an independent kingdom was doomed.

[8] Forty years before the grievous calamity fell Jehovah sent his prophet Jeremiah for a final witness. Hear him describe the situation: "The LORD said to me in the days of Josiah the king: 'Have you seen what apostate Israel did, how she went up every high mountain and under every spreading tree, and played the harlot there? I thought, "After she has done all these things, she will return to me"; but she did not return. And though her faithless sister Judah saw that, for all the adulteries that apostate Israel had committed, I put her away, and gave her a writ of divorce, yet her faithless sister Judah was not afraid, but likewise went and played the harlot, polluting the land with her wanton harlotry, and committing adultery with stones and blocks of wood. In spite of all that happened, her faithless sister Judah did not return to me in sincerity, but in sheer

---

8. For how long did Jeremiah give Judah a final witness, and how did he show Israel more in the right in her course than Judah?

hypocrisy,' is the oracle of the LORD. So the LORD said to me, 'Apostate Israel has proved herself more in the right than faithless Judah.' " (Jeremiah 3:6-11, *AT*) Judah's marriage with Jehovah God was now under strain.

⁹ The foresighted God of heaven knew that the nation of Judah would not turn back. So it was principally for the benefit of a faithful remnant of Jews who would repent and turn to him that he inspired Jeremiah to continue on with these words: "Return, O backsliding [or, apostate] children, saith Jehovah; for I am a husband unto you: and I will take you one of a city, and two of a family, and I will bring you to Zion. And I will give you shepherds according to my heart, who shall feed you with knowledge and understanding. . . . At that time they shall call Jerusalem the throne of Jehovah; and all the nations shall be gathered unto it, to the name of Jehovah, to Jerusalem: neither shall they walk any more after the stubbornness of their evil heart. In those days the house of Judah shall walk with the house of Israel, and they shall come together out of the land of the north to the land that I gave for an inheritance unto your fathers."—Jeremiah 3:14-18, *AS*.

¹⁰ As suggested in this very prophecy, the destroyers of Judah and Jerusalem came out of the north, out of Babylon. In Jeremiah's day Baby-

9. For whose benefit did Jehovah through Jeremiah offer an invitation to return to the heavenly husband of Judah?
10. What had now become Jerusalem's rival, and what did Satan move its king to want to do at Jerusalem?

lon had become the dominant world power under Emperor Nebuchadnezzar, having overthrown Assyria in 632 B.C. and then defeated the hosts of Egypt at the battle of Carchemish in 625 B.C. (Nahum 3:7, 18; Jeremiah 46:1, 2) Babylon, the seat and mother of devil religion from the days of Nimrod, was Satan the Serpent's rival against Jerusalem, the seat of Jehovah's worship. Hence Satan the Devil moved Babylon's king to want to ascend the heights of Jerusalem, destroy her temple, show himself superior to her royal stars or princes, and display himself as a match for Jehovah, and so be like the Most High God.—Isaiah 14:4, 13, 14.

[11] In the sixth year before Jerusalem's end came the prophet Ezekiel saw by vision the desecrations committed in God's temple at Jerusalem. In vision he was brought to the north gate leading to the temple's inner court, where the apostates had set up an image of resentment that caused divine resentment. "So I raised my eyes to the north, and lo! north of the altar-gate, at the entrance, stood this image of resentment. Then he said to me, 'O mortal man, do you see what they are doing? Do you see the great abominations which the house of Israel are doing here, forcing me away from my sanctuary? You shall see still greater abominations than these.' " Then Jehovah showed him an inner temple chamber where depicted on the walls were all kinds of detestable forms of reptiles and beasts, and before them

11, 12. What visions of the temple's desecration were given Ezekiel?

seventy older Israelites of influence were burning incense. Shocking, such a thing in Jehovah's nominal temple? But look over there at the north-ward gate of his temple. Listen to those women sitting there weeping for that Babylonian god, Tammuz, Nimrod deified under another name.

[12] Now into the temple's inner court, please! See those twenty-five Israelites between the tem-ple vestibule and the bronze altar. With their backs toward Jehovah's temple, they are facing the sun in the east and worshiping it, like regular Babylonians and Egyptians. (Ezekiel 8:3-16, *AT*) Those apostates never asked themselves Paul's question: "What agreement does God's temple have with idols?" If Jesus Christ had been there he would have said as he did respecting the de-filed temple of Jerusalem in his day: "Your house is abandoned to you." It was no fetish which could save Jerusalem from destruction.—2 Corin-thians 6:16 and Matthew 23:38, *NW*.

[13] For a third time now Nebuchadnezzar king of Babylon came up against Jerusalem and laid siege to it. In 607 B.C., in the eleventh year of wicked Zedekiah's reign, Jerusalem fell and was destroyed, together with her gorgeous temple. The sacred implements of worship were carried from it and deposited in the temples of Babylon, and the surviving Jews were carried off into exile. Those that tried to stay on in the land finally fled down to Egypt. Now for seventy years the land of Judah and Jerusalem lay desolate without man or domes-

---

13. How did Jerusalem's fall and desolation come, and for what cause?

ticated beast. With that year 607 B.C. the theocratic kingdom in Judah was overturned, and a king of David's line no longer sat on the "throne of Jehovah". So that year the "appointed times of the nations" began, seven of them, amounting to 2,520 years, which makes the entire period end in the fall of 1914 (A.D.). We do not digress here to call attention to the significance of the date 1914. Millions of this present generation are painfully aware of World War I, which broke out that year and since which year this world has never been the same. The point not to forget is this: What caused the destruction of Jerusalem and her temple and the slaughter and exile of her people in 607 B.C. was apostate religion. Jehovah God does not let himself be mocked with it, no more now than he did back there.—2 Kings 25:1-26; Luke 21:24, *NW;* Daniel 4:16, 23, 25, 32.

[14] One of the most outstanding features of later Bible prophecy is that a faithful remnant would return from exile and captivity to the place where God had placed his name and would there serve him again in unbreakable devotion. Over a century before this the prophet Isaiah had foretold the Jews' exile in Babylon and said: "Unless the LORD of hosts had left us a handful of survivors, we should have become like Sodom, we should have resembled Gomorrah." Sodom and Gomorrah had been wiped out long ago by a rain of fire and sulphur from the skies. In further assurance that

14. What spared the Israelites from being like Sodom and Gomorrah, and from where was the assembling to take place, and to where?

a little group would stay faithful and be restored to the Promised Land Isaiah said: "A remnant will return—the remnant of Jacob—to the Mighty God. For though your people, O Israel, be like the sand of the sea, only a remnant of them will return. . . . On that day will the LORD once more raise his hand to recover the remnant that remains of his people, from Assyria and from Egypt, from Pathros and from Ethiopia, from Elam and from Shinar, from Hamath and from the coast-lands of the sea. He will raise a signal to the nations, and will gather the outcasts of Israel; and the scattered daughters of Judah will he assemble from the four corners of the earth."—Isaiah 1:9; 10:21, 22; 11:11, 12, *AT;* also Micah 2:12; Zephaniah 3:13.

[15] It was foretold that Judah and Jerusalem would lie desolate seventy years, and so it was foreknown just when this devoted remnant would be set free from Babylon. This oppressive government itself would not let its prisoners go free, and hence it was necessary for Jehovah to bring about Babylon's overthrow. He did so, and by the very conqueror whom he had foretold, Cyrus the Persian: "Thus saith Jehovah to his anointed, to Cyrus, whose right hand I have holden, to subdue nations before him, . . . he shall build my city, and he shall let my exiles go free, not for price nor reward, saith Jehovah of hosts." (Isaiah 45:1-13, *AS*) Cyrus and his uncle, Darius the Mede, overthrew Babylon in 539 B.C.; and in 537 B.C.

---

15. After how long a desolation of the land and how was the return of the remnant brought about?

Cyrus let the Jewish remnant return to Jerusalem to rebuild Jehovah's temple and renew his worship there. Then was the time for the remnant, restored to their beloved land, to fulfill this prophetic command by Isaiah:

16 "Thou shalt take up this parable against the king of Babylon, and say, How hath the oppressor ceased! the golden city ceased! How art thou fallen from heaven, O day-star, son of the morning! how art thou cut down to the ground, that didst lay low the nations! And thou saidst in thy heart, I will ascend into heaven, I will exalt my throne above the stars of God [Judah's kings who sat on the 'throne of Jehovah']; and I will sit upon the mount [Zion] of congregation, in the uttermost parts of the north; I will ascend above the heights of the clouds; I will make myself like the Most High. Yet thou shalt be brought down to Sheol [the grave], to the uttermost parts of the pit. They that see thee shall gaze at thee, they shall consider thee, saying, Is this the man that made the earth to tremble, that did shake kingdoms; that made the world as a wilderness, and overthrew the cities thereof; that let not loose his prisoners to their home?"—Isaiah 14:4, 12-17, AS.

17 Thus seventeen centuries after Nimrod its first king, Jehovah God vindicated himself against Babylon and demonstrated his universal sovereignty. He broke the power of that seemingly in-

16. What command given in prophecy through Isaiah did the remnant then fulfill?
17. How did Jehovah thus vindicate himself over Babylon, and what did he say to the remnant regarding their mother's divorce?

vincible third world power over his people. To the remnant in Babylon he said: "Thus saith Jehovah, Where is the bill of your mother's divorcement, wherewith I have put her away? or which of my creditors is it to whom I have sold you? Behold, for your iniquities were ye sold, and for your transgressions was your mother put away."

[18] Their national organization, their mother, had been put away, not because of Jehovah's breaking his covenant and starting divorce proceedings, but because of the iniquities and transgressions of her children against the Law covenant. Hence the honest-hearted remnant repented and turned to Jehovah the great husband of their organization. They prayed for a renewal of his husbandly relations with them in their homeland. So at the end of the seventy years of desolation Jehovah's prophetic command applied to their mother organization: "Shake thyself from the dust; arise, sit on thy throne, O Jerusalem: loose thyself from the bonds of thy neck, O captive daughter of Zion. For thus saith Jehovah, Ye were sold for nought; and ye shall be redeemed without money." Then telling them to leave Babylon and its contaminations, he said: "Depart ye, depart ye, go ye out from thence, touch no unclean thing; go ye out of the midst of her; cleanse yourselves, ye that bear the vessels of Jehovah. For ye shall not go out in haste, neither shall ye go by flight: for Jehovah will go before you; and the God of Israel

---

18. Why had Jehovah put away their mother, but at the end of her desolation what commands did he give affecting the remnant?

will be your rearward."—Isaiah 50:1 and 52:2, 3, 11, 12, *AS*.

[19] For his own name's sake Jehovah restored his people. At the end of the seventy years' desolation in 537 B.C. about 50,000 Jews departed from Babylon with the vessels which Babylon had robbed from Jehovah's temple at Jerusalem. Their return was primarily to restore his worship at the place where he had chosen to put his name. Realizing now the chief importance of pure religion in the life of the nation, the Jews, together with proselytes of good will, at once went to rebuilding the temple of God their Deliverer on its old location. The altar was first set up in the inner-court space and, as it was the seventh Jewish month, the joyous feast of tabernacles was celebrated for the seven days of it. Then, after considerable interference by their enemies over many years, they finally brought the entire temple to completion under their Jewish governor Zerubbabel and in the sixth year of the reign of the Persian king Darius. The prophets Haggai and Zechariah greatly encouraged them to this successful conclusion.—Ezra 2:64 to 3:13; 6:14, 15.

[20] All this interests us today, for it foreshadowed the restoring of a faithful remnant from mystic Babylon and the renewal of the pure worship of Jehovah God in these modern days.

---

19. How was Jehovah's worship restored to the land of Judah and the temple completed?
20. Because of foreshadowing what does this interest us today?

CHAPTER XIV

The Spread of Hinduism

THE first hints that the nation of Israel had any connections with India, the land of Hinduism, were the ivory, apes and peacocks which King - Solomon imported in his fleet of Tarshish ships, in the eleventh c e n t u r y B.C. (1 Kings 10:22; 2 Chronicles 9:21) The Hebrew and Sanscrit words for peacock and ape bear a relationship to one another. For instance, the Hebrew word *koph* corresponds with the Sanscrit word *kapi* and means both the tailless ape and the tailed monkey. In India the monkey is worshiped as a god. But it was by becoming a province of the Persian empire that the land of Israel had more of a tie with the land of Hinduism, for the Persian empire was finally expanded to include one hundred and twenty-seven provinces and to extend from Ethiopia on the southwest over to India on the far east, and so was a land bridge between India and Israel. When in the fifth century B.C. in the reign of Xerxes the Great the decree was issued by his Prime Minister Haman for all Jews throughout the empire to be massacred on the 13th day of the 12th month (Adar) of that

1. According to Bible history what connections did the land of Israel have with India, Jews there being affected in Xerxes' reign?

year, it included any Jews who might be in the Indian province. Prompt courageous action by Queen Esther and her Jewish cousin Mordecai turned the tables on Haman and saved the day for the imperiled Jews.—Esther 1:1; 8:9.

[2] Since 1947 that part of India where the Hindu religion predominates is called Hindustan. The beginnings of Hinduism are thought to be shrouded in darkness, but the evidence is that it sprang from Babylon, Nimrod's royal capital. When Jehovah God defeated the intentions of the people in building the city and tower of Babel by confusing their language, they scattered, dropping the idea of Babylon as a world capital for holding all the people together in oneness of language as well as of political allegiance. Some of these moved eastward and settled on the sub-continental Indian peninsula. Though they carried a changed language with them, they still bore the traditions of the false religion which they had held in common at Babylon. They knew of the global deluge of Noah's day. They knew how he and his immediate family had survived in the ark and given a new start to the human race. Through Noah, who practiced the revealed religion of Jehovah God, they knew of the divine promise in Eden, that the seed of the woman was to suffer a heel wound from the Serpent who had tempted Eve, but the seed was to triumph at last over the Serpent and crush his head. Noah was still living in the days of the tower-building fiasco.

---

2. Where did Hinduism have its real start, and how did it take root in India?

[3] Nimrod was in rebellion against Noah who worshiped Jehovah as God. From all the religions that have been built around Nimrod, he was put to a violent death, whether at the instance of Noah is not known. Nimrod by his political and hunting exploits had made himself a god in the eyes of his subjects. When he died, his wife Semiramis had him deified, claiming he had not died but was transferred to immortal heavenly life among the stars. To him she applied the Edenic promise of the seed that was to have his heel bruised, and she was the woman who had produced this seed for mankind's delivery from the Serpent. So the settlers of India carried this tradition of false religion with them from Babylon, as well as other distortions of the truth concerning the true God, the deluge, man's fall into sin and mankind's future destiny.

[4] To illustrate, take the Indian triad or trinity, called *trimúrti,* meaning "three forms". It is composed of Brahma the Creator, Vishnu the Preserver, and Siva the Destroyer. Together, the three compose the one god Brahm. Brahma is the supreme god of the Hindus, but actually he is little worshiped, and it is said that in all of India there are only two temples devoted to him. But in him the Hindus preserved some conception of the true Creator, his perfections, his graciousness, for the name was of Hebrew derivation. It is simply the Hebrew word *Raham,* meaning "the merciful or compassionate one", with the digamma (soft V-sound) in front. Because one's intestines tremble at times in compassion, it came also to mean

---

3. What traditions of false religion did those settling in India carry with them?
4. How is this illustrated in Brahma and Vishnu of the Hindu trinity?

"the womb, or, bowels". So Brahma was viewed as the great "womb" from which all forms of life that are conceived in the womb came. The name corresponds to *Er-Rahman,* meaning "The all-merciful one", the name which the Turks apply to their god. As for Vishnu the Preserver, he is famed for having miraculously preserved one righteous family at the time that the world was flooded. His name is the Sanscrit form of the Chaldee *Ish-nuh,* with the digamma prefixed, and which means "the man Noah" or "the man of rest". How appropriate that one of Vishnu's ten avatárs (or descents from heaven and incarnations) should be that of a fish which survives through water!

[5] The eighth and most celebrated of the incarnations or avatárs of Vishnu was that in the person of Krishna. His name has nothing to do with "Christ", which is a Greek word and means "Anointed". Krishna is the Sanscrit word meaning "black", and was the name given to Vishnu's incarnation either because the body he assumed was black or because Vishnu's distinguishing color was black, as that of Brahma was red and that of Siva was white. The infant Krishna, or *black* god, is represented in India at the breast of the goddess Devaki and is shown with woolly hair and marked Negro features. How well this matches Nimrod who was the son of Cush, whose name means "black"! In sculptures in one of the oldest of the Hindu pagodas Krishna is shown trampling upon the serpent's head and also in another pose as wrapped about by the serpent and being bitten at the heel by it. Krishna's body is black, but a

5. What does Krishna's name mean, and how was he represented as being the seed of the woman?

halo of glory is about his head. This would picture the woman's seed as coming through the Hamitic branch of Noah's family instead of through the Shemitic branch which Noah blessed. Krishnaism, it must be said, does not appear in the Vedas, the most ancient Hindu scriptures.

[6] As to Siva, the third member of the triune Brahm, he is pictured not only as the Destroyer but also as the Reproducer or Re-creator, because what is destroyed must be re-created, death being thought to be a passing of a person to a new form of life. Hence Siva is worshiped under the form of the linga, the phallic emblem of the male reproductive organ. This contradiction of qualities in Siva is based on the Hindu idea that there is no annihilation, but there is merely a transformation, a passing from one condition into another because of the supposed immortality of the human soul. So Siva is styled the Bright or Happy One, just as when people in Christendom say that "death is a friend", in flat contradiction to Paul at 1 Corinthians 15:26, where he calls death the "last enemy". Siva's name does not occur in the Vedas, but he is fully described in the sacred Puranas. The Hindus are thus seen to have had the trinity doctrine many c e n t u r i e s before Christendom adopted it. A triangle is a symbol of it to them. Christendom b o r r o w e d the doctrine from the same Babylonish sources as did the Hindus.

[7] The Vedas are the four Books of Knowledge of the Hindus and form their "Scriptures". The essential teaching of the Vedas is the soul's one-

6. As for Siva, the third member of the Hindu trinity, what contradiction of qualities are represented in him, and on what basis?
7. What are the Vedas, and what do they teach on creation, liberation and the soul?

ness with what they conceive to be the deity or godhead. Hindu philosophy is that this tangible universe of which we are a part is a creation that is to dissolve and return to what is called its "seed state". Time, space and the forces of cause and effect do not belong to eternity. However, there are great world cycles (*yuga*) and in these cycles names and forms repeat themselves. The final goal of the soul is liberation, and its liberation lies in going beyond or out of reach of this world-cycle process. Souls are without beginning and without end and so can attain this liberation. As the *Katha Upanishad* says: "The soul is not born, nor does it die. It has not come from anywhere nor has it produced anything. It is unborn, eternal, everlasting, ancient; it is not slain though the body is slain. If the slayer thinks of slaying the soul, and if the slain person thinks that the soul is dead, both have missed the truth. The soul slays not nor is slain. The soul, smaller than the small and greater than the great, is hidden in the hearts of all living creatures." How very much this resembles the definition of the human soul given by Christendom's clergy!

[8] What, then, produced the finite, material forms of creation? The *Upanishad* says it was ignorance or *maya*. This power resided in the deity, Brahman, the Ultimate Reality, and it projected the material universe and all the material forms it displays. This great, formless, sexless, changeless spirit pervades all these forms. It appears as finite forms subject to the various experiences of existence. As the real soul is immortal, it goes through countless incarnations, passing from one material

---

8. What produced the finite, material forms, and how or by what process does the soul gain eventual liberation?

substance or body at death and passing into another. With each birth or transition the soul adds a little more to its self-merit. Finally it goes beyond the power of this illusory law of cause and effect and thereby attains immortality and freedom in the real sense. When it does this, it combines or merges with the great spirit, the deity, the Ultimate Reality. Every soul is therefore potentially divine. The free soul cannot be deluded by the mere appearance of things. But after the death of the body, the soul, which has been freed from ignorance, desire and attachment to material things, becomes swallowed up in the Supreme Spirit and thus attains complete liberation. So reincarnation is a process leading toward perfection of soul.

[9] The Hindu swamis point out that "Hinduism is noted for its catholic and universal outlook", and that "the *Bhagavad Gita* declares that all religions are strung on the Lord like pearls on a necklace. In whatever way people offer their worship to the Lord, He accepts it. All religions lead to the same Truth. Ramakrishna repeatedly said that the different religions are only different paths leading to the same spiritual experience of peace and blessedness. . . . The Hindu attitude toward other religions is that of respect and not of mere tolerance, much less of rivalry". However, we must observe that this was not demonstrated in the sanguinary race and religious riots that followed the establishment of Hindustan and Pakistan in 1947. Believing in reincarnation, they claim that "a Hindu accepts Christ, too, as an incarnation".

---

9. What view is Hinduism said to take of all religions? But how was this contradicted?

[10] But how strange and inconsistent this, since Jesus Christ taught doctrines which are utterly contradictory to such Hindu philosophy! If there is "Absolute Reality", then there must be absolute truth, and this allows no room for contradictions such as exist between the hundreds of religions. Jesus Christ assured us through his apostles that "it is impossible for God to lie" and that "he remains faithful, for he cannot deny himself". "With him there is not a variation of the turning of the shadow."—Hebrews 6:18; Titus 1:2; 2 Timothy 2:11-13 and James 1:17, *NW*.

[11] Jesus Christ did not say his heavenly Father was an all-pervasive, dormant or sleepy spirit, but described him as the most active person in all the universe. Said he: "My Father has kept working until now, and I keep working." (John 5:17, *NW*) Also his Father does not absorb souls into himself. All souls or living creatures that he judges worthy of eternal life he maintains in a soul-existence separate from himself, but in harmony with himself and dependent upon him. Those whom he judges undeserving of life in the new world he destroys. Hence Jesus said to his followers: "Do not become fearful of those who kill the body but can not kill the soul; but rather be in fear of him that can destroy both soul and body in Gehenna [the place of annihilation]." He did not agree that all religions were just different paths leading to the same truth and same spiritual experience of peace and blessedness. He warned his followers: "Go in through the narrow

10. Why is a Hindu inconsistent in claiming to accept Christ as an incarnation, in view of the absolute truth? 11. How did Jesus Christ describe his heavenly Father, the destiny of human souls, and the matter of many religions?

gate; because broad and spacious is the road leading off into destruction, and many are the ones
going in through it; whereas narrow is the gate
and cramped the road leading off into life, and
few are the ones finding it." (Matthew 10:28;
7:13, 14, NW) All this multitude of religions has
worked, not for peace, harmony, unity, mutual
happiness, but for division and disorder and war;
and "God is a God, not of disorder, but of peace".
—1 Corinthians 14:33, NW.

¹² Hindu belief and practice are therefore seen
to be saturated with animism, that is to say, the
belief that all natural objects and the universe itself possess a soul; that all objects have a natural
life or vitality and are endowed with a soul. To
the Hindu mind it is hard to get the idea of a
personal God with an individual existence. But
the Hindu will have to admit that, say, the house
in which he lives was built by some human creature with an individual body of a definite form.
The house did not put itself together because it
was pervaded by some everywhere-existing soul.
It took the intelligence and ability of some individual person to put it up. If that is the case with
such a small simple thing as a house, then how
much more so would it be the case with the immense visible universe which shows such superhuman power and intelligence? Clinging to his
idea that the great spirit pervades everything, the
Hindu will insist that the deity is made up of all
things of the universe. The house in which you
live is therefore deserving of as much honor as
you, or even more honor than you, because it is a

12. Why does belief in animism make it hard for Hindus to get the idea of a personal God? Why are they
wrong in worshiping what they make?

part of the godhead or deity. But, we ask, how can that be, when man is the builder of the house? How could the thing he makes be greater or more worshipful than himself? The apostle Paul stated the rule: "He who constructs it has more honor than the house. Of course, every house is constructed by someone, but he that constructed all things is God."—Hebrews 3:3, 4, *NW*.

[13] Under the influence of animism the Hindu will retort: "But the house is not inanimate, for it can think and has life. Only the trouble is that our senses are so dull, we cannot pick up the waves of its vitality and thought. This is why the Hindu has worshipful respect for the house or other object." But this contradicts proved science in this electronic age when men can visualize even the construction of the atom, and can measure microwaves. A house as a whole, or the parts making it up, does not possess any of the five senses which we humans have. It does not have any brain and hence cannot be or do what the credulous Hindu believes. Why, if the deity or godhead is the sum of all things and all things make up god, then why worship and pray to anything at all? If each individual thing is only a part of god, how can it answer for the whole god? If all corrupting, corroding things are part of god, it follows that god is in that same condition, corrupt, diseased, ill and feeling pain, because all the human family who are part of god are in such a condition. Claiming that all this is mere ignorance (*maya*) does not remove it, no more than the Christian Scientist by similar reasoning removes evil. We humans

---

13. How are the Hindus unreasonable in claiming all objects have thought and life, are part of god and are to be worshiped for that?

are superior to cows, monkeys, and other animals and also objects like wood and stone images, and so if man is obligated to worship them because they are a part of the godhead, why do they not in turn worship man for the same reason? Even in a human family, is it the father that must worship his daughter, or is it the daughter that must show deep respect for the father who transmitted life to her? So the Hindu reasoning is lopsided. It is unreasonable. It is not based upon fact.

[14] To be practical now: What has Hinduism done for that vast portion of mankind among whom it predominates? Hindu society is divided up into four castes: (1) the *Brahmins,* the custodians of learning and spiritual tradition; (2) the *Kshatriyas,* the kings and military protectors; (3) the *Vaisyas,* the agriculturalists, cattle-raisers and tradesmen; and (4) the *Sudras,* the servants and manual laborers. There are 3,000 divisions of these main castes, and then 10,000 further subdivisions. Being of any caste is hereditary. *Karma,* or causality, determines one's birth into this or that caste; that is, what one did in the previous life determines what one is in one's present incarnation. For many ages the *Brahmins,* to exalt and fasten themselves as a priestly, half-divine class to whom the other castes should bow down, have taught that the other castes came from the arms and body and feet of Brahma but that they alone came from the mouth of Brahma the Creator.

[15] From this we see that a hierarchical, political and economic system has been bound to the Hindu

---

14. What has Hinduism done to the society of its believers, and what determines this division of society?
15. What kind of system has thus been bound on the Hindu people, and how was some relief constitutionally provided in 1948?

people from which they cannot get loose, because it is claimed to be religious. Rebellion and refusal to submit to the rules and restrictions of it causes persons to become outcastes, which puts them in a position shunned by all caste members, as "untouchables". Till recently there were forty million of such in India. In December, 1948, the Hindustan Constituent Assembly adopted an article in the new Indian Constitution which outlaws "untouchability" and permits the outcastes to leave their ghettos, use village wells, bathe in the rivers and enjoy other privileges as citizens. By the new draft Constitution there must be no discrimination because of religion, race, caste or sect.

[16] There are thought to be 330,000,000 gods and goddesses, and these are worshiped in some 10,000 temples, in many cases with images and rites which shock the decency of moral, self-respecting people. While to Brahmins the ultimate goal *nirvana* means the soul's merging into the universal spirit Brahm, to the lower castes *nirvana* means a life of abandonment and joy in another world. Hinduism has been carried to many countries and has gained converts, so that today about 12 out of every 100 persons are Hindus. But now, with all other religions of Babylonish origin, Hinduism has reached the crisis and is destined to pass away with this world. The expecting of a new incarnation or materialization of their god Vishnu the Preserver as a man called Kalkin will prove to be a forlorn hope and will leave Hindus disillusioned as this world goes into destruction with Siva unable to re-create it.

16. How have deities and temples multiplied, what is *nirvana* taken to mean by some, and how will Hinduism result in disillusionment?

CHAPTER XV

Buddhism, a Salvation by Psychology

ABOUT the time that the city of Jerusalem was undergoing its seventy years of desolation and the Jews were languishing in exile in Babylonia, that is, in the sixth century B.C., a religious reform movement was started in India. The prime mover of it was a Hindu who came to be called Buddha. That he was actually a historical person, critics have expressed a doubt. The Buddhist scriptures contain what most persons would regard as fantastic legends about his birth. For instance, that when the dream foretelling his birth was interpreted, an earthquake occurred, thirty-two miracles took place, including healing the blind, deaf, dumb and lame in the Sakya kingdom, and the fires in all hells were put out. Then when the boy was born to Queen Maya, he was able to stand up and be worshiped by gods and men, then to take seven steps to the north and at the seventh step to stop and call out with a lion-like roar, "I am the chief of the world." When, after the queen mother died, his aunt took the infant to the temple, he recited three verses to remind her no god in that temple was equal to himself, and as soon as he arrived, all the temple idols fell down at his feet. These legends were no doubt spun out of the realms of unreality in order

1. What religious reform was begun in India in the sixth century B.C., and what legends make the actuality of its founder doubtful?

203

to impress the students of Buddhism with what an unusual person he was even from birth.

[2] By a careful comparison of the Buddhist scriptures in the Pali language (Buddha's Indian dialect) with longer-known Sanscrit writings on the subject, researchers have come to the following conclusions regarding him. His personal name was supposed to be Siddhartha, meaning "He whose aim is accomplished". He was an Indian prince of the Sakya tribe and of its Gautama clan. Sometimes he is called Sakyamuni, "the wise man of the Sakyas," but more frequently Gotama (Pali) or Gautama (Sanscrit). After he was "enlightened" with his philosophy, he was called Gautama the Buddha, meaning "Gautama the awake or enlightened". Prior to this enlightenment he was called the Bodhisattva, meaning "one destined for enlightenment". Long protected from sights of sorrow and suffering, he finally came upon an old man, a seriously sick man, a dead body, and a religious self-mortifier. This led him to wondering why evil and suffering existed. About thirty years of age he abandoned his family for a religious life of trying to solve this mystery for himself. In the very week that his wife presented him with their first son he deserted them. After a farewell look at them sleeping he fled past his sleeping female minstrels and rode off into the night. That was in 533 B.C.

[3] So he renounced his pampered palace life and became a pauper. He adopted the yellow robe, which reminds us how the Roman Catholic car-

2. By what various names is he called, and why? And what led him to take up a religious life?
3. What features of Buddhism did he now establish, and how did he eventually come by his enlightenment and become Buddha?

dinals later adopted the yellow robe until one of them had an unfortunate encounter with a despised Jew, after which the cardinals changed to red. He shaved his head and became called the "Shaved-head" and established an order of shaved-head monks like himself, just like the later shaved-head monks of Christendom. Besides his razor, he carried with him a begging-bowl and instituted an order of religious beggars. To probe into the secret of the cause of human suffering, old age and death, he inflicted tortures on himself and also tried going into a trance by not breathing. All this did not work. So he turned to a course of moderation, or what he called the Middle Way of temperance. Finally, after seven years of fruitless search, he sat down under a bo tree or wild fig tree at Gaya, determined to keep sitting there until he ascertained the truth. For four to seven weeks he remained there, and then, one night, his enlightenment came and he became Buddha.

[4] Had Gautama had the inspired Hebrew Scriptures, which began with the prophet Moses nine hundred years before this and which were by now almost complete, he would not have had to go to all this personal trouble to work up a personal philosophy on how and why wickedness, suffering and death invaded mankind. So what Gautama considered his "enlightenment" was not according to sacred Hebrew writings. What was his revelation? That all suffering is caused by desire and hence when a person stops craving anything, peace comes to his restless soul. Thus we see that he came to this conclusion by a process of psychol-

4. Why was his "enlightenment" not in harmony with Hebrew Scripture, and how did he sum up his discoveries in four propositions?

ogy. His idea was that salvation from pain and conscious misery comes from no outside gods but from controlling one's own mind and through it the body. He summed up his discoveries in four simple propositions: (1) All living is painful. (2) Suffering is due to craving or desire. (3) When desire ceases, there comes release from suffering. (4) The way to the ceasing of suffering is by the Eightfold Path of "right view, right intention, right speech, right action, right livelihood, right effort, right mindfulness, right concentration".

[5] What was right to Buddha was set forth in commandments, the five that are obligatory upon all men being, not to kill any living creature; not to steal; not to commit adultery; not to lie, slander, or swear; and to avoid drunkenness. Five other commandments were binding upon those devoting themselves to a religious life to attain nirvana directly, namely, to abstain from food out of season, that is, after midday; to abstain from dances, theatrical representations, songs, and music; to abstain from personal ornaments and perfumes; to abstain from a lofty or luxurious couch; to abstain from taking gold or silver. But if we injure no one by our acts, no wrong has been done; and if our acts are an inconvenience to only ourselves, no one else has any right to regard us as transgressors. According to his philosophy no act is sin, but a bad act produces a bad result and so it is to be avoided. Badness must be regarded as to whether it hurts another person. If it injures only one's self, it does not matter, for each one is his own responsible master. So it

5. What were his five obligatory commandments, and what his five optional ones, and how did he reason sin away?

would be no crime to commit adultery if the husband of the woman consented, because no one is injured.

⁶ As for the way this material universe came about: It arose from empty space according to unchangeable natural laws, an EVOLUTION. The precipitate or condensing or settling of this formed matter, an evil from which springs a constant change of birth, according to unchangeable laws fixed in that evil. The cause of evil is ignorance; this is the original cause from which creatures are born. So to Buddha there was no personal Creator. In order to get out of difficulties he resorted to the doctrine of transmigration of the human soul, which he thus clothed with an immortality. Nirvana was gained when we got past all this series of rebirths. Nirvana was to be viewed not as annihilation, but as a consummation and fulfillment of effort. It was the completion of our becoming one successive thing after another, so that we got beyond all states of conscious, personal being. This was earned by a practice of moral virtues and the habit of intellectual virtues.

⁷ By transmigration and reincarnation we were rising on the steppingstones of our dead selves. By self-control we refrained from pampering desire. Our big work in e x i s t e n c e was that of self-naughting. The final goal, nirvana, was when the whole work of self-naughting had been accomplished. Buddha's system, therefore, was a way of attaining salvation from all existence by means

6. To him, how did the material universe come about, and how was nirvana attained?

7. To him, what was our big work in existence, and what the final goal, and so what kind of system of salvation was his?

of developing self-righteousness according to his standards. Nirvana was the final escape, a despiration or a drawing breath no more.

[8] So Buddha placed human life on a low level and had contempt for the human body. Referring to its nostrils, ears, eyes, mouth, etc., he spoke of it as "this nine-holed frame, this body foul, this charnel house". His estimate of womankind was also low, and he unwillingly admitted woman to a low position in his order. Being so negative and pessimistic, his philosophy did not make for social progress. Having found his philosophy, he went out preaching it and he sent out his followers as missionaries. He died at the age of eighty, suffering intensely from having overeaten pork. His followers did not consider his death as a death but the mere "shattering of the bodily investment" of his soul. His body was cremated, and the bones were preserved for sacred relics. His bones were held in veneration and in time were worshiped. Temples attached to them were raised and images of Buddha were installed at them. Though Buddhism is claimed to be not a religion but a philosophy, yet all the outward formalities were paid to his memory and his images that make up religious worship. He developed into a member of a Buddhist trinity! There is a triple-bodied Buddha which is called *Trikáya* (meaning "having three bodies") ; and in Japan a three-headed god, San Pao Fuh. After Buddha's death many thousands of monasteries of monks after his order were set up. They retired from the world and indulged in prayers, using the rosary and prayer wheel or mill.

---

8. How did he estimate human life and womankind, how was his death regarded, and how did a religion develop around him?

[9] Buddhism spread in India, its birthplace, and it predominated there until the tenth century A.D. It was blended with Hinduism, and Buddha was degraded in rank and declared to be a lesser incarnation of the Hindu god Vishnu. Image worship and relic worship took the place of what Buddha had taught. By its missionaries Buddhism was carried to Ceylon, Burma, Siam and Tibet. Afterward it reached its greatest growth in China and Japan, but is now reported to be declining in Japan. Lhasa, the capital of Tibet, became the Rome or Mecca of Buddhism, the city's name meaning the "Place of God". Here the Dalai Lama has had his residence, amid the convents and cells of the Buddhist monks. He is the ecclesiastical sovereign of Tibet and is the supreme pontiff or pope of the regions of central, eastern and southeastern Asia. He is considered an incarnation of Buddha. Buddha's teachings were at first transmitted by word of mouth, but later they were recorded in his own language, Pali, to form the Pali Canon; but there are Chinese and Tibetan versions. It consists of three "pitaka" or "baskets", the Sermon basket, the Discipline basket, and the Doctrinal basket.

[10] Wherever the missionaries went, they compromised with the local religions, so that Buddhism has become very changed from what its founder taught. The godless Buddha himself became a god, "the great god Buddh." The ceremonies in connection with this form of religion

9. How was Buddha finally degraded in India, to where did Buddhism spread, and how were Buddha's teachings transmitted?
10. How did it become a very complicated form of religion, a prototype of what dominant religion in Christendom, and in what respects?

have become very complicated. In many respects they are a prototype of the mightiest religious system in Christendom. There are the chanting of prayers, the rosary, candles, incense, priestly vestments, crosses, miter, cope and chaplet, holy water, the confessional, litanies, fasts, processions, worship of saints, and relics. These are so much like those of the Roman Catholic Church that when Jesuit priests first carried their missions into Buddhist lands they exclaimed that "there was not a piece of dress nor a priestly function nor a ceremony of the court of Rome, which the Devil had not copied in this country".

[11] As the Buddhist system preceded by many centuries the organizing of the Roman Catholic system in the third century A.D., the priests were doubtless stating the matter in reverse. Before the pope of Rome Buddhist monasteries existed. The Dalai Lama of Tibet ruled as the Supreme Pontiff or Pope of Buddhism before the Franciscan Friar Odoric visited Tibet about A.D. 1328. Vows of celibacy, poverty and obedience are taken by Buddhist priests the same as by the Roman Catholic. As for the life of a *bhikku* or monk, he was to keep from all sexual intercourse, put away home relationship, and care not for the world's favor or disapproval. He shaved his head, carried an almsbowl in which he accepted his food from charitable givers; he avoided all luxury, wore a robe (of yellow) over his rags, and viewed his body like a loathsome wound, and did not seek a comfortable place for his sleep. How does this compare with the practice of the Roman Catholic monks?

---

11. How were those surprised Jesuit priests actually stating the matter of copy religion in reverse?

[12] Parallel with the above, one delegate to the 1893 Parliament of Religions at Chicago, a convert to Protestant religion, was reported in *The American Sentinel* of August that year as saying: "There is a remarkable correspondence between Romish worship and Hindoo worship. Romanism is but a new label on the old bottles of paganism containing the deadly poison of idolatry. Often the Hindoos ask us, when seeing the Romish worship, 'What is the difference between Christianity and Hindooism?' In India we have not only to contend with the hydra-headed monster of Idolatry, but also the octopus of Romanism."—*The Battle of Armageddon,* page 263.

[13] Neither let anyone think that the doctrine of purgatory was discovered first by Pope Gregory the Great (595-604 A.D.). The Buddhists were ahead of him by hundreds of years on this doctrine. They had their hells and heavens. For a vivid description of their purgatory, take this excerpt from one of the five Nikāyas of the Pali canon, the Añguttara-Nikāya, as translated in the Harvard Classics (Volume 45, pages 701-704). According to this, the soul of one who does evil with his body, voice and mind, goes after death of the body to a "place of punishment, a place of suffering, perdition, hell". There the soul undergoes fiery torture as described below:

> Then, O priests, the guardians of hell inflict on him the torture called the fivefold pinion: they force a heated iron stake through his hand; they force a heated iron stake through his other hand;

12. How is the case parallel when comparison is made between Romanism and Hinduism?
13. How can it be shown that Pope Gregory the Great was not ahead of the Buddhists in his discovery of "purgatory"?

they force a heated iron stake through his foot; they force a heated iron stake through his other foot; they force a heated iron stake through the middle of his breast. . . . Then, O priests, the guardians of hell harness him to a chariot, and they make him go forward and they make him go back over ground that is blazing, flaming, and glowing. There he experiences grievous, severe, sharp, and bitter pains; but he does not die so long as that wickedness is unexhausted.

Then, O priest, the guardians of hell make him ascend and make him descend an immense, blazing, flaming, and glowing mountain of live coals. . . . Then, O priests, the guardians of hell take him feet up, head down, and throw him into a heated iron kettle that is blazing, flaming, and glowing. There he cooks and sizzles. And while he there cooks and sizzles, he goes once upwards, once downwards, and once sideways. There he experiences grievous, severe, sharp, and bitter pains; but he does not die so long as that wickedness is unexhausted.

Then, O priests, the guardians of hell throw him into the chiefest of all hells. . . .

Compare this with the Catholic poet Dante's famous poem entitled "The Divine Comedy" of three parts, Hell, Purgatory and Paradise.

[14] Unquestionably Buddhism is linked with demonism. It is one more effort on the part of the demons to misrepresent Jehovah God as a fiend and bring reproach on his creation of the material universe. His work is perfect, but man cannot penetrate it to its full depths. "He has made everything beautiful in its season; but he has also implanted ignorance in their mind, so that man-

14. In what base effort is Buddhism linked with demonism?

kind cannot discover the work which God has done from beginning to end."—Ecclesiastes 3:11, *AT*.

[15] God created man, not a "foul body", but "in the image of God created he him". (Genesis 1:27) Because of selfishly disobeying the law of his Creator, the first man fell from his perfection and was driven from his perfect paradise home, to rear the human family in sin, imperfection and subjection to death. Buddhism's humiliation of the flesh in an effort to gain self-merit corresponds with the "philosophy and empty deception according to the tradition of men" against which the apostle Paul warns in these words: "Let no man deprive you of the prize who takes delight in a mock humility . . . Why do you, as if living in the world, further subject yourselves to the decrees, 'Do not handle, nor taste, nor touch,' respecting things that are all destined to destruction by being used up, in accordance with the commands and teachings of men? Those very things are, indeed, possessed of an appearance of wisdom in a self-imposed form of worship and mock humility, a severe treatment of the body, but they are of no value in combatting the satisfying of the flesh."—Colossians 2:8, 18, 20-23, *NW*.

[16] In this day when human psychology proves itself unable to scheme out any salvation for men, and the philosophies of men are being exposed as vanity, it is time for Buddhists and all others to turn to Jehovah God for true enlightenment and a complete escape from the evils of this world into his righteous new world of peace.

---

15. How was Buddha's philosophy of the abasement of the flesh the kind of philosophy against which the apostle Paul warned?
16. What is it now time for Buddhists and psychologists to do for real enlightenment and escape from evil?

CHAPTER XVI

Confucianism, a System of Morality

IT WAS in the middle of the sixth century B.C., while the Babylonian empire was still dominating the earth, that the Chinese whom we know as Confucius was born, 551 B.C., or just twelve years after the reputed birth date of Buddha. Confucius was, of course, not his real name. Because he was of the family of Kung, he came to be called "Kung-fu-tsze", which means "Kung the Master" or "Kung the Teacher". But two thousand years later, or in the sixteenth century A.D., some Roman Catholic Jesuit priests who had been living in China recommended to the pope of Rome that this Chinese should be added to the list of the saints of the Roman Catholic Church. In making their recommendation the Latin transliteration "Confucius" was the nearest that they could get to the way his name "Kung-fu-tsze" was pronounced.

[2] At his birth the name his father gave him was Kin and he added another name at the same time, Chung Ni. But because of the philosophy which he developed on human conduct and social relations he is famous throughout the world under the name Confucius. So we shall refer to him under that name.

1, 2. When was Confucius born, and how did he come to be so named?

[3] In our twentieth century, according to the theory of some, it was corruption in the Chinese government that led to the overthrow of the Nationalist Republican regime by the Communist forces in 1949. In the time of Confucius it was also disorder and corruption in government that led him to interest himself in the science of government. The feudal system of government obtained then, a government of lords and vassals. The feudal lords were continually fighting among themselves, with the result that the people were suffering greatly and were burdened with taxation. At the early age of seventeen Confucius in a local government position showed ability in the settling of disputes. It was at this time, when he was adjusting the rival claims of some herdsmen, that he uttered one of his principles for which he is widely known. He showed the herdsmen how foolish it was for them to quarrel and then said: "Do not do to others what you would not want them to do to you."

[4] This has been said to be the negative way of stating the Golden Rule laid down by Jesus Christ in his sermon on the mount: "All things, therefore, that you want men to do to you, you also must likewise do to them; this, in fact, is what the Law and the Prophets mean." (Matthew 7:12, NW) By his referring to the Law and the Prophets Jesus located the statement of the principle of his Golden Rule back a thousand years before Confucius, for in the law of the prophet Moses (1512 B.C.) the Most High God inspired this rule: "Thou shalt love thy neighbor as thyself: I am

3. What led to his interest in the science of government, and what widely known principle did he utter early?
4. How does this principle compare with Jesus' "Golden Rule"?

Jehovah." (Leviticus 19:18, *AS*) The Golden Rule of Jesus, which spells love for one's neighbor, is for *positive* action in doing good to your neighbor. But the rule of Confucius is one of *negative* reciprocity of one person toward another. It has in mind, not good, but evil and wrongdoing, and it holds a person back from doing anything for his neighbor for fear he may do his neighbor hurt or wrong.

[5] The death of his beloved mother when he was twenty-four years old profoundly affected Confucius. For twenty-seven months he mourned at her grave. In keeping with this he resigned his public office, but he continued his studies. His married life now took a turn for the worse and, to become a traveling teacher, he left his wife and son. He journeyed through the states of China and instructed all ranks of people and gained fame as a reformer of the morals of his people and as a teacher of proper conduct of humans one toward another. In his fifties his great opportunity came. He was invited to serve as a magistrate in his native kingdom of Lu, in what is now Shantung Province, and because of efficient service he rose finally to be minister of justice. He proved himself an efficiency engineer. The success of the administration of the state of Lu roused the jealousy of the neighboring princes. They conspired to estrange the Duke of Lu from his minister Confucius. At length after four years of conscientious public service Confucius resigned from office quite heartbroken. He departed, in search of some ruler who was a virtuous man and from whom he could

---

5. How did he come to be a traveling teacher, what success did he have in applying his theories, and what did he compile?

get sincere co-operation in carrying on good government according to his plans and theories. He believed that good government was the foundation for all reform. Thirteen years of searching for his ideal ruler proved unsuccessful. Finally he came back to his home state, Lu, not to engage in politics but to carry on his scholarly activities. These remaining four years till his death at seventy-two he occupied in completing his work on compiling and editing the Classics, the sacred books of the Chinese.

⁶ Confucius looked back on the past as the "good old days". He had great respect for the traditions and ancient customs of his people. His effort was to bring his generation back to the careful observance of these, rather than to introduce any new religious system. He tried to regulate the manners and habits of the people, even going into such details as to how they should sleep in bed. He believed that regard for formality and outward politeness expressed true nobility of heart. So he brought together for ready use and reference all the various ceremonies into one general code of rites, set forth in the *Li Ki King,* or the Book of Rites. In this book every formality in a person's every relationship in life is so strictly regulated that it tended to make a Chinese an automaton that was set in motion by the regulations of the *Li Ki King.* Hence it bears a resemblance to the Jewish Talmud, which is based on the traditions of the Jewish religious fathers. Concerning the religious leaders who were sticklers for such traditions and the minute regulation of the com-

6, 7. Rather than start a new religious system, what did he try to do, and how does his Book of Rites compare with the Talmud?

mon people Jesus said: "They bind up heavy loads and put them upon the shoulders of mankind, but they themselves are not willing to budge them with their finger. All the works they do they do to be viewed by men; for they broaden the scripture-containing cases that they wear as safeguards, and enlarge the fringes of their garments. They like the most prominent place at evening meals and the front seats in the synagogues, and the greetings in the market-places and to be called 'Rabbi' by men."—Matthew 23:4-7, NW.

[7] Also to show that sincerity of heart is not always expressed by outward formality, Jesus said to those traditionalists: "And so you have made the word of God invalid because of your tradition. You hypocrites, Isaiah aptly prophesied about you, when he said: 'This people honors me with their lips, yet their hearts are far removed from me. It is in vain that they keep paying respect to me, because they teach commands of men as doctrines.'"—Matthew 15:6-9, NW.

[8] Confucius made the aim of all living to be the attaining of human virtue by the observance of the five fundamental laws governing the relations (1) between ruler and subject, (2) parents and children, (3) husband and wife, (4) friends and brothers, and (5) the practice of five principal virtues: humanity, justice, order, uprightness, and sincerity or good faith. He had great regard for what compares with the fifth of the Ten Commandments which God gave by Moses: "Honour thy father and thy mother, that thy days may be prolonged in the land that Jehovah thy God giveth

---

8. How did Confucius aim for men to gain human virtue, and for the principle of which of the Ten Commandments did he have great regard?

thee." (Exodus 20:12, *Da*) While the writings of Confucius dwell sparingly on the duties of husbands toward their wives, they most rigidly stress the duties and unquestioning submission of children to their parents. It is upon this principle of a child's obedience that Confucius' entire system, moral and political, rests.

[9] A family is a unit of a nation and is the simplest illustration of how a nation should be run. According to this simple illustration the Chinese emperor stood as the father of all his subjects and so was entitled to their passive childlike obedience. As children are subject to their parents, the citizens are subordinate to and dependent upon the emperor, who is the representative father of the political state.

[10] Thus, against independence and equality of men according to the democratic principle, Confucius placed subordination and dependence. This political idea has served the selfish aims of governmental despots very well. This is what has made Confucius such a popular figure with the former governments of China, whether of native or of Tartar origin, for many centuries. While it has operated to preserve China as a nation on its land for two thousand years, it has checked China's progress. It has turned the Chinese common people to being slavish, insincere in their outward acts and fainthearted. These features cannot be made up for by the formal politeness, the gentleness of behavior and the

9, 10. How did the applying of the illustration of a family to rulership serve despots well, and how has it affected the Chinese?

TEMPLE OF HEAVEN AT PEIPING

good order of conduct. Doubtless for this reason progressive Chinese of today say that nothing has hurt China more than Confucianism.

[11] During the Chou dynasty, during which Confucius lived, ancestor worship was highly developed, but only one's own ancestors were worshiped. Ancestor worship was made as important as worship of Heaven. Confucius encouraged this practice but condemned the worship of other people's ancestors as flattery. He said: "As the foundation of things is Heaven, so the foundation of man is the ancestors." Confucius did not talk about spirits, and even detested the worship of them. Whether he recognized the existence of a personal god has been questioned. We find no positive proofs of it in the religious ceremonies which he observed and in certain expressions which he made, such as, "He who offends against Heaven has none to whom he can pray," and, "There is a Heaven that knows me." (Analects III,

11. What worship did Confucius encourage?

13, and XIV, 13) He did in effect deny a personal Creator.

[12] In the matter of physical science he maintained that "out of nothing there cannot be produced anything (*ex nihilo nihil fit*)". Instead of putting an efficient Cause before the material creation, he argued that material bodies must have existed from eternity and that the cause and also the principle for the being of such things had existed along with the things themselves. Hence this cause is just as eternal, infinite, indestructible, omnipotent and omnipresent as the material things themselves, and the blue sky or heaven (*Tien*) is the central point of it. Particularly at the equinoxes, offerings should be made to Heaven (*Tien*). But when Heaven is thus referred to by the Chinese, it does not carry along with it the meaning of a place for human souls to take up residence after the death of the body, nor does it stand for a personal god.

[13] Though Confucius' teaching does not directly speak of immortality of the human soul, such a thing is at least suggested in the worship that is paid to ancestors and in the absence of the word *death* from Confucius' philosophy. The Chinese say that, when a person dies, "he has returned to his family." According to Confucius, the spirits of the good were allowed to visit their old habitations on earth or to visit such ancestral places or halls as were designated by their descendants, in

ANCESTRAL TABLET

12. How did he account for creation's existence?
13. What indicates that he believed in immortality of human souls?

order to receive homage and, in turn, to confer
what good influences they could. Hence the duty
of performing sacred rites in such places. If any
living person neglected such duty toward dead
ancestors, his spiritual part would after death of
the body be deprived of the high state of bliss that
flows from the homage which descendants pay to
their ancestors.

[14] By all this we can measure how deep the
darkness was which shrouded the world lying outside of Jehovah's devoted people who held the
truth concerning the promised Seed of God's
"woman" and who were the recipients of Jehovah's unfolding revelations upon the divine purpose having to do with the Seed and recorded in
His inspired Word. As the apostle Paul says, the
worldly nations, including China, were "at that
particular time without Christ, alienated from
the state of Israel and strangers to the covenants
of the promise, and you had no hope and were
without God in the world".—Ephesians 2:12, NW.

[15] Confucius assembled the religious literature
of China. His name is associated with nine Chinese classical books. Five of these are called king,
meaning canonical book, and the other four shu.
Three of the king were compiled by Confucius.
One entitled "Spring and Autumn" was composed
by him as a supplement to the third king, and it
is the only work coming directly from his hand.
In this composition, which contained the annals of
his native state of Lu, Confucius was quite immoral, from the standpoint that he hid and twisted
facts in order to please his patron. He suppressed

14. How does all this display the darkness which
shrouded the world?
15. What religious literature did Confucius assemble
or write?

the facts about certain princes and about some of his relatives. The fifth *king* was compiled by Confucius' disciples from his teachings. It is the Book of Rites and was a textbook especially of ceremonial and etiquette, in which Confucius' teachings hold an important place.

[16] The four *shu* were written by his disciples. Among these was the *Meng-tse-shu,* which was the work of his great disciple Meng-tsé (called "Mencius"), who lived a century after Confucius and who ranks among the Chinese next to Confucius as a philosopher and moralist, "a second sage." His statement, "Heaven hears as the people hear," compares with the Roman *vox populi, vox dei,* meaning, "the voice of the people is the voice of god." Another disciple who attained to greater popularity than that of Mencius was Chu Hsi, or Chucius, of the twelfth century A.D. He tried to add to Confucianism by trying to solve the problem of evil. So wide was the general influence of Chucius' writings that some have said that Confucianism ought to be called "Chucianism".

[17] After Confucius died in 478 B.C. the veneration for him grew to such an extent that it amounted to worship. The man who did not teach a personal god became a god to the millions of Chinese. In every district or department a temple was erected to his honor. There are no idols, but ancestral tablets take the place of such in the gilded shrines. In the center is that of Confucius and on the sides are those of twelve of his most celebrated disciples, six on each side. Incense is burned, and even a whole ox, skinned, and a pig and goat are offered to him. The Mandarins once

16. Among his disciples, who were Mencius and Chucius?
17. How did he become a god to the millions of Chinese?

officiated as priests. An offering is made of material for clothing, coarse silk, and this is finally burned that it might become "spirit silk" in the other world. So the raw material is sent to Confucius. Formerly sacrifice used to be offered before his tomb. As late as A.D. 1906 the same sacrifice was made to him as to Heaven. The attempt by the Empress Dowager that year to deify him failed. In 1912 the Chinese Republic brought to an end the imperial worship of Heaven.

[18] What has Confucianism done for mankind? Or what has it failed to do? It has failed to do away with oppression, violence and corruption in man-made government. It has looked back to the ancient past as a sort of Golden Age and so tried to preserve its cult or form of worship and its social living. Its man-made moral philosophy has failed to supply the answer to the question of righteous government over mankind. Confucianism is not the real science of government, for it has absolutely no prophetic vision of the great theocratic government of Jehovah God. His government is the kingdom to which all his prophets pointed forward and of which the prophet Daniel, a contemporary of Confucius, said to the king of Babylon: "In the days of these kings shall the God of the heavens set up a kingdom which shall never be destroyed; and the sovereignty thereof shall not be left to another people: it shall break in pieces and consume all these kingdoms, but itself shall stand for ever."—Daniel 2:44, *Da; AS.*

---

18. Why is Confucianism not the real science of government?

CHAPTER XVII

The Sacred Secret of the Seed Solved

STANDING before the king of Babylon to recall and interpret his forgotten dream, the
Hebrew prophet Daniel said: "There is a God
in the heavens who reveals secrets, and he makes
known to King Nebuchadnezzar what shall be in
the end of the days." Then by divine help Daniel
cracked the secret message concerning God's kingdom which Babylon's magicians, enchanters, sorcerers and Chaldean wise men had failed to crack.
At that King Nebuchadnezzar prostrated himself
before Jehovah's prophet and said: "Truly, your
God is the God of gods, and the Lord of kings;
and he is a revealer of secrets, inasmuch as you
have been able to reveal this secret." (Daniel 2:27,
28, 47, *AT*) To the same degree the sacred secret
spoken in the garden of Eden concerning the
seed of the woman the same God in the heavens
is able to reveal at his own due time. His own
acts of revelation throughout the millenniums of
time since then indicated that it was his kindly
purpose to clear up the secret when the time was
ripe for it. Centuries afterward his Prophet greater than Daniel said: "There is nothing hidden that
will not become manifest, neither anything carefully concealed that will never become known and

1. With what power demonstrated in Daniel's day, how
can Jehovah God vindicate his own ancient secret given
out in Eden?

225

never come into the open." (Luke 8:17, *NW*) In this way Jehovah vindicates his own ancient secret.

[2] In fulfillment of Jehovah's revelations to his prophets but to the amazement of the ancient world, the mighty Babylonian empire fell before the Medes and Persians. In vindication of his prophecy by Daniel, the Persian empire fell before the onrush of the Greek imperialists. The Grecian empire, in turn, fell before the beastly aggressions of the Romans. The Jewish remnant who were delivered from Babylon and restored to their homeland in Palestine felt the world domination of these successive empires. In 63 B.C. Jerusalem came under the imperial sway of pagan Rome. In 37 B.C. Herod, appointed by the Roman Senate to be king of Jerusalem, took the city by storm. An Edomite, but professing to be a proselyte to the Jews' religion or Judaism, Herod renovated the temple at the holy city and built it up into a most gorgeous structure. It was during Herod's reign at Jerusalem and while Augustus was Caesar at Rome that the sacred secret of the Promised Seed began to break.

[3] The last of the Hebrew prophets, Malachi, had spoken, and for four hundred years since him no inspired prophet had risen in the land of Israel. In the meantime the Israelites or Jews had gone over to speaking Aramáic, and many of them were also speaking Greek. It was now toward the end of Herod's reign, and a birth took place which,

---

2. The domination of what world powers did the Jewish remnant feel in Palestine, and during whose rule did the secret begin to break?

3, 4. (a) How had there been a lapse in Hebrew prophets and a change in the Jews' language? (b) What birth of special pedigree now occurred?

when it came to his ears, shook his composure. Whose birth?

⁴ It was the birth of the One who was to be the Seed for ruling the new world. God by his revelations had already given clues for identifying the Seed, so that we should make no mistake about him. He was to be, not just any descendant of Noah's son Shem, but his descendant through faithful Abraham, Isaac and Jacob. Of the twelve tribes of Jacob (Israel), he was to be of the tribe of Judah, and according to Jehovah's covenant with King David for an everlasting kingdom he was to be a descendant of this king, a "son of David".

⁵ Since the overthrow of the kingdom of Judah by Babylon in 607 B.C., no king of David's line had sat upon the "throne of Jehovah" at Jerusalem. No one was to sit upon the divine throne in the everlasting kingdom until the "appointed times of the nations", which began in that year, were fulfilled 2,520 years later, in 1914 (A.D.). This was why the wicked Edomite Herod was then king in Jerusalem. In harmony with the royal covenant made with David, and according to the secret clue given at the prophecy of Micah 5:2, the One to become the Seed was to be born at David's own city, Bethlehem in Judah. But first our attention is drawn north to Nazareth. Why?

⁶ At this Galilean city lived a Jewish virgin descended from King David through his son Nathan. She was promised in marriage to Joseph. He was a carpenter but a descendant of David

---

5. By what allowance was Herod then king in Jerusalem, and where, during his reign, was the Seed to be born as a man?
6. Who was the child's mother, and when and where was the child's coming birth announced to her?

through his son Solomon and born at David's city, Bethlehem. Before ever Joseph took his virgin fiancée to his home to take up housekeeping with her, something miraculous occurred. But about six months before that an angel from heaven, announcing himself as Gabriel who stands near before God, had announced to the priest Zechariah, husband of her aged cousin Elizabeth, that these two were to become the parents of a prophet to be named John. Now the angel Gabriel materialized a human body and appeared privately to Mary, but not for any unclean purpose like that of the "sons of God" who became disobedient spirits in Noah's day and intermarried with the daughters of men. (1 Peter 3:19, 20; Genesis 6:1-4) Of Gabriel's visit we read:

[7] "And when he went in before her he said: 'Good day, highly favored one, Jehovah is with you.' But she was deeply disturbed at the saying and began to reason out what kind of greeting this might be. So the angel said to her: 'Have no fear, Mary, for you have found favor with God; and, look! you will conceive in your womb and give birth to a son, and you are to call his name Jesus. This one will be great and will be called Son of the Most High, and Jehovah God will give him the throne of David his father, and he will be king over the house of Jacob forever, and there will be no end of his kingdom.' But Mary said to the angel: 'How is this to be, since I am having no relations with a man?' In answer the angel said to her: 'Holy spirit will come upon you, and power of the Most High will overshadow you. For that reason also what is born will be called holy,

---

7. What do we read of Gabriel's visit with her on that occasion?

God's Son. And, look! Elizabeth your relative has also herself conceived a son, in her old age, and this is the sixth month for her, the so-called "barren woman"; because with God no declaration will be an impossibility.' Then Mary said: 'Look! Jehovah's slave girl! May it take place with me according to your declaration.' At that the angel departed from her."—Luke 1:26-38, *NW*.

[8] One day Joseph learned that his virgin fiancée was pregnant. As he was considering a private divorce to save her from being stoned to death as an unfaithful girl, Jehovah's angel in a dream assured Joseph that Mary's conceiving had been by the power of God's holy spirit or active force: "You must call his name 'Jesus', for he will save his people from their sins." The name "Jesus" means "Jehovah is salvation". This conception came in vindication of Jehovah's prophecy at Isaiah 7:14: "Look! the virgin will become pregnant and will give birth to a son, and they will call his name 'Immanuel', which means, when translated, 'With us is God.' " So at the customary time Joseph consummated the marriage by taking her to his home, but he had no relations with her until the birth of this miraculous son had taken place.—Matthew 1:18-25, *NW*.

[9] Did Mary's conception of Jesus by holy spirit make her the woman prophesied at Genesis 3:15: "I will put enmity between thee [the Serpent] and the woman, and between thy seed and her seed; it shall bruise thy head, and thou shalt

---

8. What was Joseph instructed to do regarding Mary, and in fulfillment of what prophecy did Jesus' birth from a virgin come about?
9. Did Mary's conception of Jesus make her the woman meant in Genesis 3:15, and how do we know the woman's identity?

bruise his heel"? From what we have learned in
the preceding chapters your answer, to be Scriptural, will be No. Just as the serpent in the secret
promise at Genesis 3:15 was not a literal serpent,
so the woman would correspondingly not be a literal woman of flesh and blood. The real serpent
was the once glorious spirit creature, the "covering cherub" in Eden. Likewise the woman is a
heavenly, spirit creation, namely, Jehovah's heavenly organization of holy spirit creatures. Made
up of devoted spirit sons, this organization is united to him and subject to him as a wife to a husband, and he addresses her as being her husband.
For long centuries she had been barren of this
promised seed, like Abraham's ninety-year-old
wife Sarah, but now the time was here for him
to show he was her life-giving husband and
to give her the Seed he had promised her. (Isaiah
54:1-5, *AS*) She was once symbolized by Jerusalem, whose kings sat on the "throne of Jehovah".
So the apostle Paul speaks of her this way and
says: "The Jerusalem above is free, and she is
our mother." And then he quotes Isaiah 54:1 in
support. (Galatians 4:26-28, *NW*) The enmity between this "woman" above in heaven and the
original Serpent Satan the Devil is portrayed in
symbols at Revelation 12:1-9, 17. Read it.

[10] But of her member-sons which one was this
symbolic woman, this heavenly organization, going to bring forth in subjection to her husband
to be the Promised Seed? Jehovah chose his only-
begotten Son, the Word, the beginning of his creation. His "woman" submissively yielded him up to

10. Which one of her member-sons did she produce to
be the Seed, and how did he point to her being his
mother?

leave heaven and his spiritual existence up there and to have his life transferred down to earth and to be born as a man from Mary. That is why Jesus said: "I am from the realms above." "From God I came forth and am here. Neither have I come of my own initiative at all, but that One sent me forth." And when someone in a crowd of listeners said, "Your mother and your brothers are standing outside seeking to speak to you," he said: "Who is my mother, and who are my brothers?" "And extending his hand toward his disciples he said: 'Look! my mother and my brothers! For whoever does the will of my Father who is in heaven, the same is my brother, and sister, and mother.'" (John 8:23, 42; Matthew 12:46-50, *NW*) These disciples became his spiritual relatives, children of his heavenly mother, God's organization.

[11] Hence Jesus' birth on earth was not an incarnation. When the angel Gabriel announced John's birth to Zechariah and Jesus' birth to Mary, that was an incarnation of the angel Gabriel, for Gabriel still remained a spirit person. For the time being he merely clothed himself with a carnal or fleshly body in order to appear to human eyes. But not so God's only-begotten Son. He emptied himself of all things heavenly and spiritual, and God's almighty spirit transferred his Son's life down to the womb of the Jewish virgin of David's descent. By this miracle he was born a man. (Philippians 2:7, *AS; NW*) He was not a spirit-human hybrid, a man and at the same time a spirit person. He was not clothed upon with flesh over an invisible spirit person, but he WAS flesh.

---

11. Why was Jesus' birth as a man no incarnation, and why cannot Mary be called the "mother of God"?

Listen to John 1:14 (*CB*): "And the Word was made flesh, and dwelt among us, and we saw his glory—glory as of the only-begotten of the Father —full of grace and of truth." On this account Gabriel told Mary: "The Holy One to be born shall be called the Son of God." (Luke 1:35, *CB*) Since this Holy One's life was transferred from heaven and had been in existence immeasurable time before Mary was born, and since Gabriel said the child would be called "the Son of God", Mary cannot Scripturally be called the "mother of God", as some call her.

[12] Mary's time to give birth to the human Son of God drew near. In compliance with the decree of Caesar Augustus for all persons to get registered at their native place Joseph left Nazareth and took Mary with him the more than sixty miles south to Bethlehem, 2,550 feet above sea level, and five miles south of Jerusalem. Now came the event long awaited. Luke's verified account says: "And she gave birth to her son, the firstborn, and she bound him with cloth bands and laid him in a manger, because there was no place for them in the lodging-room. There were also in that same country shepherds living out of doors and keeping watches in the night over their flocks. And suddenly Jehovah's angel stood by them and Jehovah's glory gleamed around them, and they became very fearful. But the angel said to them: 'Have no fear, for, look! I am declaring to you good news of a great joy that all the people will have, because there was born to you today a Savior, who is Christ the Lord, in David's city. And this is a sign for you: you will find an infant

---

12. Where did Jesus' birth come about and how there, and how was it announced, and to whom?

bound in cloth bands and lying in a manger.' And suddenly there came to be with the angel a multitude of the heavenly host, praising God and saying: 'Glory in the heights above to God, and upon earth peace among men of good-will.' " —Luke 2:1-14, *NW*.

[13] The timetable, checked against the prophecy of Daniel 9:24-27 concerning the coming of "Messiah the Prince", indicates that this was the year 2 B.C. But was the day December 25 after the northern winter had set in? From what we observed in chapter VII, December 25 was the traditional birthday of Nimrod, the false seed of the woman. The inspired Scriptures do not give the birth date of Jesus, and it does not matter, for

---

13. What year was Jesus born, and what about the shepherds indicates it was not December 25?

neither Jesus nor God his Father nor the inspired
apostles instructed us to celebrate Jesus' birthday.
The only birthday celebrations that the Holy
Scriptures mention are those of pagans, those of
Egypt's Pharaoh and of Herod Antipas who
marked his birthday by having John the Baptist's head chopped off. (Genesis 40:20; Matthew
14:6; Mark 6:21) Christ's disciples of the first
century shunned birthday celebrations as being
pagan, unchristian! The Scriptures are against
Jesus' birthday as being the wintry day of December 25. *December* means tenth month, and the
tenth Jewish month Tebeth was a rainy and cold
month, especially at Bethlehem's elevation of
2,550 feet above sea level. It could not have been
this disagreeable wintertime, for the account says
shepherds were living out of doors watching over
their flocks by night. In wintertime there was no
pasturage in the fields for the sheep and already
during the eighth month they were withdrawn
from the field and housed for the winter.

[14] What is more, Jesus once said: "Keep praying that your flight may not occur in wintertime."
(Matthew 24:20, *NW*) So there is the extreme
unlikelihood that Joseph would take his wife
Mary, then "heavy with child", for that journey
of over sixty miles (airline miles) through moun-
tainous terrain averaging 3,000 feet above sea
level in a rainy, wintry month. Besides, it was the
time of the registration required by Rome and
which called for a lot of traveling by everyone.
The Roman authorities would not be so unwise
as to require subjugated peoples, especially re-
belliously minded Jews, to submit to the hard-

14. How do travel conditions, Daniel's prophecy on the
seventy weeks, and John's birth indicate it was not
December 25?

ships of winter travel to comply with Caesar's decree. The politic Romans would be discreet enough
to take advantage of the time when Jehovah's
law required the Jews to travel to Jerusalem,
namely, in the seventh month, for the celebration
of the feast of tabernacles from the fifteenth to
the twenty-first of that month. So it was about the
beginning of the eighth Jewish month (*Bul*, meaning "rain") that Jesus was born. He was killed
on Nisan 14 in the spring of the year, or, April 1,
A.D. 33, Gregorian calendar, and, according to
Daniel 9:24-27, Jesus was then thirty-three and
a half years old. So if we measure back a half
year from Nisan 14 or April 1, it locates Jesus'
actual birthday about October 1. His second
cousin John the Baptist was born about six months
earlier. According to the time that John's father
served at Jerusalem's temple as priest, in the "division of Abijah", John was born toward the beginning of April.—1 Chronicles 24:1-10; 2 Chronicles 23:4; Luke 1:5-27, 36.

[15] Jehovah God did not reveal the birth of his
Son on earth to his enemies, the seed of the Serpent. He made humble, peaceful, God-fearing Jewish shepherds to be the witnesses of his Son's lowly birth. By his angel Jehovah announced that
this babe in the manger whom the shepherds went
to see was the One destined to be the Christ or
Messiah, the anointed King of the new world with
enduring peace on earth. In this way Jehovah God,
who first gave out the sacred secret about the
Seed of his "woman" or heavenly organization,
solved the mystery of it for us by identifying
the Seed.

---

15. To whom did God reveal the birth of his Son, and
how did he thus solve the long-standing sacred secret?

CHAPTER XVIII

World Religion and the Seed of Mystery

THE first contact that the child Jesus had with world religion was when he was visited by the magi or astrologers from eastern parts, and this quickly led to a murderous attempt on his life by the seed of the Serpent. These magi or astrologers were not sent by the Most High God. He had no dealings with magicians or astrologers. These were associated with Babylonish religion, and Jehovah's law concerning astrologers or stargazers commanded the Jews: "There must be none among you who burns his son or his daughter alive, or who practises divination or soothsaying, no augur, no sorcerer, no one who weaves spells, no medium or magician, no necromancer. Anyone given to these practices is abominable to the Eternal." (Deuteronomy 18:10-12, *Mo*) "The soul that shall go aside after magicians, and soothsayers, and shall commit fornication with them, I will set my face against that soul, and destroy it out of the midst of its people." (Leviticus 20:6, *Dy*) But Lady Babylon had dealings with magicians, for God said to her: "Let now the astrologers, the stargazers, the monthly prognosticators, stand up, and save thee from these things that shall come upon thee." (Isaiah 47:13) Hence God did not notify these star-gazing magicians or as-

1. Why was it not by Jehovah God that the magi or astrologers were sent to the child Jesus?

236

trologers that his Son had been born on earth,
and thus serve the purpose of the seed of the
Serpent. He notified Jews who worshiped him,
and that by his angel or by his holy spirit.

[2] The original Serpent and his demons have the
power to cause luminous orbs or bodies to appear
to the vision of those subject to their influence.
Jehovah's angel instructed the shepherds to go
direct to Bethlehem and gave them a sign for
identifying the babe. The eighth day from that
the babe was circumcised the same as any Jewish
boy. On the fortieth day the days of Mary's puri-
fication were up, and so she and Joseph went to
the temple at Jerusalem to make the sacrifice for
Mary's cleansing, according to Moses' law. (Leviticus 12:1-8) Hence they brought the babe Jesus
there. Then by his spirit God identified the babe
there to aged Simeon and the prophetess Anna.
(Luke 2:21-38) But there is no record that anybody else saw the star which the magi or astrologers claimed they saw from the east. Furthermore, their "star" did not lead them direct to
Bethlehem. "Look! astrologers from eastern parts
came to Jerusalem, saying: 'Where is the one born
king of the Jews? For we saw his star when we
were in the east and we have come to do him
obeisance.' " At hearing this King Herod was disturbed. So he asked the Jewish priests and scribes
where Christ was to be born. They quoted Micah
5:2, saying: "In Bethlehem of Judea; for this is
how it has been written through the prophet, 'You,
however, O Bethlehem of the land of Judah, are
by no means the most insignificant city among
the governors of Judah; for out of you will come

2. How did the sending of the astrologers to visit the
child differ from that of the shepherds and the notify-
ing of Simeon and Anna?

forth a leader [or, governor] who will shepherd my people, Israel.' "

³ Then Herod sent the astrologers to Bethlehem, saying with the cunning of the Serpent: "When you have found it report back to me, that I, too, may go and do it obeisance." On the way the star appeared to them again and went ahead and stopped over where the young child now was. They did not go into a stable but went into a house and there found the child and paid respects to it. If the "star" had been from God, why did it not lead them there in the first place? So now, because this star had let murderous Herod in on the matter, God did step in, just as when he warned the Philistine king Abimelech by a dream not to harm Abraham's wife. He did not leave the astrologers to the influence of that star any longer, for, we read, "because they were given divine warning in a dream not to return to Herod, they withdrew to their country by another route." (Genesis 20:2-8) After their leaving, Jehovah's angel warned Joseph to take the child and its mother down to Egypt at once: "for Herod is about to hunt the young child to destroy it."

⁴ Herod, finding himself outwitted by the astrologers, now arranged a dragnet of destruction to catch the Seed of God's "woman". He had all the boys in and about Bethlehem killed according to the age limits he had calculated from the astrologers. All this proves that the "star" was part of a plot of the Serpent to destroy the Messianic

---

3. When sending the astrologers to Bethlehem what request did Herod make, and how did God block their complying with it?

4. What did Herod then do, and what does this prove concerning the star, the astrologers, and astrology itself?

Seed, and that God had not sent the wise men either to Herod or to the child Jesus by means of the star. It proves that astrology or trying to gain information on the lives of people by consulting the stars is Babylonish. It is of the Serpent, Satan the Devil, and is condemned by God's Word.—Matthew 2:1-17, *NW*.

⁵ When brought out of Egypt, the child was taken, not back to the danger zone Bethlehem, but up to Nazareth. There he was brought up. He became a carpenter like his foster father Joseph. His cousin John was a priest's son, and it was God's law for a young priest to enter into his full duties at thirty years of age. But, in place of taking up priestly service at the temple in Jerusalem, John began preaching out in the wilderness of Judea, saying: "Repent, for the kingdom of the heavens has drawn near." Those who repented in view of the Kingdom's nearness he baptized in water.

⁶ The religion of the Jews had been corrupted by the leaders, for these followed the philosophies and traditions of men instead of God's plain Word. Because they were natural offspring of Abraham, they thought they were sure of a place in the kingdom of heaven. But when John saw the religious Pharisees and Sadducees coming for baptism, he showed they came from among the seed of the Serpent: "You offspring of vipers, who has shown you how to flee from the coming wrath? So then produce fruit that befits repentance; and do not presume to say to yourselves, 'As a father we have Abraham.' For I say to you that God is

5. Where was Jesus brought up, and why there, and into what activities did John enter at the proper time?
6. Why did John greet the Pharisees and Sadducees as he did, and of what did he warn them?

able to raise up children to Abraham from these
stones." Then he warned them the Promised Seed
was coming and he would make a separation between the wheat and chaff, those who accepted
God's revelations on the true Seed of Abraham
and those who clung to traditions.—Matthew
3:1-12, *NW*.

[7] How different when Jesus came from Nazareth to be baptized by John in the Jordan river!
For Jesus John did not have the greetings for a
sinner. He did not wish to give Jesus the appearance of a sinner by baptizing him. He tried to
prevent Jesus, saying: "I am the one needing to
be baptized by you, and are you coming to me?"
Jesus had no sins to confess to John and so he
was not being baptized in repentance over sins.
Why, then, did he submit to baptism? In order to
symbolize his complete devoting of himself to God
to do God's will in behalf of the kingdom of the
heavens which John was preaching. He told John:
"Let it be, this time, for in that way it is suitable
for us to carry out all that is righteous."

[8] So John submerged Jesus beneath the Jordan stream to symbolize Jesus' immersion into
the will of God. He raised Jesus out of the water
to symbolize how Jesus was raised up out of death
to his own will and was now made alive to God's
will as this would be further revealed to him. It
was here that God's "woman" or spiritual organization brought Jesus forth as a spiritual Son of
God, the heavenly Seed, for we read: "After being baptized Jesus immediately came up from the

---

7. Why did John at first object to baptizing Jesus, and
what was the reason why Jesus got baptized?
8. How was the water baptism an appropriate symbol
for Jesus, and how was it that as Christ he began his
work?

water; and, look! the heavens were opened up, and
he saw descending like a dove God's spirit coming
upon him. Look! also, there was a voice from the
heavens that said: 'This is my Son, the beloved,
whom I have approved.' " There Jehovah God acknowledged Jesus as the Seed of his "woman", begotten by his spirit to a heavenly destiny. Luke's
account adds: "Furthermore, Jesus himself, when
he commenced his work, was about thirty years
old, being the son, as the opinion was, of Joseph."
(Matthew 3:13-17 and Luke 3:21-23, *NW*) Thus
Jesus began his work as the Christ or Messiah.
Christ means "Anointed One", and immediately
after his water baptism Jesus had been anointed
with God's holy spirit.

⁹ John the Baptist did not offer one sacrifice on
God's altar at Jerusalem as the son of the Levite
priest Zechariah. Instead, he baptized the body of
the Christ who was offering himself as a sacrifice
of far greater value than that of bulls, goats and
sheep. It was a perfect human sacrifice that could
atone for the sin of the world, the sin inherited
from Adam. As we have seen, much had been
written about the Promised Seed, indicating God's
will for him. Now he had come and been baptized
to symbolize his dedication to do God's will in
this world. What this meant for him we read:

¹⁰ "Hence when he comes into the world he says
[quoting Psalm 40:6-8, *LXX*]: ' "You did not desire sacrifice and offering, but you prepared a
body for me. You did not approve of whole burnt-
offerings and sin offering." Then I said, "Look!
I am come (in the roll of the book it is written
about me) to do your will, O God." ' After first

9, 10. As what was Jesus' body which John baptized to
serve, and how was Jesus' coming to serve this purpose
foretold in the Psalms?

saying, 'You did not desire nor did you approve of sacrifices and offerings and w h o l e burnt-offerings and sin offering'—sacrifices which are offered according to the Law—then he actually says, 'Look! I am come to do your will.' He does away with what is first that he may establish what is second. By the said 'will' we have been sanctified through the offering of the body of Jesus Christ once for all time."—Hebrews 10:5-10, *NW*.

[11] This meant that the old Law covenant which was first and which had merely animal sacrifices was being done away with in order for a new covenant to be established on a better sacrifice, a sacrifice of Jesus' perfect humanity. The Law covenant had been added to God's great covenant with Abraham concerning the Seed for the blessing of all the families of the earth. It had been added for only a time, till the Seed arrived concerning whom the promise had been made. Now that Seed had arrived. God's "woman", his heavenly organization of loyal spirit creatures, had brought forth this Seed. So it was time for God to dismiss the woman servant with whom he had been married by means of the Law covenant, namely, the national organization of natural Jews or Israelites. This dismissal had been foreshadowed when Abraham dismissed his servant girl Hagar and her son Ishmael whom she had borne to him in hope that he might prove to be the promised seed of Abraham. But Abraham kept his real and original wife, Sarah, who now at last in her old age bore him Isaac, who was a picture of the real Seed of Abraham.

---

11. What did this mean for the Law covenant and the organization under it, and how was this foreshadowed with Abraham's women?

[12] To make this Seed of Abraham like the stars of heaven for multitude, Jehovah God made Jesus' faithful followers to be his spiritual brothers. For the purpose of making these the spiritual brothers of Jesus a new covenant had to be established over Jesus' sacrifice of his perfect human body, according to God's will. By this means they became God's spiritual sons, children of his "woman", his heavenly, spiritual organization. For this reason the apostle Paul, who was one of these children, could exultantly exclaim: "The Jerusalem above is free, and she is our mother. Now we, brothers, are children belonging to the promise the same as Isaac was. Wherefore, brothers, we are children, not of a servant girl, but of the free woman. For such freedom Christ set us free. Therefore stand fast, and do not let yourselves be confined again in a yoke of slavery."—Galatians 4:26, 28, 31; 5:1, *NW*.

[13] By offering up in sacrifice the human body which God had prepared for him when he was born as a man, Jesus Christ proved himself to be the High Priest of Jehovah God. No, not a priest of Aaron's family of the tribe of Levi, for Jesus was the Son of David and hence of the royal tribe of Judah. But he was a High Priest like Melchizedek, the ancient king of Salem. Jesus was made such, not by birth into the priestly tribe of Israel, but by God's own oath, when Jehovah said, at Psalm 110:4: "Jehovah hath sworn, and will not repent: Thou art a priest for ever after the manner of Melchizedek." (*AS*, margin) The apostle

---

12. By means of the new covenant how was the seed of Abraham to be made like the stars, and whom does Paul show the seed's mother to be?
13. How, despite his tribal extraction, did Jesus become a High Priest as well as Heir of the Kingdom?

Paul proves this vital point and adds: "Also, to the extent that it was not without a sworn oath, (for there are indeed men that have become priests without a sworn oath, but there is one with an oath sworn by the one that said respecting him, 'Jehovah has sworn, and he will not feel regret: "You are a priest forever," ') to that extent also Jesus has become the one given in pledge of a better covenant." (Hebrews 7:20-22, *NW*) By being born as the Son of David Jesus became the permanent Heir of the covenant God made with David for the everlasting kingdom. By being sworn into God's priesthood and offering up a perfect human sacrifice Jesus was made a High Priest like Melchizedek, king of Salem, hence a Royal Priest. His followers, his spiritual brothers, are made royal priests with him. They are what the new covenant over Jesus' sacrifice results in.

[14] Hence when Jesus was baptized by John to symbolize he had quit the carpenter work at Nazareth and was dedicating himself to do God's will as written for him in the sacred Scriptures, Jesus had a most important assignment of service set out for him by God. To carry it out faithfully would be real worship of God, true religion according to God's revealed will. To test his resoluteness to do this he was at once led by God's spirit into the wilderness. There the Serpent, Satan the Devil, tried to swerve him from his course by an appeal to fleshly appetite and love of self-display. But the Tempter failed to stir up such things in Jesus.

---

14. So from then on what would be real worship of God for Jesus, and how was his devotion to it tested at the start?

[15] Finally, from an unusually high mountain, the Devil showed him all the kingdoms of the earth, those of India, those of China, the Roman empire, and suchlike. "And the Devil said to him: 'I will give you all this authority and the glory of them, because it has been delivered to me and to whomever I wish I give it. You, therefore, if you do an act of worship before me, it will all be yours.' " But Jesus was not interested in the politics of this world. He was not accepting from the Serpent control over any worldly governments with the idea of reforming them. How could he do so, when this required him to be a worshiper of Satan the Devil?

[16] Jesus was interested in the everlasting kingdom for which God had made the covenant with King David. Of this kingdom covenant God had now anointed Jesus to be the permanent Heir. Never would Jesus abandon Jehovah's universal sovereignty and go over to devil religion, thus forfeiting his soul in order to gain worldly kingdoms doomed to destruction. So in rebuff of the Devil's contemptible offer Jesus said: "It is written, 'It is Jehovah your God you must worship, and it is to him alone you must render sacred service.' " Beaten, the great Serpent slunk away, failing to induce Jesus into any bargain and compromise with him. Never did Jesus let the Serpent get his coils about him. Near the end of Jesus' earthly life, when the Serpent was about to bruise his heel, Jesus said to his apostles: "The ruler of the world is coming. And yet he has no hold on me."—Luke 4:1-13 and John 14:30, *NW*.

15, 16. (a) What offer of world control did Satan then lay before Jesus and on what terms? (b) Why and how did Jesus turn it down?

CHAPTER XIX

The Poor Transferred to Abraham's Bosom

STANDING trial for his earthly life before Rome's governor for Judea, Jesus summed up his life's purpose on earth by saying to Pontius Pilate: "My kingdom is no part of this world. If my kingdom were part of this world, my attendants would have fought that I should not be delivered up to the Jews. But, as it is, my kingdom is not from this source. . . . For this purpose I have been born and for this purpose I have come into the world, that I should bear witness to the truth. Everyone that is on the side of the truth listens to my voice."—John 18:36, 37, *NW*.

² The conspiracy among the religious Pharisees and Sadducees had turned Jesus over to the Roman authorities for execution on a torture stake. The Sadducees were high in the priesthood and also had members in the Supreme Sánhedrin at Jerusalem which had condemned Jesus to death. They rejected tradition and insisted on the letter of what scriptures they accepted. They denied fate and said God was not interested in the doings of men and that it rested with us to be good or bad. They did not believe in angels or spirits. They taught that the human soul dies with the body and

1. How did Jesus sum up his life's purpose on earth before Pilate?
2. Whose conspiracy had turned Jesus over for execution, and what were the beliefs and practices of these religious sects?

denied the resurrection of the dead. The Pharisees believed in the human traditions handed down by the religious fathers and placed these on a level with God's written Law and prophecies, if not above them. They believed in the predestination of men, or fate. They were fond of showy hypocritical formalities and were filled with a sense of their own self-righteousness by observing manmade commands. Influenced by Babylonish Greek philosophy, they believed in the immortality of the human soul and that under the earth there are rewards or punishments for the soul. Only good souls would be sent back to the earth's top again, such souls to enter into other human bodies, but the bad souls suffer everlasting punishment. In this belief they resemble the Greek philosopher Pythagoras on the transmigration of the soul. Both these Jewish religious sects had the common people under their power and control.—Josephus' *Antiquities,* Book 18, chapter 1, ¶¶ 3, 4; *Wars,* Book 2, chapter 8, ¶ 14.

[3] So the Jewish religious leaders considered themselves clothed with righteousness as with fine white linen. They believed themselves in line for God's kingdom and applied to themselves the purple promises. Being, besides, the natural descendants of Abraham, they felt themselves to be the Abrahamic seed which God promised for blessing all families and nations. So they feasted on their educational privileges in connection with the religious system of Israel. They looked down upon the common people as mere earthlings, "people of the earth," accursed, fit to associate only with dogs and not deserving of a resurrection. They

3. How did they view themselves in contrast with the common people, and so from what did the people need to be made free?

ground the people down with heavy religious burdens and exploited them for self-profit. The nation had once been freed from exile and captivity in ancient Babylon, but now these apostate religious leaders had brought the Jews into a new religious bondage. So the apostle Paul who was once a Pharisee himself could compare the religious organization with the Egyptian servant girl Hagar and say: "She corresponds with the Jerusalem today, for she is in slavery with her children." (Galatians 4:25, *NW*) So, even though in their native land, the Jewish people, especially the faithful remnant among them, needed to be made free. Jesus pictured that they would be made free from their oppressors, in a parable he gave in the hearing of the self-righteous, money-loving Pharisees. He said:

⁴ "A certain man was rich, and he used to clothe himself with purple and linen, enjoying himself from day to day with magnificence. But a certain beggar named Lazarus used to be put at his gate, full of ulcers and desiring to be filled with the things dropping from the table of the rich man.

 Yes, too, the dogs would come and lick his ulcers. Now in course of time the beggar died and he was carried off by the angels to the bosom position of Abraham.

⁵ "Also the rich man died and was buried. And in Hades he lifted up his eyes, he existing in torments, and he saw Abraham afar off and Lazarus

4-6. What were the details of Jesus' parable on rich man and beggar?

in the bosom position with him. So he called and said: 'Father Abraham, have mercy on me and send Lazarus to dip the tip of his finger in water and cool my tongue, because I am in anguish in this blazing fire.' But Abraham said: 'Child, remember that you received in full your good things in your lifetime, but Lazarus correspondingly the injurious things. Now, however, he is having comfort here but you are in anguish. And besides all these things, a great chasm has been fixed between us and you people, so that those wanting to go over from here to you people cannot, neither may people cross over from there to us.'

6 "Then he said: 'In that event I ask you, father, to send him to the house of my father, for I have five brothers, in order that he may give them a thorough witness, that they also should not get into this place of torment.' But Abraham said: 'They have Moses and the Prophets; let them listen to these.' Then he said: 'No, indeed, father Abraham, but if someone from the dead goes to them they will repent.' But he said to him: 'If they do not listen to Moses and the Prophets, neither will they be persuaded if someone rises from the dead.' "—Luke 16:14, 19-31, *NW*.

7 The rich man, every reader can see, pictured the highly favored, self-important religious leaders, who find their counterpart today in the religious clergy of Christendom. The beggar, whose name "Lazarus" means "God is helper", pictured that Jewish remnant who hungered and thirsted for truth and righteousness and who depended upon the religious leaders for spiritual nourishment. They got very little of that, just crumbs, for they were served with religious traditions of

---

7. Whom did this rich man and Lazarus picture?

men rather than with God's written Word. They were looked down on as spiritually ulcerous, whom only "dogs" would stoop so low as to lick in order to give comfort.

⁸ Death to beggar Lazarus and then to the rich man pictured a change in the condition of these classes. By means of God's angels the beggar class were transferred to Abraham's household to feast with him at his table, leaning upon his bosom. This meant becoming free from dependence on Jewish religious leaders and now becoming the children promised in God's covenant with Abraham. As Abraham here pictures Jehovah God himself, this meant becoming the spiritual children of this heavenly Father. This did not occur in hell, Sheol or the grave, for Jesus did not say the beggar Lazarus was buried. This blessed change of state came to the faithful Jewish remnant in this life. But how? By Jesus' priestly ministerial work.

⁹ Jesus followed up John the Baptist and preached God's kingdom throughout the land wherever he could gain an audience. In the synagogue at his home town Nazareth he took the roll of Isaiah's prophecy and read to his townsmen the prophecy concerning the liberation work he would do for the people, in these words: "Jehovah's spirit is upon me, because he anointed me to declare good news to the poor, he sent me forth to preach a release to the captives and a recovery of sight to the blind, to send the crushed ones away with a release, to preach Jehovah's acceptable year." With that as his text Jesus began to

8. What did Lazarus' death picture, and then his transfer to Abraham's bosom?
9. How did Jesus announce his work of liberation at Nazareth, but with what response from the Nazarenes?

preach to them, saying: "Today this scripture that you just heard is fulfilled." But when he told them the straight truth the religious people there in that synagogue rioted and rushed him out of town and tried to stone him to death. (Luke 4:16-30, *NW*) Those Nazarenes did not accept the liberation he offered by means of the truth. So they did not become his disciples.

[10] Later he said to believers: "If you remain in my word, you are really my disciples, and you will know the truth, and the truth will set you free." (John 8:31, 32, *NW*) Abraham's son Isaac was born from the free woman, his wife Sarah. Jesus, whom Isaac pictured, is free as the Son of God's free "woman", His organization, and all his followers who become children of the Greater Abraham with him are also free, being children of Jerusalem above, the free "mother". So by Jesus' preaching the Kingdom truth the faithful remnant died to their hitherto diseased beggar state of slavish dependence upon Jewish religious leaders and became part of Abraham's true seed. Five hundred years previous a Jewish remnant had come out of captivity in ancient Babylon. Now again a remnant got free from a religious bondage like that of Babylon.

[11] The religious rich man class died to their former advantageous condition and came into torments instead of comforts. If dead and buried, how could they experience torments? This class died to the service of Jehovah God and showed themselves to be the visible seed of the Serpent, for they persecuted and opposed Jesus and his

10. How did a remnant now get free from a bondage like that of Babylon?
11. To what did the rich man class die, and in what way were they buried in Hades?

disciples who were serving God. The rich man class were buried in Hades, Sheol, or hell or the grave (all equivalent terms) in that they were rejected from God's service and were just as inactive in it as persons in the grave are inactive, buried in earthly things.

¹² But is there a blazing fire of torment in Hades? Not in the literal Hades or grave. But in their dead and buried condition the religious rich man class were subject to fiery torment. How? By exposure to the teaching of God's Word by Jesus and his disciples. Jesus separated the rich man class like chaff or straw from the wheat. "What is the straw to the wheat? saith Jehovah. Is not my word like fire? saith Jehovah." (Jeremiah 23:28, 29, *AS*) How they must have been scorched when Jesus denounced them as hypocrites, vipers! as in Matthew, chapter 23! They howled against Jesus and finally procured his death. After Jesus' death and resurrection and his ascension they objected to the activities of his disciples and felt torment at their preaching and teaching the people. They did not see themselves favored with any of the blessings of the true sons of Abraham, but they saw the faithful Jewish remnant enjoying these as Christ's disciples, and this tormented them. When the feast day of Pentecost came and the holy spirit was poured out in fulfillment of Joel 2:28, 29, it was poured, not upon this rich man class, but upon Christ's disciples. It was these disciples filled with the spirit who preached the message of God's kingdom and who became alive and active in His service. It was not the rich man class who were thus being used. They were left inactive toward God's service as if buried stiff

12. How, then, did they experience fiery torment there?

in the grave or Hades. But how they did writhe under the torment of the disciples' educational work among the common people!—Acts 2:2-47; 4:1-22; 5:33-40; 7:54-60.

[13] In what way, then, did they want the Lazarus class to dip the tip of their finger in water and cool the tongue of those tormented in the blazing fire? Since water is used as a symbol of the Scriptural truth, they wanted the Lazarus class to leave the bosom of God's favor and compromise the truth and present the message of God's Word in such a way as not to torment them any further. It would also ease the pain of their religious susceptibilities if the faithful remnant would quit preaching God's Word altogether, and let the religious leaders do the only instructing, in the traditional way. But the Greater Abraham's reply to their plea reminds us how truly Jesus' sermon on the mount worked out: "Happy are you poor, because yours is the kingdom of God. Happy are you who hunger now, because you will be filled. Happy are you who weep now, because you will laugh. But woe to you rich persons, because you are having your consolation in full. Woe to you who are filled up now, because you will go hungry. Woe, you who are laughing now, because you will mourn and weep." (Luke 6:20, 21, 24, 25, NW) That was the way things had reversed themselves for the beggar and the rich man.

[14] God's righteous judgments have reversed matters that way, and his judgments are unalterable.

---

13. In what way did they want the Lazarus class to dip the finger tip in water and apply it to their tongue, but was this granted?
14. What did the great chasm between symbolize, and what did the rich man mean in wanting Lazarus to be sent to his five brothers?

"Thy judgments are a great deep." (Psalm 36:6) They stand as a "great chasm" to divide the rich man class far from the bosom of divine favor and from the Lazarus class. This chasm of judicial separation cannot be crossed or bridged from either side. In view of that, the rich man class prayed God to send the remnant to his "five brothers", that is, his allies and religious associates, that he "may give them a thorough witness". By this the rich man class indirectly acknowledged that the remnant are Jehovah's witnesses. But do they really want these witnesses of Jehovah to testify the Kingdom message to their allies and religious brothers? No; but to compromise the message and present their message in such a manner as not to put these religious brothers in a "place of torment" the same as the rich man class is in. Do not expose false, traditional religion, and do not proclaim "the day of vengeance of our God".—Isaiah 61:2.

¹⁵ But their religious brothers and allies in the Jewish organization have "Moses and the Prophets". So "let them listen to these", is the Greater Abraham's reply. The remnant of Jehovah's witnesses are under divine command and anointing to preach Moses and the Prophets. They are not allowed to take away from such nor add to such. So if the rich man's brothers are real sincere Jews wishing to escape the fiery condemnation of the Scriptures, let them listen to the message of the Law and the Prophets and discern that these point them to Christ, the Seed of God's woman.

---

15. What did those brothers have that made sending Lazarus unnecessary, and so what were they responsible to do?

[16] But the rich man class insist that they know better than Abraham. Moses and the Prophets are not enough! What their brothers need is a sign besides, someone to come to them from the dead. Then they will believe! But the Greater Abraham, Jehovah God, replied the same as his Son Jesus Christ: "A wicked and adulterous generation keeps on seeking for a sign, but no sign will be given it except the sign of Jonah the prophet. For just as Jonah was in the belly of the huge fish three days and three nights, so the Son of man will be in the heart of the earth three days and three nights. . . . look! something more than Jonah is here." And: "Unless you people see signs and wonders, you will by no means believe." (Matthew 12:39-41 and John 4:48, NW) Because the rich man's "brothers" were wicked and adulterous for not exercising faith but wanting to *see* something before believing, no sign was to be given them. Having Moses and the Prophets, those brothers are responsible to search these inspired Scriptures and see that Jehovah's witnesses are telling the truth. If they refused to believe Moses and the Prophets, they could not be persuaded by someone's resurrection.

[17] So when the Greater Abraham resurrected Jesus from the dead on the third day, did God send him to the "rich man" class or to the "five brothers" of such? No! God did not make these religious hypocrites witnesses of the resurrection of his Son, for he knew they would not even then believe, but would pervert the facts. Indeed, they

16. What did the rich man's reply now indicate, and why was his suggestion not to be followed and Lazarus sent?
17. To whom then did God send the resurrected Jesus, and why to them?

were the very ones that bribed the soldiers who had been guarding the sealed tomb where Jesus' corpse was buried to say that his body had been stolen from it by his disciples while these soldiers were asleep at their posts. (Matthew 28:11-15) Hence the Greater Abraham sent the resurrected Jesus to the Lazarus class, for these would prove faithful witnesses of this crucial resurrection truth. Said the apostle Peter, one of the Lazarus class: "We are witnesses of all the things he did both in the country of the Jews and in Jerusalem; but they also did away with him by hanging him on a stake. God raised this One up on the third day and granted him to become visible, not to all the people, but to witnesses appointed beforehand by God, to us, who ate and drank with him after his rising from the dead. Also he ordered us to preach to the people and to give a thorough witness that this is the One decreed by God to be judge of the living and the dead. To him all the prophets bear witness."—Acts 10:39-43, NW.

[18] In proof that the "rich man" or his "five brothers" would not be "persuaded if someone rises from the dead", we have this record about the preaching of Peter and John: "Now while the two were speaking to the people the chief priests and the captain of the temple and the Sadducees came upon them, being annoyed because they were teaching the people and were plainly declaring the resurrection from the dead in the case of Jesus." (Acts 4:1, 2, NW) There was no relief from torment for the rich man class back there. Likewise there is none for their modern counterparts now.

18. What action against apostles shows the five brothers would not be persuaded by anyone's resurrection?

CHAPTER XX

The "Sacred Secret of This Godly Devotion"

CHRIST Jesus established the congregation of his followers to be a firm pillar of witness and a support of the truth of the sacred secret of God. But warning was sounded well in advance that many would leave the true congregation and would form a counterfeit organization to twist the sacred secret, as Nimrod and Semiramis had done at Babylon. The apostle Paul warned the young disciple Timothy of this, in these words: "I am writing . . . that you may know how you ought to conduct yourself in God's household, which is the congregation of the living God, a pillar and support of the truth. Indeed, the sacred secret of this godly devotion is admittedly great: 'He was made manifest in flesh, was declared righteous in spirit, a p p e a r e d to angels, was preached about among nations, was believed upon in the world, was received up in glory.' However, the inspired utterance says definitely that in later periods of time some will fall away from the faith, paying attention to misleading inspired utterances and teachings of demons, by the hypocrisy of men who speak lies, marked in their conscience as with a branding iron."—1 Timothy 3:14 to 4:2, NW; Dy; CB; AS.

1. What features did Paul describe about the "sacred secret of this godly devotion", and what warning did he sound in connection with it?

[2] Take note of these features about the sacred secret, from which hypocritical men were to apostatize. "He was made manifest in flesh, was declared righteous in spirit." This feature came to be true when Christ Jesus was resurrected from the dead on the third day. In the flesh he was condemned by men as a sinner, blasphemer, coworker with Beelzebub, and a seditionist against the Roman empire. So at the loud demand of the Jewish chief priests, officials, rulers and scribes Jesus was hanged upon a torture stake until dead, the charge being posted above him "Jesus the Nazarene the King of the Jews". Men, that is, his few followers then, could not vindicate him of the false charges. But God could do so, declaring him to be righteous. How? By raising him from the dead as he had hinted in His promise in the garden of Eden. The Serpent was to bruise the heel of the woman's Seed, but the Seed, in turn, was to crush the Serpent's head. How could this be except God healed him from the bruise at the heel? Jesus had not died for his own sins, meriting his destruction, but had died in place of sinners, taking their place. To this effect it is written: "Christ by purchase released us from the curse of the Law by becoming a curse instead of us, because it is written: 'Accursed is every man hanged upon a stake.'" (Galatians 3:13, NW) Hence because Jesus was no sinner but was faithful till death God could raise him up.

[3] But with what kind of body was Jesus to be raised from the dead? God had prepared a fleshly

2. Why did Jesus need vindication after his death, and who could vindicate him?
3. As a sacrificer only with what kind of body could Jesus be raised in his vindication, and with what body was he raised?

body for him in com-
ing to earth, and in or-
der to have something
acceptable to God to
sacrifice he must sac-
rifice this perfect hu-
man body. This he did
on the stake. To sacri-

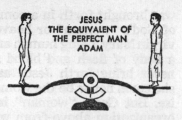

fice something means to give it up, to suffer the
loss of it, to renounce it for something else. Hence
Jesus on being restored to life could not have that
body back again in order to live in it. To do so
would be taking back the sacrifice. God was equal
to the situation. After Jesus' baptism when the
holy spirit was poured out upon him God begot
him by his spirit to be his spiritual Son and said:
"This is my Son, the beloved, whom I have approved." It follows that at his resurrection from
death he must be brought forth a spirit Son, no
longer flesh. Is this mere self-deception, or do we
have inspired witness to this effect? We have Peter who saw him a number of times during the
forty days after his resurrection. What have
you to tell us, Peter? "Christ died once for all
time concerning sins, a righteous person for unrighteous ones, that he might lead you to God,
he being put to death in the flesh, but being made
alive in the spirit." Made alive how, did you say,
Peter? "In the spirit." This, too, is how he "was
declared righteous in spirit". Hence Jehovah's
High Priest did not withdraw his human sacrifice,
but it still remained for mankind's eternal benefit.
—1 Peter 3:18, *NW*.

⁴ By this resurrection as a spirit person Jesus

---

4. So when was Jesus brought forth in a complete sense
as the woman's seed, and how does Paul show this?

was brought forth in a complete sense as the Seed of God's "woman" or heavenly organization. The virgin Mary, being human and able only to produce a body of flesh and blood from her womb, could never bring forth Jesus as a spirit creature. So she could never be the woman of the Edenic promise. But God's "woman" in heaven, his spiritual organization above from which Jesus came forth to become a man for thirty-three and a half years on earth, was the mother that produced him for God's loving purpose, "the Jerusalem above." Of his full spirit birth at his resurrection we read: "We are declaring to you the good news about the promise made to the forefathers, that God has entirely fulfilled it to us their children in that he resurrected Jesus; even as it is written in the second psalm, 'You are my son, I have become your Father this day.' "—Acts 13:32, 33, *NW*.

⁵ Almighty God raised his Son Jesus Christ from the dead an immortal spirit person, never able to return to corruption. So to make himself visible and appear to his disciples for the forty days after his resurrection that they might be his witnesses, Jesus materialized different bodies on various occasions to show he was alive but no longer a human creature. (See Mark 16:11, 12, *Dy; CB; Kx*.) Because of being now a spirit, he could ascend to heaven and appear in God's presence up there.

⁶ As his disciples watched Jesus ascend heavenward on the fortieth day, his materialized body disappeared within a cloud and the two materialized angels standing by said: "This Jesus who

---

5. By what means did Jesus manifest himself to his disciples after his resurrection?
6. With what did Jesus ascend and enter into God's presence, and for whom did he first apply it?

was received up from you into heaven will come thus in the same manner as you have beheld him going into heaven." They did not say he would come back in the same form or body as the disciples had seen ascend. "Flesh and blood cannot inherit God's kingdom, neither does corruption inherit incorruption." (Acts 1:1-11, *NW;* 1 Corinthians 15:50, *NW*) As Israel's high priest entered into the Most Holy of the temple, not with the fleshly bodies of the bull and goat but only with their blood which represented their life, so the High Priest Christ Jesus ascended not with the fleshly body he had sacrificed but with the value of the perfect human life he had sacrificed. This he presented to God in his heavenly residence for all those who were to believe on him afterward. In this way, too, he "appeared to angels" in heaven. This human life value he applied so as to put the new covenant into force for his followers on earth who were to become members of the seed of Abraham, spiritual children of Jehovah God.—Hebrews 13:11, 12; 9:11, 12, 24-26, *NW.*

 7 On the passover night just before his death Jesus arranged for a yearly memorial of his death. He passed the cup of wine to his eleven faithful apostles, the traitor Judas having left, and he said: "Drink out of it, all of you; for this means my 'blood of the covenant' which is to be poured out in behalf of many for forgiveness of sins." "This cup means the new covenant by virtue of my blood, which is to be poured out in your be-

---

7. When did Jesus inaugurate the new covenant, and begin to be "preached about among nations"?

half." (Matthew 26:27, 28 and Luke 22:20, *NW*) Ten days after his ascension into the presence of God to hand over the value of his human sacrifice, namely, on the feast day of Pentecost, Jesus Christ the Mediator inaugurated that new covenant toward his disciples on earth. He applied to them the benefits of this paid-over sacrifice. He evidenced this by pouring out the holy spirit upon them, anointing them as he had been anointed from heaven. Under the power of that spirit Peter said that day: "This Jesus God resurrected, of which fact we are all witnesses. Therefore because he was exalted to the right hand of God and received the promised holy spirit from the Father, he has poured out this which you see and hear. Actually David did not ascend to the heavens, but he himself says, 'Jehovah said to my Lord, "Sit at my right hand, until I make your enemies a stool for your feet." ' " (Acts 2:1-4, 32-35, *NW*; Psalm 110:1, *AS*) Thus Jesus glorified began to be "preached about among nations".

[8] From that Pentecostal day forward God's woman, "the Jerusalem above," began to bring forth other members of Abraham's seed, and thus the Lazarus class was received more fully into Abraham's bosom to be associated with Jesus Christ the principal one of the seed. "Now the promises were spoken to Abraham and to his seed. It says, not, 'And to seeds,' as in the case of many such, but as in the case of one, 'And to your seed,' who is Christ. Moreover, if you belong to Christ, you are really Abraham's seed, heirs with reference to a promise." (Galatians 3:16, 29, *NW*) So Abraham's seed began to become like the

---

8. When did God's woman begin to bring forth other members of Abraham's seed, and how many of them did the Jewish nation furnish?

stars of heaven for multitude. It was first sixty years after this, when the apostle John was given the vision to write the Bible's last book, The Revelation, that the till then unknown number of that multitudinous seed of Abraham was revealed to be 144,000 to be associated with the Lamb of God, Jesus Christ. (Revelation 7:1-8; 14:1, 3) But not that many of the Jewish nation believed on Jesus as the Christ, the Son of David and Seed of Abraham, and were brought into the new covenant. Only a remnant of the natural Jews did, some thousands of them, and these became spiritual sons of God, children of his "woman".—John 1:11, 12.

⁹ So we see that the servant woman to whom Jehovah God had been married by the Mosaic Law covenant did not produce the seed of Abraham. God dismissed her as Abraham did Hagar and her son Ishmael. The Law covenant by which God had been married to her he canceled by nailing it to the stake on which his Son Jesus died. (Colossians 2:13, 14) Thirty-seven years later, in the year 70 (A.D.), earthly Jerusalem which symbolized this dismissed servant woman was destroyed again, this time by Imperial Roman legions, in further proof of God's judgment of dismissal against her. (Luke 19:41-44; 21:20-24) But he retained his true "woman", his theocratic organization above, whom he now made fruitful with many children, as he had promised.

¹⁰ How, then, was Jehovah God going to complete the foreordained number of the Seed of Abraham, if the natural Jews did not supply the

9. What did God do with the "woman" who failed to produce the seed, and how was this action manifested?
10. When did Jesus begin to be "believed upon in the world", and why and how?

required number of believers? This was a feature
of the sacred secret that God kept hid for many
generations. It was this: the remaining needed
members were to be taken from among the non-
Jewish nations, the nations of the world. To this
end Jesus Christ the woman's Seed was not only
to be "preached about among nations" but also
to be "believed upon in the world". According to
Daniel 9:27, after a full week of years from when
Jesus was baptized and was anointed with God's
spirit and became Christ, this feature of the mystery was to be made manifest. Seven years from
A.D. 29 brings us to A.D. 36. In that year it was
that the apostle Peter, not the rich man class, was
sent to preach to the Gentile nations, that Jesus
might be believed upon in the world. Under divine
direction he went to Caesarea, entered a Gentile
home, and preached to the Italian centurion Cornelius and all the uncircumcised Gentiles he had
gathered in his house. They believed what Peter
preached about Jesus. Then, just as at Pentecost,
"the holy spirit fell upon all those hearing the
word." In evidence they, too, began speaking with
foreign languages and glorifying God. Then Peter
commanded them to be baptized in water to symbolize their dedication of themselves to God by
belief in Jesus Christ.—Acts 10:9-48, *NW*.

[11] So now these uncircumcised Gentile believers,
whom the Jewish rich man class looked upon as
Gentile dogs, began to be received into Abraham's
bosom. Jehovah, the Greater Abraham, begot
them to be his spiritual children, sons of his "free
woman". They, too, were taken into the new covenant. Here, then, the congregational "body of

11, 12. (a) So whom now did the congregational "body
of Christ" begin to include? (b) What did Paul say
about the sacred secret so long hidden?

Christ", of which Jesus is the Head, began to include uncircumcised Gentile believers. Thus believing Jews and believing Gentiles were united in the one "body of Christ". So this long-hidden feature of the sacred secret was solved. After the apostle Paul had worked hard and suffered much to bring many uncircumcised Gentiles to a knowledge of this secret he said:

[12] "I in my turn am filling up what is lacking of the tribulations of the Christ in my flesh on behalf of his body, which is the congregation. I became a minister of this congregation in accordance with the stewardship from God which was given me in your interest to preach the word of God thoroughly, the sacred secret which was concealed from the past systems of things and from the past generations. But now it has been made manifest to his holy ones, to whom God has been pleased to make known what are the glorious riches of this sacred secret among the nations. It is Christ in union with you, the hope of his glory. He is the one we are publicizing, admonishing every man and teaching every man in all wisdom, that we may present every man complete in union with Christ."—Colossians 1:24-28, *NW;* see also Ephesians 3:4-9.

[13] By its union with Jesus Christ its Head the congregation was joined to the Seed of God's woman and was therefore a secondary part of that Seed. In great enmity the Serpent and his seed were determined to destroy the true Christian congregation which possessed the clean and undefiled religion, the worship of Jehovah God revealed through Jesus Christ.

---

13. In what way was the congregation a secondary part of the woman's seed, and so whose enmity did it incur?

CHAPTER XXI

The Falling Away from Christianity

THE virgin congregation of the first century underwent much persecution at the instigation of the Serpent's seed, and yet it grew and spread to all nations. This not proving successful at all, the Serpent determined upon a more cunning strategy, the perverting of the truth by apostates inside the congregation. Jesus warned of this. In his parable he foretold that Satan the enemy would sow weeds, imitation Christians, among the wheat, "the sons of the kingdom," particularly after the twelve apostles fell asleep in death.—Matthew 13:24-30, 36-43, *NW*.

[2] Peter drew an illustration from the history of the Israelite people and said that as false prophets arose among them, "there will also be false teachers among you. These very ones will quietly bring in destructive sects and will disown even the owner that bought them, bringing speedy destruction upon themselves. Furthermore, many will turn out of the way and follow their acts of loose conduct." (2 Peter 2:1-3, *NW*) In farewell warning to the overseers from the congregation at Ephesus Paul said: "I know that after my going away oppressive wolves will enter in among you and will not treat the flock with tenderness, and from among you yourselves men will rise and speak

1. Failing by persecution, what strategy did Satan determine against the congregation, and how did Jesus forewarn of this?
2. How did Peter and Paul warn of this same thing?

twisted things to draw away the disciples after themselves. Therefore keep awake." (Acts 20:29-31, NW) Was it any wonder that Jude found it necessary to write the Christians to "put up a hard fight for the faith that was once for all time delivered to the holy ones"?—Jude 3, NW.

[3] About thirty years later, or about two years before the end of the first century, John, the only surviving apostle, disclosed how far apostasy had progressed, saying: "Young children, it is the last hour, and, just as you have heard that antichrist is coming, even now there have come to be many antichrists; from which fact we gain the knowledge that it is the last hour. They went out from us, but they were not of our kind; for if they had been of our kind, they would have remained with us. But they went out that it might be shown up that not all are of our kind." That was why he urged them to continue remaining in union with the heavenly Father and with his Son.—1 John 2:18, 19, 24, NW.

[4] Time proved the accuracy of these prophetic warnings. During the next century the faithful Christians concerned themselves with assembling the inspired writings of Jesus' disciples that thus they might have all these together with the Hebrew Scriptures and so have the complete Bible. These they began binding together in codex form, that is, in book form with separate pages and with lids. The professed Christians may not have become prominent in worldly affairs, but many of

---

3. Toward the end of the first century how far did the apostle John show the apostasy had by then progressed, and what did he urge?
4. With what worthy endeavor did Christians occupy themselves in the second century, but with what did their leaders become infected?

them began to yield to the popularity of the Greek philosophy. They showed they placed such Babylonish philosophy above the Holy Scriptures, for they endeavored to wrest the Scriptures to harmonize with such Grecian philosophy, so compromising the truth. In the latter half of this second century Theophilus, the so-called "bishop" of Antioch in Syria, came into prominence and betrayed himself as tainted with popular paganism. Writing in Greek in defense of his religion he introduced into his doctrine the word *trias* (τριάς), which means "triad or trinity".

[5] A contemporary of Theophilus in Northern Africa, a Latin writer named Tertullian, of the city of Carthage opposite Italy, wrote in defense of his religion and introduced into his writings the word *trinitas*, which means "trinity". From then on trinitarian doctrine came to infect the belief of professed Christians more and more. Such doctrine is altogether foreign to true Christianity. The word *trias* (τριάς) is not even found in the inspired Christian Greek Scriptures, and the word *trinitas* is not found in even the Latin translation of the Bible, the Vulgate.

[6] Then there was Origen (A.D. 185-254) of Caesarea, famous for his Biblical criticism and his *Hexapla*. He yielded to the philosophy of Plato on the human soul's immortality. He was therefore led to believe in the "pre-existence of human souls, and their incarceration in bodies for offenses previously committed". (Mosheim's *Institutes of Ecclesiastical History*) Babylonish Hinduism this!

---

5. What did Tertullian introduce into his Latin religious writings and was there any basis for this in the Greek or the Latin Bible?
6. On what pagan doctrine did Origen of Caesarea yield?

THE LABARUM

[7] Due to the apostasy from the simplicity of the original Christian faith the professed Christianity became more popular as it compromised with the accepted pagan philosophies of the world. The real fusion of paganism and apostate Christianity, however, came in the first quarter of the fourth century. Constantine was fighting for control of Rome. So he turned his military might against Maxentius who had usurped the government of Italy and Africa. It took three battles to conquer him. During this military campaign for worldly political office Constantine claimed he saw a cross flaming in the heavens, beneath the sun, and displaying this inscription, *In hoc signo vinces,* that is, "By this sign you will conquer." The following night Christ is said to have appeared to him and to have ordered him to take for his standard an imitation of the fiery cross seen in the heavenly vision. So he had a standard made in this form, which was called the *labarum.*

[8] The Roman Catholic Hierarchy claim this was a sign from heaven which led to Constantine's conversion to the Christianity of the day. But faithful upholders of the Holy Scriptures can take no such view of the matter. Jesus told his own countrymen, the Jews, "Unless you people see signs and wonders, you will by no means believe," and he called them an adulterous and wicked gen-

---

7. Under what circumstances was it that Constantine claims he saw the flaming cross in the heavens, and so what standard did he adopt?
8. Why are the Roman Catholic Hierarchy Scripturally wrong in claiming this was a sign from heaven to convert Constantine?

eration because of always wanting a sign. Hence
he said no sign would be given but the sign of the
prophet Jonah who came out of the belly of the
huge fish. It is absolutely unscriptural, therefore,
to argue that Jesus would stultify himself and
send a sign from heaven to a pagan in order to
convert him to Christianity, and especially when
that pagan was shedding blood with carnal weapons in order to gain political supremacy in the
aggressive Roman empire. That was not the way
that the Italian centurion Cornelius was converted.

⁹ Moreover, after his victory over his political
opponent Maxentius, Constantine was declared by
the Roman Senate to be Augustus and also Pontifex Maximus, on October 28, 312. By this Constantine became the Chief Priest of the pagan
Roman religion, which was far different from
getting baptized to indicate his conversion to
Christianity. The fact is, he was not baptized till
he fell sick twenty-five years later, in 337, the
year he died. Constantine was a pagan worshiper
of the sun god, and the symbol of this false god
was the cross or the letter T, the initial letter of
the false god Tammuz. If what Constantine saw
in vision was a cross, then it was the sign of his
god, for Jesus Christ was not hanged upon a cross
but was hanged upon a simple stake. It was from
Constantine's time onward that the symbol of the
apostate Christianity which he professed to accept
was the cross.

¹⁰ In January, 313, Constantine published the

---

9. What pagan title did he accept showing he was not
converted, and why could it have been only a pagan
cross he saw in his vision?
10. What religious fusion did Constantine seek, and
what council did he call in 325 and for the settlement
of what?

memorable edict of toleration in favor of the Christians. He was politician enough to see that the religious organization of which he was Pontifex Maximus was headed for shipwreck and that the apostate Christianity of his day was a powerful religious movement in his empire. So he endeavored to get a fusion of the two religions, by a compromise from each side. He succeeded. The bishop of Rome was not Pontifex Maximus then. Constantine was, and as such this unbaptized Roman emperor called a council for the settlement of the religious issue which was dividing the professed Christians and troubling his empire. He called it to meet A.D. 325, not at Rome, but at Nice, in Asia Minor. Only 318, about one-sixth of the bishops called, came. The bishop of Rome did not preside. The emperor as Pontifex Maximus did. The sessions were not in Latin, but in Greek.

[11] After wrangling two months pro and con on the trinity, the unbaptized emperor, Constantine, not the bishop of Rome, decided that this should be the doctrine of the professed Christian church. The Nicene Creed upholding the trinity was drawn up in Greek, not Latin, and was enforced by the sword of the state. However, it is not enforced by the "sword of the spirit, that is, the word of God". (Ephesians 6:17, CB; Dy) Arius, who had wielded the "sword of the spirit" to prove that the trinity was not Scriptural or Christian, was banished, and the emperor sided with Athanasius. From this developed the Athanasian creed which states: "And the catholic faith is this: that we worship one God in Trinity, and Trinity in Unity; neither confounding the persons, nor dividing the substance.

11. Who decided which religious doctrine should prevail, and what does the Athanasian creed say on this doctrine?

. . . So the Father is God, the Son is God, and the Holy Ghost is God. And yet there are, not three Gods, but one God." You understand?

[12] Constantine was really the first Roman Catholic pope. The Roman Senate placed him among the gods, and the apostate Christians of the East reckoned him among the saints. This, despite the fact that after his vision of the cross he killed his son, his second wife, several others of his relatives, and some of his most intimate friends. To fuse apostate Christianity more solidly with paganism, Constantine assigned the bishops political positions and thus wedded the church with the political state. So these bishops proved they did not have the pure apostolic religion, for the disciple James writes: "Religion clean and undefiled before God and the Father, is this: to visit the fatherless and widows in their tribulation: and to keep one's self unspotted from this world. Adulterers, know you not that the friendship of this world is the enemy of God? Whosoever therefore will be a friend of this world, becometh an enemy of God." —James 1:27; 4:4, *Dy; CB*.

[13] It was the Augustine born twenty-nine years after the Nicene Council who popularized the doctrine of the immortality of the human soul among the professed Christians, despite objections by those who clung to the Holy Scriptures. Thus Augustine put pagan Plato ahead of Christ. In the following century Vigilius of Thapsus, south of Carthage, made a citation in his Latin writings which has become verses 7 and 8 of 1 John, chap-

12. Despite what murderous record was Constantine religiously glorified, and how did his bishops show they had no apostolic religion?
13. How did Augustine put Plato ahead of Christ, and how did the forgery at 1 John 5:7, 8 have its beginning?

ter 5, namely, "For there are three that bear record *in heaven, the Father, the Word, and the Holy Ghost: and these three are one. And there are three that bear witness in earth,* the spirit, and the water, and the blood: and these three agree in one." The words "in heaven, the Father, the Word, and the Holy Ghost: and these three are one. And there are three that bear witness in earth" are not found in any Greek manuscript till a thousand years after Vigilius; nor were they found in Jerome's Latin *Vulgate,* nor in any Latin manuscript before the ninth century, nor are they quoted by any of the Greek ecclesiastical writers. The words are recognized as a forgery and spurious and so have been omitted from modern Bible translations. But for centuries they have been used as the main support of the "trinity".

[14] Constantine's successors followed his example in adopting the title Pontifex Maximus until Gratian, emperor of Rome of the Western Empire. (A.D. 375-383) He refused to assume the title and the insignia of Pontifex Maximus, a dignity till then considered as annexed to that of emperor. So in 378 the bishop of Rome, Damasus, took over the title, and now this title, borrowed from a pagan cult, is one of the chief designations of the pope or pontiff of Vatican City.

[15] Bishop Leo I (A.D. 440-461) was the first who tried to be a totalitarian pope in the modern sense. He tried to establish the "apostolic chair" as a spiritual supremacy over every branch of the Catholic religious organization and to establish for its occupant the exclusive use of the title of

14. How did the pagan title Pontifex Maximus undergo a change of hands?
15. How did Leo I try to be a pope in the modern sense?

Papa (Pope) of the whole Catholic organization. In support of this he tried to prove that the bishop of Rome is the apostolic successor of Peter. Strong opposition to this was organized in both the East and the West. The general council in Ephesus, A.D. 449, treated Leo's envoys with indignity and threatened them with violence. It is said that Leo I originated the fasts of Lent and Pentecost.

[16] Gregory I (A.D. 595-604) was the first to discover "purgatory". It was by means of the apparitions and visions which he related in his dialogues that he first discovered it. He claimed his discovery was because "the end of this world was at hand, and the nearer we came to the other [world] the more we discovered it!"

[17] A.D. 533 Emperor Justinian addressed the bishop of Rome as the head among all the bishops of the Eastern and Western congregations of the empire. Addressing Pope John II, he said: "The victorious Justinian, the devout, the fortunate, the renowned, the triumphant, the ever august, to John, the most holy archbishop of the fostering city of Rome, and patriarch.—Rendering honor to the Apostolic See and to your Holiness . . . we do not permit that any question be raised as to anything which concerns the state of the churches, however plain and certain it be, that be not also made known to your Holiness, who is the Head of all the holy churches. . . ."—*Thy Kingdom Come,* pages 70-72.

[18] Thus in the course of the apostasy from true

---

16. What did Gregory I discover, and by what means?
17. A.D. 533 as being what did Emperor Justinian address John II?
18. (a) In what division of the professed believers did the apostasy result? (b) What blasphemy is committed against the "Holy Father"?

Christianity there developed a division into the clergy and the laity, reaching its culmination in an exalted hierarchy with the pope at its head. He was called the "father of fathers" (*pater patrum*) and "holy father", in absolute violation of Jesus' command: "Call none your father upon earth; for one is your father, who is in heaven." (Matthew 23:9, *Dy; CB*) In harmony with his own command Jesus never let anyone call him "father" upon earth. Sometimes he addressed others as "Son", "Daughter," and "Children". (Matthew 9:2; Mark 10:24; Luke 8:48; John 13:33; 21:5) But he never received or accepted the spiritual title "Father" from them. He reserved that term only for his heavenly Father. Only once does the expression "Holy Father" occur in the entire Bible. That is where Jesus prayed to God and said: "Holy Father, keep them in thy name whom thou hast given me." (John 17:11, *Dy*) It is blasphemy for any religious potentate who claims to be the "Vicar of Christ" to demand and to receive the title "Holy Father". This practice bespeaks rank apostasy.

[19] The Roman Catholic cardinal, John Henry Newman, composer of the song "Lead, Kindly Light", is outspoken enough to admit that the Roman Catholic system has disobeyed God's command to avoid becoming infected with pagan religion and getting snared by it. He admits that she has continually made compromises with demonism. In 1878 he published his *Essay on the Development of Christian Doctrine*. In chapter 8 he asks concerning the Roman Catholic Church:

---

19. How did Cardinal Newman admit that the Roman Catholic system has continually made compromises with demon worship?

"Had it the power, while keeping its own identity, of absorbing its antagonists, as Aaron's rod, according to St. Jerome's illustration, devoured the rods of the sorcerers of Egypt? Did it incorporate them into itself, or was it dissolved into them? Did it assimilate them into its own substance, or, keeping its name, was it simply infected by them?" Then in disbelief of Jehovah God's warning Newman answers:

> "Confiding then in the power of Christianity to resist the infection of evil, and to transmute the very instruments and appendages of DEMON-WORSHIP to an evangelical use, and feeling also that these usages had originally come from primitive revelations and from the instinct of nature, though they had been corrupted; and that they must invent what they needed, if they did not use what they found; and that they were moreover possessed of the very archetypes, of which paganism attempted the shadows; the rulers of the Church from early times were prepared, should the occasion arise, to adopt, or imitate, or sanction the existing rites and customs of the populace, as well as the philosophy of the educated class."

Then, betraying the fusion of apostate Christianity with paganism, this British cardinal continues:

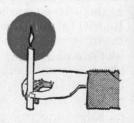

> "The use of temples, and these dedicated to particular saints, and ornamented on occasions with branches of trees; incense, lamps, and candles; votive offerings on recovery from illness; holy water; asylums; holydays and seasons, use of calendars, processions, blessings on the fields;

sacerdotal vestments, the tonsure, the ring in marriage, turning to the East, images at a later date, perhaps the ecclesiastical chant, and the [song] Kyrie Eleison [Lord, have mercy], are all of pagan origin, and sanctified by their adoption into the Church."—Pages 355, 371, 373, Edition of 1881.

[20] Michael Williams, once a leading defender of Roman Catholicism in America, contributed an article to the Brooklyn *Eagle* (New York) under date of February 21, 1943, and in it he quoted the following statement made by the late Pope Pius XI to newspapermen in Rome:

"The Head of the Catholic Church would consider it his duty to deal with the Devil himself, to say nothing about any mortals who, hypothetically, or in reality, were merely agents of the Dictator of Diabolism, if reasonable grounds existed to support the hope that such dealings would protect, or advance, the interests of religion among mankind."

This statement, coming from the pope who made concordats with the Fascist dictator Mussolini in 1929 and the Nazi Fuehrer Hitler in 1933, is proof that the spirit of Catholicism is the same today as in the time of Constantine. In stark naked contrast to the refusal of Jesus on the mount of temptation to make any bargain with the Devil for worldly political power, the Catholic spirit is one of compromise with demonism, Babylon's religion, for world control.

----

20. How did the late Pius XI show that the spirit of Catholicism is still one of compromise with demonism for world control?

CHAPTER XXII

Islam, Mohammed's Religion of Submission

JOHN the Third (A.D. 561-574) was pope of Rome when the founder of Islam was born. He was Kutam, the son of Abdallah, but before his call to religious reform he came to be named Mohammed, meaning "the Praised One". His system of religion (or, *din*) is generally called after this name, "Mohammedanism," but those who practice it prefer to call it "Islam", which means "resignation" or "entire submission", because it teaches man's entire duty is submission to God's will. Its adherents are called Moslems.

² The Mohammedan era dates from 622, the year of Mohammed's flight or *hegira* from Mecca to Yathrib, which was then renamed in his honor Medinat al nabi, "city of the prophet," or, short, Medina. Mohammed was born at Mecca A.D. 570, or possibly 562 "the year of the elephant". He belonged to the family of Hashim, which claimed lineal descent from Ishmael, Abraham's son by Hagar, the Egyptian slave girl of Abraham's wife Sarah. Except that Mohammed was a caravan conductor, little is known of his early life until he married his employer, Khadijah, a wealthy widow fifteen years his senior. By her he had seven children.

1, 2. Who was Mohammed? What is his religion called, and why?

278

[3] Disturbed by the idolatrous practices of the people about him who were infected with animism, tending to polytheism, Mohammed desired to bring them to a higher level of belief and practice. He periodically sought solitude for meditation. It was while he was in a cave outside of Mecca that he felt his call to be a prophet came to him. At once he began to preach that there was just one God, the Creator, Allah, and that there were rewards for believers in him in paradise and punishment for the wicked in the traditional "hell". The gist of his message was, "There is no god but Allah; and Mohammed is his prophet." His ideas he got largely from the impression which both Judaism and the apostate Christianity of the sixth century had made upon him. From stories he heard at the lips of Christian apostates he supposed that their trinity was made up of Jehovah, Mary and Jesus. It is doubtful if he read any of the Bible itself to get the truth.

[4] Three years before he fled from Mecca to Medina his wife Khadijah died. He now acquired a number of wives, whether for political reasons or for sexual gratification. The wars he waged against the Jews in Medina and in other parts of Arabia were marked by great cruelty on his side, also the conflicts which he carried on against several Arabian tribes allied with the Meccans. In 630 he broke his treaty of peace with Mecca, and suddenly, without any formal declaration of war, he surprised that city at the head of 10,000 men. The city magistrates were obliged to submit

3. What was the gist of his message? Where did he get his ideas?
4, 5. (a) How was his religion established in Arabia? (b) When and where did he die, and what writings did he leave behind?

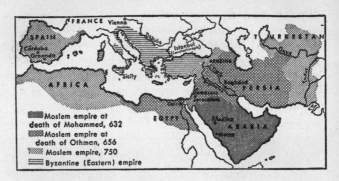

Moslem empire at death of Mohammed, 632
Moslem empire at death of Othman, 656
Moslem empire, 750
Byzantine (Eastern) empire

to him and they acknowledged him not only as the secular ruler but also as the plenipotentiary of the Deity.

[5] Through this victory the religion of Mohammed was put in a secure position in Arabia. After this he went out and defeated the enemies who came against him. He sent his envoys to neighboring lands and commanded their submission. He did not win their sincere conversion to Islam, and his war with the Byzantines ended unfavorably. On June 8, 632, he died at Medina, in the lap of Ayesha, his favorite wife. As his religious writings he left behind him the Koran (meaning "Recitation"), which he claimed to be God's word transmitted to him through the angel Gabriel. However, what writings he left did not satisfy all the needs of his followers, and hence much Islamic teaching was built up after his death.

[6] Mohammed's first successor (caliph) was his father-in-law Abu Bekr. All first four of the orthodox caliphs were friends of Mohammed, namely, Abu Bekr, Omar, Othman and Ali. The office,

6. How was the religion spread by his successors, and how far?

dignity and dominion of a caliph was called a caliphate. In course of time rival caliphates were established by dissenters. Under Omar the spread of Mohammedanism by the literal sword was unbelievably swift. The Syrian capital Damascus fell in 635; Jerusalem in 636. Persia yielded the Euphrates region in 637, and Egypt yielded her submission in 640. Before Omar fell at an assassin's hand in 644 he had pushed the power of the Moslems to India's very borders.

[7] Also westward the Mohammedan armies swept, and all northern Africa came into their hands, and even Spain. It was first in 732, a hundred years after Mohammed died, that they met a decisive defeat at Tours, France, by Charles Martel, the grandfather of Charlemagne. But the Moslem power continued to threaten Christendom. In Spain the Western Caliphate of Córdoba lasted till 1301. In 1492 the last kingdom of the Mohammedan Moors, at Granada, was conquered by the Spanish King Ferdinand V. Eastward, the Mohammedan Turks besieged Vienna in 1529 and again in 1683.

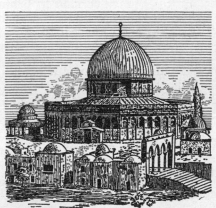

MOSQUE OF OMAR, FROM THE NORTHWEST

7. How did the Mohammedan armies threaten Christendom?

⁸ Islam spread clear into China. In 1258 the Mongol Hulagu came and sacked Baghdad and wiped out the caliph and his family. Moving westward, he was checked by the Egyptian Mamelukes and forced to retire to Persia. But fifty years later the Mongols embraced Islam and made it the state religion. One of their descendants, Bāber, founded a great Moslem empire in India, and today we have as one result the Moslem Republic of Pakistan. In the sixteenth century, after the conquest of Egypt, the sultans of Turkey assumed the title of Caliph. It continued in their line till March 2, 1924, when the new Turkish Republic abolished it. Moslem wars against the infidels or unbelievers were called *jiháds,* holy wars. The last jihád was called by the Ottoman Caliph of Turkey, in 1914, when that country joined the German Kaiser in World War I. It proved a complete failure, and Palestine was lost to Turkey. Still Mohammedanism predominates there today, and the Mosque of Omar still stands in Jerusalem where once the temple of Solomon stood. *Mosque* means a "house of prayer" for the Moslems.

⁹ When the Jews rejected Mohammed's fiery preaching, he substituted Mecca for Jerusalem as the holy city toward which Moslems turned to pray. This flattered the people of Mecca, which was already a city of pilgrimage for those who came there to worship the black meteorite stone in its Kaaba or cubical receptacle. Against the worship of this Kaaba stone Mohammed had once preached, but now, compromising, he made it a part of his religious system, so that one of the

8. How did Islam spread in Asia, and what is its position in Palestine now?
9. What did Mohammed make the chief holy city? Why, and how?

duties laid on each Moslem was to make at least one pilgrimage to Mecca during his lifetime and do religious acts toward the stone, including kissing it seven times. Such pilgrimages had the effect of binding the Mohammedan world together.

[10] Mohammed was exalted to be the seventh, the last and the greatest of Allah's prophets. Those preceding him were Adam, Noah, Abraham, Moses, Solomon and Jesus. Adam was said to have repented of his sin in Eden and to have obtained the forgiveness of Allah without the need of any propitiatory sacrifice and to have been made God's first prophet and then gone to heaven. Of the above prophets each one, with the exception of Solomon, was specially commissioned to proclaim new laws and a new dispensation, which did away with the preceding ones. Thus Mohammed did away with the dispensation inaugurated by Jesus Christ. He declared for the unity of God or Allah, and pronounced the trinity of Christendom, which made Jesus Christ the second person of a triune god, a blasphemous fiction of false priests. God was declared to have no offspring, and hence Jesus was not accepted as the Son of God. Of the need of a human sin offering to free mankind of the disability of inherited sin and death there is no mention in the Koran.

[11] The Koran or Mohammedan Bible is made up of 114 suras (chapters), each comprising a single revelation. It is a conglomeration of legends drawn from unscriptural Jewish traditions and from other sources, and of laws. Despite all its contradictions and its conflict with proved sci-

10. What rank does Islam assign Mohammed as prophet, and how does it view Jesus?
11. Of what is the Koran composed, how do Moslems treat it, and yet why does this not prove it true or right?

ence it is greatly reverenced by devout Moslems
and is constantly read by them. But their sincere
acceptance of it as the last word of God through
Mohammed does not make it true or right. Before
Mohammed Paul the Christian apostle had written: "Let God be found true, though every man
be found a liar, even as it is written [at Psalm
51:4]: 'That you might be vindicated in your
words and might win when you are being
judged.'" (Romans 3:4, NW) God cannot lie or
contradict himself but speaks the eternal truth.
Since he is accepted as having raised up Noah,
Abraham, Moses and Jesus as prophets and hence
to have spoken by them, he would not by a later
prophet than them contradict what he had earlier
said by them, even though his revelation by each
of these successive prophets did introduce a new
dispensation by each prophet. He would always
harmonize with himself.

[12] In the garden of Eden while the sinner Adam
was listening God foretold that he would raise up
a Seed to his woman and that this Seed would
be bruised at the heel by the Serpent but would,
in turn, bruise the Serpent's head. Noah carried
this divine Edenic prophecy across the Flood, and
his great-grandson Abraham came to the knowledge of it. Then God disclosed to Abraham that
the Promised Seed would be through him, saying:
"In thee shall all families of the earth be blessed."
(Genesis 3:15; 12:3) Abraham had first a son by
Hagar, the Egyptian servant girl, and years later
a son by his true wife Sarah. Hagar's son was
named Ishmael, and Sarah's, Isaac. But God rejected the older Ishmael from being the son in

---

12. What promise was passed on from Eden to Abraham and how was it amplified to him?

whose line of descent the Promised Seed was to come. He said to Abraham: "What will be called 'your seed' will be through Isaac." And at the time that Abraham proceeded to offer up Isaac as a sacrifice in obedience to God's command, God swore by himself and said to Abraham: "In thy seed shall all the nations of the earth be blessed." –Genesis 21:12; 22:15-18; Hebrews 11:17, 18, *NW*.

[13] Since Mohammed was a descendant of Abraham, not through Isaac, but through Ishmael, he could not be the prophet through whom all nations are to be blessed. Mohammed claimed that the writers of the Christian Greek Scriptures falsified the record about Jesus, but this claim is not borne out. We have papyrus manuscripts containing the writings of Christ's disciples that go back as far as the second century A.D., and these testify to the genuineness of the Christian Greek Scriptures as we have them today. The Christian apostle Peter definitely identified Jesus Christ as the Promised Seed of Abraham in whom all nations of the earth are to be blessed. And the apostle Paul, referring to God's promise to Abraham concerning the Seed writes: "Now the promises were spoken to Abraham and to his seed. It says, not, 'And to seeds,' as in the case of many such, but as in the case of one, 'And to your seed,' who is Christ." (Acts 3:19-26; Galatians 3:16, *NW*) Since there is but the one promised Seed, and since Christ Jesus is that one Seed, there could not be another and a later seed, such as Mohammed, who, besides, is not descended from Abraham through Isaac.

---

13. Why could Mohammed not be the Seed of the Abrahamic promise?

[14] Moses, who wrote the above records about Abraham and Isaac, is accepted as one of God's prophets. Certainly, then, he did not falsify. God revealed to Moses more of the depth of the meaning of his name *Jehovah.* That name occurs in the entire collection of the Hebrew Scriptures 6,823 times, but the Koran hides that holy name. Allah is not his name, for *Allah* means "the God". That is what he is. That is his title but is not the name he gives himself when speaking with Moses: "This is my name for ever, and this is my memorial unto all generations." (Exodus 3:6-15, *AS*) Jehovah God has promised yet to sanctify his holy name before all nations, including the Mohammedan nations; and yet the Koran ignores that fact.—Ezekiel 38:23; 39:7, *AS*.

[15] At Mount Sinai, where the Ten Commandments were given, Jehovah told Moses, who was acting as mediator for the Israelites or Jews: "I will raise them up a prophet from among their brethren, like unto thee; and I will put my words in his mouth, and he shall speak unto them all that I shall command him. And it shall come to pass, that whosoever will not hearken unto my words which he shall speak in my name, I will require it of him." (Deuteronomy 18:15-19, *AS*) The Moslems claim that this promised prophet was Mohammed. But how could that be? Mohammed was not a Jew, of Moses' brethren. He was of the nation of Ishmael whom Jehovah had rejected from having a part in the promise concerning Abraham's seed, and he did not speak in Jehovah's name. Centuries before Mohammed was born,

14. Though the Koran accepts Moses, how does it treat God's name?
15. Why could Mohammed not be the prophet greater than Moses?

Peter spoke to Moses' brethren the Jews and applied God's prophecy concerning the Greater Moses to Jesus Christ and identified him as the promised Prophet.—Acts 3:20-23.

[16] The Koran denies that this Jesus was impaled on a torture stake till dead, but the apostle Peter addressed the Jews who had demanded that Jesus be impaled and to them Peter said in their courtroom: "In the name of Jesus Christ the Nazarene, whom you impaled but whom God raised up from the dead, . . . there is no salvation in anyone else, for there is not another name under heaven that has been given among men by which we must get saved." (Acts 4:10-12, *NW*) So that excludes Mohammed's name, too.

[17] The Koran rejects the sacrifice of Jesus Christ as a ransom for mankind to gain life in the new world. In doing so it denies Jesus is Jehovah God's High Priest who sacrificed his human life for obedient mankind. It ignores, too, the new covenant which was put into force over Jesus' sacrificial blood, whereas the prophet Jeremiah had foretold that new covenant centuries previous. How, then, can the Koran take Moses as God's prophet and yet nullify the prophetic significance of the Law covenant which Moses mediated with Israel and which had animal sacrifices and a priesthood all foreshadowing the priesthood of Jesus Christ and his atoning sacrifice? The Koran is inconsistent in doing so and makes God deny himself.—Leviticus 16:1-34; Jeremiah 31:31-34; Hebrews 3:1; 9:1-28.

---

16. How does Peter exclude Mohammed's name as vital to salvation?
17. How is the Koran inconsistent in accepting Moses and yet denying the priestly and mediatorial work of Jesus?

[18] Moslems claim to accept what Jesus said concerning the "comforter" or "paraclete". But only in order to apply this to Mohammed. Says A. Yusuf Ali, in his footnote comment[416] on Sura III.81:

> In the New Testament as it now exists, Muhammad is foretold in the Gospel of St. John 14:16; 15:26; and 16:7: The *future* Comforter cannot be the Holy Spirit as understood by Christians, because the Holy Spirit already was present, helping and guiding Jesus. The Greek word translated "Comforter" is "Paracletos", which is an easy corruption from "Periclytos", which is almost a literal translation of "Muhammad" or "Ahmad".

And in his footnote comment[5438] on Sura LXI.6, he says:

> *"Ahmad"*, or *"Muhammad"*, the Praised One, is almost a translation of the Greek word *Periclytos*. In the present Gospel of John 14:16; 15:26; and 16:7, the word *"Comforter"* in the English version is for the Greek word "Paracletos", which means "Advocate", "one called to the help of another, a kind friend", rather than "Comforter". Our doctors contend that Paracletos is a corrupt reading for Periclytos, and that in their original saying of Jesus there was a prophecy of our holy Prophet *Ahmad* by name. Even if we read Paraclete it would apply to the holy Prophet who is "a Mercy for all creatures" (xxi. 107) and "Most kind and merciful to the Believers."

[19] This would locate the coming of the "comforter" or "helper" six centuries after Jesus gave the promise. But according to the above-cited verses of John Jesus promised to send the comforter to his apostles there with him, and not to

---

18. How do Moslems apply Jesus' promise concerning the "comforter"?
19. Why could this promise not mean Mohammed?

non-Christian Moslems centuries later. Jesus did not say it would be a person in flesh. He told them it was God's spirit, "the spirit of the truth," and that it would "bring back to your minds all the things I told you"; "the spirit of the truth which proceeds from the Father, that one will bear witness about me, and you, in turn, are to bear witness, because you have been with me from when I began." He later told them they would be baptized with it "not many days after this". (John 14:26; 15:26, 27; 16:13-15 and Acts 1:4, 5, *NW*) So how could this mean Mohammed who lived centuries after these apostles?

[20] On the day of Pentecost, ten days after Jesus ascended back to heaven, he did pour out the holy spirit upon those apostles, and they began speaking with foreign tongues and performing miracles. And Peter, under inspiration by that spirit, declared that Jesus, at his Father's right hand in heaven, had poured it out on them. (Acts 2:32-36) Certainly Mohammed did not bring back to their minds all the things Jesus had told them, for Mohammed denies the most vital things Jesus said. Mohammed is not found to be a personification of the "spirit of the truth" but is found denying the truth of Jehovah God as spoken through his prophets Noah, Abraham, Moses, Solomon and Jesus. And the apostle Paul said that if, later, even an angel from heaven should bring a message different from what he preached to them, let him be accursed. This allows for no angel Gabriel to send Mohammed later and nullify that message. —Galatians 1:8, 9.

[21] Among the fundamental things which prove

20, 21. Why is Mohammed not the comforter?

that Mohammed did not express the "spirit of the truth" is his teaching of the immortality of the human soul. That is a Babylonish false doctrine, the foundation of which was laid by Satan the Devil when deceiving Eve in the garden of Eden. Yet it was on the basis of this false doctrine that Mohammed framed his teachings concerning the hell of seven stories where human souls are tormented after death, as well as his doctrine that Adam is in heaven, the lowest of the heavens. But Jesus said: "No man has ascended into heaven but he that descended from heaven, the Son of man." And at Pentecost Peter said that not even faithful King David was up there, but was sleeping in his tomb awaiting the resurrection of the dead. (John 3:13, NW; Acts 2:25-35) God does not fiendishly torment souls in hell. He destroys the wicked and resurrects those asleep in death.

[22] Mohammed's religion has not prevailed over all religion, as predicted, even though it has such an appeal because it is an easy or light religion that makes concessions to human weakness. It claims one-ninth of the world's population, or 250 million adherents. But it is divided into 72 sects or denominations, and today it is threatened like Christendom by the world menace of international communism. In this the final crisis of this old world Islam has no message to offer distressed humanity regarding God's kingdom of the Seed of his woman for the blessing of all who turn to the one living and true God, Jehovah. Let Moslems as well as people of Christendom take heed to Jehovah's words at Isaiah 8:20, AS. Let them study His Word in the Holy Bible and thus enjoy the morning light of the new world.

---

22. How does Islam fail man? What is recommended?

CHAPTER XXIII

Christendom Rejects
the Kingdom of the Seed

IN HIS sermon on the mount Christ Jesus told
his disciples to pray this way: "Our Father
in the heavens, let your name be sanctified.
Let your kingdom come. Let your will come to
pass, as in heaven, also upon earth." In harmony
with this he instructed his disciples in the same
sermon to put the kingdom of the heavenly Father
ahead of everything else. Do not be like the pagans or heathen who worry and seek after selfish
material things of this world, but do this: "Keep
on, then, seeking first the kingdom and his righteousness, and all these other things will be added
to you." (Matthew 6:9, 10, 33, NW) He sent his disciples out on home missionary work among the people, with these orders: "As you go, preach, saying,
'The kingdom of the heavens has drawn near.'"
(Matthew 10:7, NW) His own parables were illus-
trations about the Kingdom. On the night of his last
passover with them before his death he handed his
faithful apostles the Memorial cup and said: "From
now on I will not drink again from the product of
the vine until the kingdom of God arrives."

² After the Memorial celebration he said to
them: "You are the ones that have stuck with
me in my trials; and I make a covenant with you,

---

1. What government did Jesus instruct his disciples to
pray for and to preach?
2. With what governments were they not to meddle,
and why not?

just as my Father has made a covenant with me, for a kingdom, that you may eat and drink at my table in my kingdom, and sit on thrones to judge the twelve tribes of Israel." (Luke 22:18, 28-30, *NW*) God's coming kingdom was His government by the enthroned Seed of his "woman". This was the theocratic government they were to preach and prepare for. They must not meddle with worldly kingdoms.

[3] Since Constantine's time Christendom, or that part of the world which makes a pretense of Christianity, has not done this. On "Christmas Day" of the year 800 the pope crowned the blood-stained Charles the Great (or Charlemagne) emperor of what the pope called "The Holy Roman Empire". This religious pontiff, who claimed to be Christ's vicegerent, undertook to crown the political rulers of Western Europe. Then, to make the subjects believe it was their religious duty to render unquestioning obedience to such rulers, the Roman Catholic Hierarchy taught the doctrine of the "divine right of kings". This doctrine they based on the apostle's words at Romans 13:1, "Let every soul be subject to higher powers: for there is no power but from God: and those that are, are ordained of God." (*Dy*) Scripturally these words now apply to the heavenly "superior authorities" of God's theocratic organization and not to worldly political powers like Nimrod and other totalitarian rulers.—*NW*.

[4] By thus crowning political rulers and teaching their divine right and so causing a union of the *church* (so called) and the state, the Roman Cath-

3. Whom did the pope proceed to crown as worldly rulers, and on the basis of what false doctrine?
4. What union were they thus causing, and what government were they rejecting for worldly control?

olic Hierarchy were rejecting the kingdom of the Seed of God's woman. Contrary to Jesus' example in the mountain of temptation the pope and his hierarchy were accepting control over the governments of this world at the price of falling down and worshiping Satan, who from Nimrod's time had sought and had gained world control. They forfeited their souls for worldly control.

[5] When the Protestant Reformation came in the sixteenth century, did it discontinue this alliance of church and state? No! Roman Catholic authorities call it, not a reformation, but a "rebellion". Judged by the facts, it was indeed more a sedition against the Roman pontiff than a true reformation. The great religious explosion was touched off when the Roman Catholic priest Martin Luther objected to the selling of papal indulgences for early release of human souls from "purgatory" and posted his ninety-five theses to the church door at Wittenberg, Germany, at midday of October 31, 1517. From his revolt there developed not only the Lutheran church but also the many other sects of the Protestant movement.

[6] The spiritual authority of the pope over a large part of Christendom was now broken. Many independent-minded persons took courage to establish religious organizations of their own, generally around some personal leader. To put down this rebellion against papacy the Hierarchy carried on religious wars and pushed the inquisition more vigorously than ever. From larger Protestant groups new sects broke off and generally suffered persecution from the parent organization.

5. Was the sixteenth-century religious split a true reformation, and how was it begun?
6. How did many sects arise, especially in what century, and as what kind of force have all these acted?

The land of America became the haven for many
who were suffering religious persecution to flee to.
In this land many new sects arose, especially in
the nineteenth century, so that in the year 1951
there were listed in the United States about 265
different sects. These religions acted as a great
divisive force. They could not stand for true Christianity. The apostle Paul asked: "Does the Christ
exist divided?" No; but Christendom today is a
great religious confusion and disunity. It is another Babylon or Babel.—1 Corinthians 1:13, *NW*.

⁷ That the Protestant movement was more a
rebellion against the religious supremacy of the
pope than a real reformation and a return to primitive Christianity is manifest from this fact:
These new sectarian religious systems carried
away with them the fundamental religious teachings of the mother organization, for example, the
immortality of the human soul, punishment of
souls in a hell of fiery torment under the care of
red devils, the trinity, the celebration of Christmas,
Easter, Lent, etc., the division of the people into
a titled, paid clergy and the laity, the idolizing of
heroes religious, political, military and athletic,
and many other things of Babylonish religion.

⁸ For example, the Lateran Council of 1513, under Pope Leo X, pronounced the soul's immortality
to be an orthodox article of Catholicism and
adopted the following rule: "Whereas, some have
dared to assert concerning the nature of the
reasonable soul, that it is mortal; we, with the
approbation of the Sacred Council, do condemn
and reprobate all those who assert that the intel-

7. By what things is it manifest that it was a rebellion
against papacy rather than a real reformation?
8. How was this shown in the action taken on Luther's
95 theses and the one on the immortality of the soul?

lectual soul is mortal, seeing that the soul is not only truly and of itself and essentially the form of the human body, as is expressed in the canon of Pope Clement the Fifth, but likewise immortal; and we strictly inhibit all from dogmatizing otherwise, and we decree that all who adhere to the like erroneous assertions shall be shunned and punished as heretics." But Martin Luther in his *Defense,* proposition 27, "Adversus Execrabilem Antichrist Bullam," published in 1520, said: "I permit the Pope to make articles of faith for himself and his faithful—such as 'the soul is the substantial form of the human body,' 'that the soul is immortal,' with all those monstrous opinions to be found in the Roman dunghill of decretals." It was in the 27th of his 95 theses that Luther thus denied immortality of the human soul, but his followers slashed it out together with another one, and then divided two others in two so as to keep the number of these theses up to the original 95. —*Caranza,* page 412, 1681, and Luther's Works, Volume 2, folio, pages 106, 107, Wittenberg, 1562.

⁹ Though independent of the pope, the Protestant systems are still in bondage to Babylonish religion. They did not manifest the uncompromising course that the Israelites on being led by Jehovah into the Promised Land were commanded to take toward the demon gods, idols and religious practices of the pagan inhabitants of the land, lest they be ensnared by false religion. Protestants were only partial in their religious renovation and sought to keep their respectability with this world. They, too, allied themselves with the political pow-

---

9. Why is it that the Protestant systems are still in Babylonish bondage, and how do they show friendship with this world?

ers and in some instances established new unions of church and state. They upheld the clashing political states by taking up murderous weapons and participating in mortal combat, and made themselves the handmaids of the state, obeying man rather than God. To justify themselves, they declared they would set up Christ's kingdom by Christianizing the worldly political systems.

[10] This was no true reformation. This was not a return to the primitive Christianity of the apostles and the early Christian congregation. The original Christians refused to hold political office or worship the state as represented by the deified emperor. Hence they were regarded as anarchists hoping to destroy the state, guilty of hating the human race. On this matter a standard school textbook says: "The early Christians were ready to die for their faith. They refused to worship the gods of the pagan Romans. Since they believed in peace, they would not serve in Rome's imperial armies. They openly condemned evil deeds. . . . The Roman emperors who wanted to restore the belief in the Roman gods did not look with favor upon the teachings of the Christians. . . . It was easy for Roman officials to believe that the Christians in their secret meetings everywhere were hostile to the government. Did they not stubbornly refuse to worship the spirit of the Emperor? Did they not speak of Christ as their King? The government charged that in their meetings the Christians plotted treason against Rome. Accordingly, throughout the empire officials punished and persecuted Christians at various times." —*From the Old World to the New*, Colligan-Littwin, 1932, pages 88-91.

10, 11. What course of original Christians proves the Reformation was no return to primitive Christianity?

[11] People of various religious cults in Rome would unite in common worship to the spirit of the emperor, swearing a common allegiance to it. But, to quote *The Book of Culture* (Peyser, 1934, page 549), "The Christians, however, strong in their faith, would take no such oath of loyalty. And because they did not swear allegiance to what we would to-day consider as analogous to the flag, they were considered politically dangerous." Those Christians were quiet and orderly and paid their taxes, and thus rendered to Caesar what was Caesar's, but to Jehovah God they rendered their lives and worship, the things which were God's. —Matthew 22:21.

[12] When Christendom's religious systems, Catholic and Protestant, meddle in the political affairs of the world, allying themselves with the state and fighting its controversies, it is outright spiritual adultery, harlotry! It has made Christendom a pornocracy, not a theocracy. The religious systems claim to be the "bride" promised to Christ in marriage and obligated to wait for his second coming in glory. Referring to Christ, John the Baptist said: "He that has the bride is the bridegroom." (John 3:29, *NW*) Likening Jesus to the Bridegroom, the apostle Paul wrote: "Husbands, continue loving your wives, just as the Christ also loved the congregation and delivered up himself for it, that he might sanctify it, cleansing it with the bath of water by means of the word, that he might present the congregation to himself in its splendor, not having a spot or a wrinkle or any of such things, but that it should be holy and with-

---

12. In view of what professed relationship to Christ are Christendom's religious systems guilty of spiritual harlotry?

298 WHAT HAS RELIGION DONE FOR MANKIND?

out blemish. This sacred secret is great. Now I am speaking with respect to Christ and the congregation." Expressing his concern for her continued loyalty, Paul wrote: "I am jealous over you with a godly jealousy, for I personally promised you in marriage to one husband that I might present you as a chaste virgin to the Christ. But I am afraid that somehow, as the serpent seduced Eve by its craftiness, your minds might be corrupted away from the sincerity and the chastity that are due the Christ."—Ephesians 5:25-27, 32 and 2 Corinthians 11:2, 3, *NW*.

[13] The very apostasy to Christ the Bridegroom that Paul feared, the religious systems have committed in Christendom. Based on their claims of being betrothed to Christ Jesus the Bridegroom, they have committed spiritual fornication by unscriptural connections with the political state and by selfish friendship with this world of which Satan the Devil is the god. "Adulteresses, do you not know that the friendship with the world is enmity with God? Whoever, therefore, wants to be a friend of the world is constituting himself an enemy of God."—James 4:4, *NW*.

[14] Under God's law through Moses, virgins who committed harlotry while promised in marriage to an Israelite man were condemned to be stoned to death. (Deuteronomy 22:17-21, 23, 24) Since the Mosaic law contained a shadow of things to come, let the religious systems know that a violent end like this is in store for them at God's hands. They have rejected Christ's kingdom, by not waiting to be taken into his established kingdom but run-

---

13. Why may they be Scripturally styled "adulteresses"?
14. So in view of God's law through Moses what kind of end may they expect, and what government have they rejected by their course?

ning ahead for worldly political protection, support, honors and power and allying themselves with the corrupt governments of this world. "You have begun ruling as kings without us," says Paul. —1 Corinthians 4:8, *NW*.

[15] But Christendom's flat rejection of the real kingdom of the Seed of God's woman has come in our own critical world period beginning with A.D. 1914. That year the time came for God's woman, his loyal heavenly organization, to bring forth the Seed in the role of enthroned reigning King. Why so? Because 2,520 years before that date, namely, in 607 B.C., Jehovah God used Nebuchadnezzar king of Babylon as his executional servant to destroy Jerusalem and thus overthrow the typical kingdom of God, as he had said: "I will overturn, overturn, overturn it: this also shall be no more, until he come whose right it is; and I will give it him." (Ezekiel 21:24-27, *AS*) The One whose right it is to rule in the everlasting kingdom of God is Christ Jesus the Seed of God's woman, the Permanent Heir of the covenant for the Kingdom. Since the seven "appointed times of the nations" began in 607 B.C., they must end A.D. 1914, and at that date is the time for the Heir with the right to it to be given the Kingdom. At that time the Kingdom was due to be born.

[16] In sign language the last book of the Bible pictures God's woman, his wifely heavenly organization, at the crucial date A.D. 1914. The apostle John there says: "A great sign was seen in heaven, a woman arrayed with the sun, and

15. But after what year came Christendom's flat rejection of the real kingdom, and in the face of what foreordained event?
16. How in Revelation is God's woman pictured at the date A.D. 1914, and what is there shown to take place?

the moon was beneath her feet, and on her head was a crown of twelve stars, and she was pregnant. And she cries out in her pains and in her agony to give birth. And another sign was seen in heaven, and look! a great fiery-colored dragon, with seven heads and ten horns and upon its heads seven diadems; and its tail draws a third of the stars of heaven, and it hurled them down to the earth. And the dragon kept standing before the woman who was about to give birth, that, when she did give birth, it might devour her child. And she gave birth to a son, a male, who is destined to shepherd all the nations with an iron rod. And her child was caught away to God and to his throne."—Revelation 12:1-5, *NW*.

[17] Jesus said that when a woman has given birth she forgets all her birth pangs because of the joy that a son has been born. (John 16:21) So did God's woman rejoice at the birth of this symbolic male child who was snatched from the dragon's jaws and elevated up to God's throne to rule the nations with a rod of iron? John says Yes: "And I heard a loud voice in heaven say: 'Now have come to pass the salvation and the power and the kingdom of our God and the authority of his Christ.' " (Revelation 12:10, *NW*) This joyous exclamation by God's woman or heavenly organization proves that the birth of the male child pictures God's giving the Kingdom to the Seed whose right it is to have it. Again we read: "Loud voices occurred in heaven saying: 'The kingdom of the world has become the kingdom of our Lord and of his Christ, and he will rule as king for ever and ever.' And the twenty-four persons of advanced

---

17. What descriptions in Revelation show whether God's woman rejoiced over the birth of the symbolic male child?

CHRISTENDOM REJECTS THE KINGDOM 301

age who were seated before God upon their thrones fell upon their faces and worshiped God, saying: 'We thank you, Jehovah God, the Almighty, the one who is and who was, because you have taken your great power and begun ruling as king.'"

[18] But now the question is, Did the religious systems of Christendom exult with God's woman at the birth of her royal Seed as King? The elderly ones in heaven who thanked God for taking his power and ruling by his Christ foretold that they would not do so, saying: "But the nations became wrathful, and your own wrath came, and the appointed time . . . to bring to ruin those ruining the earth." (Revelation 11:15-18, *NW*) Not in heathendom, but in the heart of Christendom was where World War I began in 1914, the birth year of the Kingdom. Of the many nations which became embroiled in that war for world domination practically all were so-called Christian nations. For his clearly demonstrated favoritism toward the Teutonic powers the pope of Rome was barred from the peace negotiations. But all the religious systems of Christendom favored one or another of the nations according to the national ties of such systems, but none God's newborn kingdom. Had they sided with God's kingdom, the rightful government of earth, the war would never have flamed into a world conflagration, with its aftermath of international distress that is with us to this day. That is what worldly, apostate religion has done for mankind! The actions of the religious systems during World War I spoke deafeningly to say, Christendom has rejected God's kingdom.

---

18. Did Christendom rejoice at this birth, and what do the facts speak deafeningly to say about her action?

CHAPTER XXIV

The Remnant Restored from Mystic Babylon

AFTER giving birth to the royal Ruler in 1914 God's woman brought forth the final remnant of her seed. They are today the special target of the Serpent, Satan the Devil. Who are they? The fact that the Wicked One has deceived the whole world makes it certain that they are unpopular.

[2] Matching God's woman, Satan the Devil has his own woman. It is by her that he produces the seed of the Serpent with which the Seed of God's woman is at enmity. We have seen that God's woman is his heavenly theocratic organization of which the true Christian congregation are spiritual children. So Satan's woman is his own organization. The disobedient angels, the sons of God who rebelled against Jehovah's universal sovereignty, are the invisible and dominant part of the organization. In Noah's day they filled the earth with violence. Today by their undetected influence they are lining up all earthly kings and their hosts to the field ominously called "Armageddon" for the universal war, "the war of the great day of God the Almighty." These superhuman, unseen spirit forces under Satan their ruler form the symbolic "heavens" of his organization.

1. After the Kingdom's birth, whom did God's woman bring forth, and whose special target of attack are they?
2. What is Satan's woman, and what are his "heavens"?

³ The Serpent also has a visible earthly seed. Jesus said that the "weeds", the imitation Christians, whom the Devil sowed in among the wheat, are the "sons of the wicked one". But all the "children of the Devil" are evident by their practice of unrighteousness and murderous hatred of God's people, like Cain who slaughtered his brother Abel. (Matthew 13:38, 39 and 1 John 3:10-12, NW) These visible agents and servants of the Devil among men form the symbolic "earth" of his wicked organization.

⁴ Together, these heavens and earth make up the world of which the Devil is ruler: "The whole world is lying in the power of the wicked one." (1 John 5:19, NW) Because the Serpent the Devil reformed his organization after the global flood of Noah's day and began its visible part with Nimrod's Babel or Babylon, the prophetic Scriptures use Babylon as a symbol of the Devil's entire organization, visible and invisible, and talk of it as such. From Nimrod's notorious Babylon it finally rose in Nebuchadnezzar's day to be the third world power to dominate the earth, adding to its nefarious deeds the destruction of Jerusalem and its temple. Mighty Babylon of earth met its overthrow at God's decreed hour. Its globe-circling counterpart, Satan's woman or world organization, will meet its disgraceful end likewise, and soon, and never rise again. "Down with you, sit in the dust, O maiden Babylon! No throne for you, sit on the ground, lady Chaldea!"—Isaiah 47:1, Mo.

---

3. What is the "earth" of his organization?
4. What constitutes his world, what is it called in prophecy, and what end is it destined to meet soon?

⁵ Sixty-eight years after it destroyed Jerusalem and took thousands of the Jews captive to its provinces, Babylon's empire fell. But the false, demon-inspired religion which it had nurtured in defiance of Jehovah God had spread to the ends of the earth. It continued on, to infect finally compromising Christendom. So the great Babylonish organization, visible and invisible, has continued dominating the vast majority of mankind. And now it, too, has had a mighty fall, from the heav-. ens themselves. When was that?

⁶ Immediately after God's kingdom was born in 1914. Christ Jesus had waited at his Father's right hand for many centuries since his ascent to heaven, and now the time had arrived for God to make Christ's enemies a stool for his feet and to send the royal rod of his strength out of the heavenly Zion. (Psalm 110:1, 2; Hebrews 10:12, 13) So down with great Babylon beneath his feet at his footstool the earth! "War broke out in heaven: Michael [his name meaning 'Who is as God?'] and his angels battled with the dragon, and the dragon and its angels battled but it did not pre-

---

5. After Babylon's empire fell, what continued on and finally infected Christendom, so continuing Babylonish domination?
6. When and how did great Babylon have a fall from the heavens?

vail, neither was a place found for them any longer in heaven. So down the great dragon was hurled, the original serpent, the one called Devil and Satan, who is misleading the entire inhabited earth; he was hurled down to the earth, and his angels were hurled down with him."

⁷ The great ruler or king of Babylon Satan the Devil and the invisible part of Babylon, his angels, were humbled to this earth, never again to contaminate heaven. Joy this for heaven, but oh how the earth, yes, the visible part of great Babylon, has felt the effects of this bitter abasement: "Woe for the earth and for the sea, because the Devil has come down to you, having great anger, knowing he has a short period of time." Enmity between the Serpent and the woman! How that enmity did burn now! "Now when the dragon saw it was hurled down to the earth [with its angels], it persecuted the woman that gave birth to the male child [the King in his kingdom]." Not able to get back to heaven and its contacts up there, the abased Devil did his persecuting by striking at the woman's remnant of spiritual children on earth. "And the dragon grew wrathful at the woman, and went off to wage war with the remaining ones of her seed, who observe the commandments of God and have the work of bearing witness to Jesus."—Revelation 12:7-9, 12, 13, 17, NW.

⁸ That description identifies who they are. Satan and his whole world wage war against them. They observe God's commandments. They bear

---

7. What did this mean for the earth, and how, since barred from heaven, did Satan carry forward his persecution of God's woman?
8. Who are the remnant of her seed identified as being, and as what have they been known since 1931?

witness to Jesus, but not just to a Jesus who came nineteen centuries ago and died and was resurrected and ascended to God's right hand in heaven. No, but to a Jesus come into the Kingdom for which he was anointed and taken into the Davidic covenant; a Jesus who as a glorified immortal spirit Son of God returns to earth to rule as its King by extending the rod of his power down here and clearing the earth of every last enemy of God. No denying it, they are witnesses whom Jehovah God has raised up. And since the year 1931 when they saw the suitability of this Scriptural name and adopted it they have been known as "Jehovah's witnesses". If they did not observe his commandments they would not be his witnesses.

⁹ In this way they copy their glorified Leader, "Jesus Christ, 'the Faithful Witness,' 'The firstborn from the dead,' and 'The Ruler of the kings of the earth'." (Revelation 1:5, NW) And to the remnant of Jesus' followers God says: "Ye are my witnesses, saith Jehovah, that I am God. Yea, since the day was, I am HE, and there is none that delivereth out of my hand: I will work, and who shall hinder it? Thus saith Jehovah, your Redeemer, the Holy One of Israel: For your sake I have sent [an army] to Babylon, and have brought all of them down as fugitives, even the Chaldeans, whose cry [or, rejoicing] is in the ships. I am Jehovah, your Holy One, the Creator of Israel, your King."—Isaiah 43:12-15, Da; Mo.

¹⁰ Similar to the faithful Israelite remnant that

9. In this capacity they copy whom, and how does Jehovah address them and promise them deliverance?
10. Of what were those of the remnant once captive, and in seeking the pure and undefiled religion what did they undertake before 1914?

left Babylon after its fall and returned to Jerusalem to rebuild the temple and restore Jehovah's pure worship there, the remnant of the seed of God's woman were once captive in Babylon. There, like the Israelites, they were contaminated with the Babylonian religion and systems of this world, including apostate Christendom. They believed many things in common with the modern Babylonians and followed their worldly customs in many things. But the end of the "appointed times of the nations" got closer as 1914 drew near. Correspondingly the time for God's kingdom to be born and for great Babylon's invisible section to be hurled down from heaven got closer. So God's spirit or invisible active force began moving on the hearts of those seeking his truth, those seeking the "pure religion and undefiled before God and the Father". Then intensive Bible study was carried on independent of the clergy of Christendom. In the last half of the nineteenth century those clergymen were still in apparent prosperity and were outwardly righteous to the Babylonians and on good terms with the political rulers and in high hopes of going to a heavenly kingdom after quitting the politics of this world. They were like the "rich man" in Jesus' parable.

[11] On the other hand, the so-called "laity" were looked down upon and held under great restraint and fed little of Bible truth. Those laymen who were trying to search for Bible truths without complete trust in the clergy and dependence upon them were especially despised, considered spiritually ulcerous and viewed as religiously poor, out

11. How were they viewed and treated like the beggar Lazarus, and who tried to keep them in Babylonish bondage?

of Abraham's favor, and fit to mix only with dogs to whom holy things should not be given. A class like the beggar Lazarus they were! The clergy and their allies tried to keep these in Babylonian bondage to themselves.—Luke 16:19-31.

[12] Under the guidance of God's spirit of freedom the magazine today known as *The Watchtower* but known back there as *Zion's Watch Tower,* began to be published in July, 1879. In the first year of its publication it pointed to the date 1914 as marked in the Bible. It sounded the warning of modern Babylon's approaching fall. It pealed forth the clarion call to flee from Babylon and be clean from it in order to bear the temple "vessels of Jehovah" which Babylon had misappropriated. (Isaiah 52:11, 12, *AS*) The better to organize, serve and activate this work of liberating God's devoted people by the power of the truth, the Watch Tower Bible and Tract Society was incorporated in Pennsylvania, United States of America, in 1884. The remnant of Jehovah's witnesses have used this legal corporation as their servant or agent ever since. But how the clerical "rich man" class of Protestantism, Catholicism and Judaism have hated, misrepresented and fought against this liberation movement of Jehovah's remnant of the seed!

[13] Then total warfare was set in motion in 1914. All elements of the population in the nation were mobilized and regimented. There was war hysteria. The Serpent remembered how he had caused Jesus

---

12. When and why was *The Watchtower* published and the Watch Tower Society incorporated, and with what reaction by remnant and clergy?
13. How, following A.D. 1914, was the Babylonian captivity of the remnant brought to a culmination, as foretold at Micah 4:10?

to be branded as a seditionist and revolutionary disturber of the peace in order to involve the Seed of God's woman with the government of Rome and 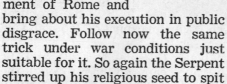 bring about his execution in public disgrace. Follow now the same trick under war conditions just suitable for it. So again the Serpent stirred up his religious seed to spit out their venom of murderous hatred against the remnant on earth, the associates of the great Seed of God's woman. By this, halt their escape from Babylon! But before this was achieved, the remnant in concerted action throughout the land distributed millions of copies of the free tract "The Fall of Babylon", on Sunday, December 30, 1917, and on the same day hundreds of public lectures on the same subject were delivered by speakers to large audiences. Now again by false religious misrepresentation the remnant were implicated with the governments of the visible section of modern great Babylon, and the free and unhampered activities of the liberty-seeking remnant were practically halted. Literature of theirs was banned, leading officers of the Society were imprisoned and oppressive measures were applied to the remnant. This was a culmination of their captivity in Babylon. They felt great pain over it and languished under the seemingly unbreakable power of their enemies. But at the time of this greatest anguish deliverance was nearing. As it had been written: "Be in pain, and labor to bring forth, O daughter of Zion,

like a woman in travail; for now shalt thou go forth out of the city [Jerusalem], and shalt dwell in the field, and shalt come even unto Babylon: there shalt thou be rescued; there will Jehovah redeem thee from the hand of thine enemies."
—Micah 4:10, *AS*.

[14] World War I ended in the fall of 1918. The captive remnant took hope. In 1919 the promised rescue came. The invincible spirit of Jehovah God moved upon them, as it did in Ezekiel's vision of the valley of dry bones (Ezekiel 37:1-28), and His message of deliverance came to them through the message of truth revealed from his Word. "You will know the truth, and the truth will set you free." In the spring of the year the work was reorganized and courageously resumed with faith in Jehovah God. "Blessed are the fearless," rang in their ears; and that was the main theme of the first postwar international assembly they held at Cedar Point, Ohio, September 1-8, 1919. What research in the Holy Scriptures there was! Restoration of primitive truth as well as uncovering of fulfilled prophetic truth was the reward, with its corresponding measure of increase of freedom in Christ. That we were in the foretold "time of the end" of this world was more keenly appreciated. In 1920 the command of Jesus given in his prophecy on the sign of the "time of the end" was seen to apply now since 1914: "This good news of the kingdom will be preached in all the inhabited earth for the purpose of a witness to all the nations, and then the accomplished end will come." (Matthew 24:14, *NW*) What made this good news

---

14. When and how did the promised rescue come, and with what increase in understanding of the Scriptures and work to be done?

different from all preceding was that this was the good news of God's kingdom as established in the hands of the Seed of his woman.

¹⁵ A Kingdom witness! By delivering it it would make us witnesses, and to save some flesh for this purpose was why Almighty God had shortened the days of the tribulation upon the Devil's organization Babylon by allowing an interval after it was hurled down from heaven to earth.—Matthew 24:21, 22; Mark 13:19, 20.

¹⁶ In 1925 came the revelation through the Scriptures that chapter twelve of The Revelation applied to the birth of God's kingdom in 1914 and that immediately following its birth the invisible wing of Babylon, Satan and his demon angels, had been cast out of heaven. Now their main target of attack was the remnant of the woman's seed, because these had been taken by Christ Jesus into the covenant for the everlasting kingdom. (Luke 22:28-30, *NW; Ro*) In that same year of 1925 there began to be brought to the remnant's notice the present application of Isaiah 43:10-12: "Ye are my witnesses, saith Jehovah, and my servant whom I have chosen; . . . therefore ye are my witnesses, saith Jehovah, and I am God." (*AS;* see *The Watchtower* of 1925, pages 9, 22, 75.) His witnesses they must intelligently prove themselves from then on. Six years of intensive work to do so followed. Then on July 26, 1931, at the international assembly in Columbus, Ohio, came the public adoption of the name "Jehovah's witnesses". By these witnesses Jehovah has made his name

15. How and why did Jehovah shorten the days of tribulation at this time?
16. What revelations were made in 1925, and when and where was the name "Jehovah's witnesses" publicly adopted?

famous throughout the world in this "time of the end", despite the mounting opposition of the modern Babylonians and their invisible king, Satan the Devil, the Serpent.

[17] Truly the remnant of the seed of Jehovah's woman have been delivered from Babylon and restored to his theocratic organization for his worship and service. The tables have been turned! In fulfillment of Jesus' parable the remnant have died like the beggar Lazarus to their former poor, oppressed condition and have plainly come into the bosom of favor of the Greater Abraham, Jehovah God. With their apostolic brother Paul they can say: "The Jerusalem above is free, and she is our mother. Wherefore, brothers, we are children, not of a servant girl [earthly, tradition-bound Jerusalem], but of the free woman. For such freedom Christ set us free. Therefore stand fast, and do not let yourselves be confined again in a yoke of slavery." (Galatians 4:26, 31; 5:1, NW) In such freedom from mystic Babylon the restored remnant are determined to stand firm and no more let themselves be snared by false religion through any compromise. In appreciation of their own God-given freedom they are working with might and main to help all people of good will to gain the same glorious freedom now before Babylon is destroyed.

---

17. How have the tables of the rich man and Lazarus classes been turned now, and what efforts for freedom are the remnant making?

CHAPTER XXV

Red Religion and the "Man of Lawlessness"

THAT anyone should gain liberty from modern Babylon is a miracle, accomplished by Almighty God's power. When the Israelite remnant marched away from the once world-mistress Babylon in 537 B.C., it almost seemed unreal to them: "When Jehovah brought back those that returned to Zion, we were like unto them that dream. Then was our mouth filled with laughter, and our tongue with singing: then said they among the nations, Jehovah hath done great things for them. Jehovah hath done great things for us, whereof we are glad. Turn again our captivity, O Jehovah, as the streams in the South." (Psalm 126:1-4, *AS*) It was a totalitarian power from which they had been set free, Babylon the third world power. The Babylon over which Nimrod the mighty hunter ruled at the beginning of its history was a totalitarian government run in defiance of the supremacy of Jehovah God. Nimrod who was popularly idolized as a mighty god claimed to be the liberator of the people from the opium of the religion of Jehovah, the God of Noah and of his son Shem. (Genesis 10:8-10, *AS*) The modern Babylon is a still greater creation of Satan the Devil run in defiance of Jehovah's universal sovereignty. It is a totalitarian organization, the mother of all totalitarian systems on

1. In view of what facts is the remnant's gaining of liberty from modern Babylon a miracle of God's power?

313

earth. There is enmity between it and God's woman, the heavenly Jerusalem or Zion; and this enmity has been heightened by Jehovah's freeing of his remnant since 1919.

² At the hurling of Satan the king of Babylon and his angels down to earth after God's kingdom was born in the heavens, the cry rang out, "Woe for the earth and for the sea, because the Devil has come down to you, having great anger, knowing he has a short period of time." The fire-red dragon's comedown meant not only total war between nations and kingdoms on a global scale; it meant not only earthquakes, pestilences, food shortages, and fearful sights, all of which Jesus said were to be a "beginning of pangs of distress" and a sign that the "time of the end" had begun for this world. (Matthew 24:3-8 and Luke 21:10, 11, NW) It meant also that totalitarian forms of government on a modern style would be set up and there would be great regimentation of the people. The purpose of Satan the red dragon was by this means to hold the people in unbreakable bondage to his organization Babylon. In the short period of time remaining till the battle of Armageddon he must turn all mankind into destruction by lining them up against Jehovah's rule of the earth by Christ Jesus his King. It enrages Satan to see the remnant of the seed of God's woman challenging the power and claims of Babylon and rendering their worship and service to Jehovah as Universal Sovereign to whom all the earth belongs. He tries to hinder people of good will from joining them.

---

2. As respects government how has the red dragon's comedown to earth meant woe for it, and how do the remnant make him enraged?

[3] One totalitarian system fears another such. One modern development that has thoroughly frightened the totalitarian religious system of the pope, yes, and all Christendom too, has been the rise of totalitarian political power in Eastern Europe. Fascist totalitarian rule was foisted upon Italy in 1922, and Nazi totalitarian rule on Germany in 1933; but the pope made working agreements with these through concordats and his priests blessed the aggressive armies of Fascism and Nazism. In fact, through the Fascist dictator the pope gained political independence for Vatican City in 1929. These political totalitarian systems were used by the pope as the "sword of the church" to fight the totalitarian system that now all Christendom fears, that of Communism. The pope well remembers that after the Communist Manifesto was issued by Engels and Marx at the end of 1847 there were great political revolutions in Europe, including Italy, and on November 24, 1848, the pope was obliged to escape in disguise from the Vatican and flee south to Gaeta. He did not return to Rome till April of 1850, surrounded by French bayonets. Another such flight from the Vatican could be forced now by international Communism directed by its capital Moscow, Russia.

[4] In November of 1917, during the throes of World War I, there came the Bolshevik counter-revolution in Russia and a Communist government was set up with Nikolai Lenin as the leading figure. The Russian Orthodox Church which had been married to the previous Czarist government

3. Why is it not the Fascist and Nazi but the Communist totalitarian political system that the pope fears?
4. How did Communism come to power in Russia, and how has the Russian Orthodox Church viewed the head of the Soviet state?

was disestablished from this union and parts of its property were confiscated. In harmony with the saying of Karl Marx religion was branded as "the opium of the people", and there was a shocking exposure of the real frauds the orthodox clergy had practiced on the illiterate and oppressed people. At the bitter persecution which was carried on against the Russian clergy protest was made by the clergy of other lands and an appeal to their government to interfere in behalf of religion. But in vain! What remains of the Russian Orthodox Church has now been made subservient to the Soviet state. After Lenin's death January 21, 1924, Joseph Stalin made successful political maneuvers and finally became the undisputed head of the Communist political bureau in August, 1926. He thus rose to be General Secretary of the Communist party of the country. In 1945 he was made Generalissimo. On March 12, 1948, a headline in the New York *Times* read: "Stalin Selected by God, Moscow Patriarch says." The "providence of God chose" this "wise leader".

[5] The movement is stigmatized by the religious leaders in the Western democracies as "godless (or atheistic) Communism". And the Communists do brag that they are godless and irreligious. But if we recall the definition of "religion" set out in our first chapter, namely, "a form or system of worship," we must conclude that the Communists are religious and indulge in worship according to the creed of their party. When we remember that Satan the Devil promised to give Jesus political power in this world if Jesus would worship him as the "ruler of this world", the Communists must have come to their position of political power only

5. How do Communists falsely brag of their system?

by grant of the "ruler of this world", Satan the Devil, for their worship of him. How and at what price the pope and other religious leaders came by their political power and influence we leave our readers to judge.

[6] Because they deny his existence, the Reds may deny they worship the Devil. But they have set up a state religion by requiring the people to give their unquestioning obedience to the political state as their highest counselor, guide, provider and protector. In this they attribute to the state what really belongs to the living and true God, Jehovah. For him they have substituted a man-made visible organization. In endeavoring to set up or sanction only national church systems in each country and make them completely subject to the political authorities, they are making the state a super-religious system that regulates the religious affairs of the subservient systems. As with children in religious parochial schools, they are most careful to indoctrinate the growing children in the articles of the Communist *credo*. As its Holy Scriptures Communism has the writings of Marx, Engels, Lenin, and Stalin, who are spoken of as inspired writers. "Inspired" by whom?

[7] Carrying our comparison farther, we note that Communism has its missionaries, whose entry into their midst countries of the Western bloc of nations are attempting to deny or prevent. It has its priesthood or hierarchy, that Politburo with all its lesser orders of functionaries for the guid-

6. How have they attributed to the state what belongs to God, made it a super-religious system, and indoctrinated children?
7. How does Communism compare with religion as to missionaries, priesthood, shrines, pilgrimages, holy days, deification, etc.?

ance of the people in Communist orthodoxy and
with power to demand and hear confessions and
to issue excommunications, to forbid heretical
literature and to censor and expurgate books,
magazines, movies, stage plays, poetic and musical compositions. It has its shrines and pilgrimages. Moscow parallels the Mohammedan
Mecca. There the Kremlin, where Stalin has had
his residence with his family, is Communism's
Vatican; and pious pilgrimages are made to the
tombs of its martyrs and venerated men. It has its
calendar of holy days, among which are May Day
and the anniversary of Lenin's death and also,
during his life, the birthday of Stalin, December 21. On that day in 1950 in the satellite land
of Albania the People's Assembly voted to erect a
statue to "the deity, Joseph Vissarionovich Stalin", and the premier declared: "The Great Stalin
is our people's glorious savior." Other flattering
titles have been paid him, glorifying him to the
place of a national god. As with Lenin, he is venerated as being the embodiment of the political aims
of Communism. The prophets of Communism
predict world victory for it.

[8] It is significant that the religion of Communism was born in the heart of Christendom. The
lands where it has its strongholds and its greatest
number of adherents are lands where there has
been union of church and state and where religious hierarchies have dominated the lives and
politics of the people, such as Russia, Italy, France,
etc. This betrays the failure of Christendom and
exposes its religion to be Babylonish, but dressed
up with Christian names. True Christianity does

8. Where was Communism born, where does it have its
strongholds, and what fact does this betray, as admitted even by the clergy?

not breed political Communism. Hypocritical religion does. Honest clergymen are forced to admit it. Said a Presbyterian preacher in Brooklyn, New York, on Sunday, February 4, 1951: Communism is an "instrument of social change born in the intolerable vacuum left by a thousand years of Christian failure to achieve a better instrument or any instrument at all".—New York *Times*, 2/5/51.

⁹ Christendom's religion in all its sectarian forms is an apostasy, a falling away from the pure, primitive Christianity based on God's holy Word the Bible. It has rejected God's kingdom set up at the enthronement of the Seed of his woman, Jesus Christ. As an organized, collective system of religion its clergy are the "embodiment of disobedience" to Jehovah God. They form a "man of lawlessness" toward him, just as Saul the first king of Israel was lawless, hypocritically setting himself up above Jehovah's law. Who this man of lawlessness or man of sin was to be was long a mystery. But now the united course of conduct of Christendom's clergy and religious leaders discloses who it is today fully developed. This composite "man" was to be revealed before the "day of Jehovah" arrived for destroying that lawless religious system.

¹⁰ "Let no one seduce you in any manner," writes the apostle Paul, "because it [the day of Jehovah] will not come unless the falling away comes first and the man of lawlessness [the embodiment of disobedience, *AT*] gets revealed, the son of destruction. He is set in opposition and lifts himself up over everyone who is called 'god' or an

---

9. As an organized, collective system of religion, what do Christendom's clergy form? What discloses this?
10. What does the apostle Paul write about the "man of lawlessness" at 2 Thessalonians 2:3-8, *NW?*

object of reverence, so that he sits down in the temple of The God, publicly showing himself to be a god. Do you not remember that, while I was yet with you, I used to tell you these things? And so now you know the thing that acts as a restraint with a view to his being revealed in his own due time. True, the mystery of this lawlessness is already at work; but only till he who is right now acting as a restraint gets to be out of the way. Then, indeed, the lawless one will be revealed, whom the Lord Jesus will annihilate by the spirit of his mouth and bring to nothing by the manifestation of his presence."

[11] The "mystery of this lawlessness" was already at work in the days of Christ's twelve apostles. As the governing body of the Christian congregation, they were the ones who were acting as a restraint upon the development of this "man of lawlessness" to full growth. They were filled with God's spirit and this helped them as a restraining power over this apostate "son of destruction", foreshadowed by the traitor Judas Iscariot who betrayed Jesus to be hanged on a torture stake to die in agony and shame. His being called the "son of destruction" means he is sure to be destroyed.

[12] So the falling away of Christian leaders from true Christianity to form a "man of lawlessness" class or system began shortly after the twelve apostles died. The apostles being thus out of the way, the composite lawless man came out into the open and followed his self-exalting, lawless course of conduct. He set himself up as an apostate

---

11. What acted in restraint of developing the "man of lawlessness" and its revelation? What fate awaits it?
12. How did this "man of lawlessness" set himself up as a god in God's temple, and what has the time come for Christ to do to him?

clergy in power over the religious interests of professed Christians. The clerical word was more powerful than the written Word of God. The clergy put the traditions and commands of men up above the laws of God and nullified them. Assuming the titles of "Reverend", "Right Reverend," "Most Right Reverend," "Divine," and even "vice-god" for the pope, they elevated themselves in their temples, cathedrals and church buildings as objects of reverence capturing the due reverence and fear away from Jehovah God and his Son Jesus Christ. They claimed to be sons of God, but they made themselves gods or spiritually mighty ones to their parishioners and flocks. So to them the words which Jesus once quoted apply: "God takes his stand in the divine assembly; in the midst of the gods he gives judgment. 'How long will you judge unjustly, and show partiality toward the wicked?' I say, 'You are gods, and all of you sons of the Most High! Yet you will die as men do, and fall like any prince.'" (Psalm 82:1, 2, 6, 7, *AT;* John 10:35) Now that Christ Jesus is present in his kingdom, the time has come for him to annihilate these apostates, now that he has exposed this "man of lawlessness".

[13] "But," continues the apostle Paul, "the lawless one's presence is according to the operation of Satan with every powerful work and lying signs and wonders and with every unrighteous deception for those who are perishing, as a retribution because they did not accept the love of the truth that they might be saved. So that is why God lets an operation of error go to them that they may get to believing the lie, in order that they all may

13. By what is the lawless one's presence accompanied, and what end awaits those who believe the lie in preference to the truth?

be judged because they did not believe the truth but took pleasure in unrighteousness." (2 Thessalonians 2:3-12, *NW*) This warns of a terrible end for people who do not love the pure truth of God's written Word but who prefer to have their ears tickled by the religious lies of these clergy "gods". If the blind people choose to be led by blind religious guides, they can expect to fall into the ditch with them.

[14] Communists with their Red religion and the clergy of Christendom—which class is the more reprehensible? The Bible answers, The religious clergy. Those who have become communists have stumbled at the hypocrisy of the clergy and have turned against their religion and its gods. But the clergy have professed to be Christian and to speak for the Most High God. So they have wielded great influence over hundreds of millions in their flocks. They have failed to use this marvelous opportunity to teach these God's Word of truth but have led them into worldly philosophy and Babylonish religion. They have guided the people into outright opposition to God's kingdom by Christ and into full support of Satan's world and its conflicts, World Wars I and II included. Showing their reprehensibility above that of all others, Jehovah's Word says of the clergy: "I sent not these prophets, yet they ran: I spake not unto them, yet they prophesied. But if they had stood in my council, then had they caused my people to hear my words, and had turned them from their evil way, and from the evil of their doings." (Jeremiah 23:21, 22, *AS*) They will therefore have the severer judgment.

---

14. As to Red religion and Christendom's clergy, which will have the severer judgment, and why?

CHAPTER XXVI

Pure Religion Alone Survives the World's End

FROM the time when he began, the purpose of Satan the Devil has been to wipe out true religion from the earth. This he is trying to do especially now when he has but a short time till the battle of Armageddon, not alone by means of so-called "godless Communism" but also by means of his hypocritical religious seed, who palm themselves off as guides to the true God. "It is therefore nothing great if his ministers also keep transforming themselves into ministers of righteousness." Both Communism and apostate Christianity work for the destruction of true faith and worship. (2 Corinthians 11:13-15, *NW*) But it is an infallible rule, "Every rotten tree produces bad fruit." Now false religion, both the pagan and the apostate Christian, must eat the fruit of its Babylonish doings over the many centuries. "For they have sown the wind, and they shall reap the whirlwind," just as the apostate Israelites did. (Matthew 7:17, *NW;* Hosea 8:7) But the true religion, which God planted, has sown the fruits of true worship according to His Word, and now it will reap the fruits of righteousness. "Riches profit not in the day of wrath: but righteousness delivereth from death." (Proverbs 11:4, 6) Hence true religion will survive.

1. For what do both Communism and apostate Christianity work, and now what must all false religion eat or reap?

² Jehovah's King who now reigns since A.D. 1914 is highly interested in religion. He is Christ Jesus, whom Jehovah has sworn in as a "priest forever after the likeness of Melchizedek". Being both King and High Priest, he uses his royal power in behalf of the interests of clean and undefiled religion. Like his prototype, King Solomon, he builds the true temple of Jehovah, the spiritual temple of which his 144,000 faithful followers are "living stones" and of which he himself is the "chief cornerstone". (Hebrews 3:1; 7:15-17; 1 Peter 2:4-9, NW) He is therefore careful about preserving the remnant of such living stones who are yet to be built into the glorious heavenly temple. For it is written concerning all of the spiritual temple class: "Happy and holy is anyone having part in the first resurrection; over these the second death has no authority, but they will be priests of God and of the Christ, and will rule as kings with him for the thousand years." (Revelation 20:6, NW) According to Jesus' parables, it is when he comes into his kingdom that he calls to account all his servants, to determine who are faithful and who are undependable apostates. Consistently, he calls before himself for judgment not only his true followers but also all those who pretend to be his servants, namely, Christendom.

³ The apostle Peter warns us: "It is the appointed time for the judgment to start with the house of God. Now if it starts first with us, what will the complete end be of those who are not obedient

2. As High Priest what is the reigning King Christ Jesus interested in preserving, and whom does he call before him for judgment?
3. How is it now the appointed time for judgment to start at God's house, and how are the remnant being saved with difficulty?

to the good news of God? 'And if the righteous man is being saved with difficulty, where will the ungodly man and the sinner make a showing?' " (1 Peter 4:17, 18, *NW*) Whatever judgment Christians may have had individually before this "time of the end", it is organizations of religion that the High Priest and King now puts on judgment with all their members. He has shown his approval of the faithful remnant, "who observe the commandments of God and have the work of bearing witness to Jesus." He has ushered them into his joy and has committed to them the interests of true religion, to proclaim world-wide the good news of the established kingdom and to declare the oncoming "day of vengeance of our God". (Matthew 24:14, 45-47; Isaiah 61:1, 2) In view of the war waged on them by the abased Serpent and his demons the remnant are indeed being saved with difficulty. Yet they will be preserved for the heavenly kingdom. But what about the make-believe Christians?

⁴ The facts prove that these latter have been rejected. The clergy, once rich in spiritual privileges, have now died to this favored condition. As respects God's real service according to his commandments for this "time of the end", the clergy are as inactive as if lying buried stiff in the cold grave. But, like the rich man in Jesus' parable, they are suffering torment, because they are feeling the heat of the preaching of God's fiery Word by Jehovah's witnesses. They weep and grind their teeth at the remnant and their fellow witnesses of good will. They pray to God, the Greater Abra-

4. What judgment is the rich man class now undergoing, what selfish request of theirs is refused, and why?

ham, that he will send the Lazarus class away
from his bosom and on a mission that will not result in fiery torment for the religious clergy or
their "five brothers", their religious allies. But the
Greater Abraham refuses this selfish request. The
clergy and their "brothers" have God's written
Word. Were they to harmonize their lives and
teachings with this they would not feel tormented.

⁵ If the clergy howl in protest at the mere
preaching of God's kingdom and his day of vengeance, what will they do when they reap the
whirlwind they have sown? When God, by his
Melchizedekian King, comes against them at the
battle of Armageddon, what a painful, inglorious
end will be theirs! "Because I will do this unto
thee, prepare to meet thy God, O Israel." (Amos
4:12) The prophecies indicate that the universal
conflict of Armageddon will strike the religious
leaders first, and even their hitherto allies will
turn on them in wrath. Christendom's clergy
claim to be at God's sanctuary, and yet they turn
their backs on his true holy house and worship
the sun god, whose pagan symbol was the cross
and who represents Satan the Devil. So when
Jehovah sends out his executional officers under
Christ Jesus he commands them: "Slay utterly
. . . and begin at my sanctuary." They will do so,
for the prophecy says: "Then they began at the
ancient men which were before the house." God
thus shows his rejection of them.—Ezekiel 9:6;
8:16-18.

⁶ The entire visible religious organization, both

5. At what group will the battle of Armageddon strike
first, and how does Ezekiel, chapter 9, show this?
6. Why will the visible religious organization suffer
first at Armageddon, and how is it pictured at Revelation 17:3-6?

pagan and apostate Christian, will suffer first at Armageddon as being most reprehensible for earth's corrupt condition. Since the flood of Noah's day this world-girdling religious organization has been Babylonish, for it has stemmed from Nimrod's Babylon. Nimrod was an apostate from Jehovah's worship and committed spiritual adultery with Satan's woman or demon organization, by forming unlawful ties with her. So the Babylonish worldly religious organization is adulterous for the same reason. In the prophecies it is pictured as a harlot, a prostitute, who has committed fornication with the kings of the earth or Satan's earthly organization. Given an apocalyptic vision of God's judgment on her, the apostle John writes: "I caught sight of a woman sitting upon a scarlet-colored wild beast that was full of blasphemous names and that had seven heads and ten horns. And the woman was arrayed in purple and scarlet, and was adorned with gold and precious stone and pearls and had in her hand a golden cup that was full of disgusting things and the unclean things of her fornication. And upon her forehead was written a name, a mystery, 'Babylon the Great, the mother of the harlots and of the disgusting things of the earth.' And I saw that the woman was drunk with the blood of the holy ones and with the blood of the witnesses of Jesus."—Revelation 17:3-6, NW.

⁷ Explaining the meaning of this symbol, the angel told John: "The waters which you saw, where the harlot is sitting, mean peoples and crowds and nations and tongues. And the woman that you saw means the great city that has a king-

---

7. Whom does the harlot here specifically symbolize, and why?

dom over the kings of the earth." (Revelation 17:15, 18, *NW*) Satan's woman or his entire organization visible and invisible is called Babylon the Great because it was symbolized by Babylon from Nimrod's time till its overthrow in 539 B.C. But the woman Babylon in Revelation, chapter 17, pictures more the VISIBLE organization of the religious heads of heathendom and Christendom. The clergy of Christendom are viewed as the visible tie between God and men; and so, too, here the symbolic woman Babylon is the visible religious tie between Satan's invisible demon organization and his visible organization, the people of the earth. Hence she pictures the religious ruling element, including the apostate "man of lawlessness" in Christendom.

[8] What about the beast that she rides? In Daniel's day the Babylonian empire was pictured as a wild beast, a lion with four wings and which tried standing on its hind feet like a man. (Daniel 7:1-4) That Babylonian empire passed. So the beast that Lady Babylon is now pictured as riding is this peace beast, formerly known as the League of Nations but now since its reappearance in 1945 the United Nations. Its having sixty member

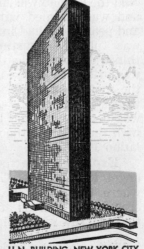

U.N. BUILDING, NEW YORK CITY

---

8. What does the beast which the harlot rides picture, and what does she blasphemously call it?

nations in 1951 was well s y m b o l i z e d in the peace beast's having seven heads and ten horns. Lady Babylon, or organized religion of this world, professes to be in favor of *pax,* peace, for this doomed world. So she plasters the peace beast with blasphemous names: she once called the now defunct League of Nations the "political expression of the kingdom of God on earth", "rooted in the gospel." Today she calls the United Nations "man's best hope for peace". She utterly rejects the now reigning Christ Jesus, "The Prince of Peace," and his kingdom.

[9] But remember: The tower of Babel project was defeated by Jehovah's confusing the tongues of the builders. Also the third world power, Babylon, fell and was divided up between the Median and Persian conquerors. Also the demon section of mystic Babylon fell defeated to earth by the war in heaven following the birth of God's kingdom up there. So, too, visible Lady Babylon, though yet quite popular with her political bedmates, must topple. The prophecies foreshadow that God will strike confusion into the ranks of his enemies and they will fight one another. First they will turn on

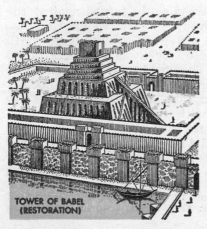

TOWER OF BABEL
(RESTORATION)

9, 10. How will God bring the harlot's ride on the beast to an end, and how does The Revelation picture this?

religion, as a useless, burdensome appendage.
Lady Babylon's deceptive cries of *Pax et secu-
ritas,* "Peace and security!" will turn to shrieks
of Treachery! Just as suddenly as when the
childbirth pang stabs through a pregnant woman's frame. (1 Thessalonians 5:1-3, *NW;* Latin
Vulgate) The "ten horns" of power on the seven
heads of the peace beast turn antireligious and
start goring her. She taught them to war against
Christ's kingdom, so why should they have any
regard for her? The angel explained to John:

[10] "The ten horns that you saw mean ten kings,
. . . And the ten horns that you saw, and the wild
beast, these will hate the harlot and will make her
devastated and naked, and will eat up her fleshy
parts and will completely burn her with fire. For
God put it into their hearts to carry out his purpose, even to carry out their one purpose by giving their kingdom to the wild beast, until the
words of God will have been accomplished."
—Revelation 17:12, 16, 17, *NW.*

[11] Those horns are already turned against the
remnant of the woman's seed whom God has
called, chosen and proved faithful; but they will
fail to destroy these, for these remain loyal to
Christ's kingdom. The angel said: "The ten horns
that you saw mean ten kings, who have not yet
received a kingdom, but they do receive authority
as kings one hour with the wild beast. These have
one purpose, and so they give their power and
authority to the wild beast. These will battle with
the Lamb [even after destroying harlot Lady
Babylon], but, because he is Lord of lords and

---

11. Do those same horns turn against the remnant, and
what does Revelation 17:12-14 show on the war waged
by the horns?

King of kings, the Lamb will conquer them. Also those called and chosen and faithful with him will do so."—Revelation 17:12-14, *NW*.

¹² When the Lamb Christ Jesus conquers and destroys these kings and former unmoral allies of Lady Babylon, it will mean the destruction of the symbolic earth, the visible organization of Satan's world. Their destruction is pictured at Revelation 19:11-21. Christ Jesus lets Satan and his demons witness the destruction of the wicked earthly organization. After that he crushes the Serpent's head and all his demon brood under his feet by hurling them into the abyss for the thousand years of his reign after the battle of Armageddon. (Revelation 20:1-3) In this way Jehovah's great executional Officer will destroy the symbolic heavens or invisible, superhuman part of Satan's organization. His expression of God's vengeance will consume them like fire. By God's Word those devilish heavens and earth have been reserved till now: "By the same word the heavens and the earth that are now are stored up for fire and are being reserved to the day of judgment and of destruction of the ungodly men. Yet Jehovah's day will come as a thief, in which the heavens will pass away with a hissing noise, but the elements being intensely hot will be dissolved, and earth and the works in it will be discovered."—2 Peter 3:7, 10, *NW*.

¹³ Christ Jesus, the King-Priest like Melchize-

12. How will the earth and heavens of Satan's world be destroyed, and how does the apostle Peter describe this?
13, 14. (a) Whom will Christ Jesus not execute there, and what will survive? (b) In view of this world's end, what advice of Peter do these prospective survivors heed?

dek, will not execute the remnant of the woman's seed nor their good-will companions who follow them out of mystic Babylon and take up the pure worship of Jehovah God, at this His footstool, the earth. In this "war of the great day of God the Almighty" He will not destroy his earthly footstool. He will preserve it to make it glorious after he has brought to ruin those who ruin the earth. Contrary to false Babylonish religious teachings on the "end of the world", the earth will survive this universal war even though God's foes are armed with atomic bombs, hydrogen bombs and other weapons of mass destruction, for ruining the earth's surface. Earth will again survive, just as it lasted through the flood of Noah's day for further inhabitation by mankind. Did Noah, his wife and their companions survive in the ark till the global flood had subsided? Yes, and so also the remnant and their good-will companions will survive, and pure religion will survive with them. They will see come true God's promise of a righteous new world after Armageddon. So now they heed Peter's advice, in view of the certain end of Satan's world:

14 "Since all these things are thus to be dissolved, what sort of persons ought you to be in holy acts of conduct and deeds of godly devotion, awaiting and keeping close in mind the presence of the day of Jehovah, through which the heavens being on fire will be dissolved and the elements being intensely hot will melt? But there are new heavens and a new earth that we are awaiting according to his promise, and in these righteousness is to dwell."—2 Peter 3:11-13, NW.

CHAPTER XXVII

New World Unity Under Theocratic Worship

FROM its very start the new world will be united. Satan's woman, his Babylonish world organization, and her gods will be gone and no more be able to entice anyone into spiritual fornication. It will be impossible then to practice spiritism either for getting advice on the future or for getting a false comfort from demons who counterfeit dead humans. The demons will all be abyssed at the grand climax of the universal war for vindicating Jehovah God as the Supreme Sovereign over all creation. There will no more be any rendering to Caesar what is Caesar's besides rendering to God what belongs to God. Caesar and his political system will lie lifeless in ashes, never again to challenge the rightful domination of the earth by the true eternal God. With Caesar all divisive national boundaries and "iron curtains" must disappear along with all the international jealousies, rivalries, customs barriers and human butchery which they have occasioned. "The earth belongs to the Eternal, and all earth holds, the world and its inhabitants; 'twas he who founded it upon the seas, and fixed it on the floods." —Psalm 24:1, 2, *Mo;* 1 Corinthians 10:26, *NW*.

² The remnant of the seed of God's woman and

1. From its very start, in what state will the new world be, and why?
2. Will difference of language and national extraction break up the unity of Armageddon survivors, and on what is the answer based?

the great crowd of companions who survive the end of this world with them will be made up of men, women and children who have come from "all nations and tribes and peoples and tongues". (Revelation 7:4-14, *NW*) Will not this difference of language and national extraction be a cause of friction and misunderstanding and again produce division? Not at all, and this we say on the basis of present-day proof. The spiritual remnant and their increasing crowd of earthly companions who are to survive the world's end are with us today. Already before the end of this divided, war-minded world these are displaying a unity the wide earth over. World War II and all related political, commercial and religious controversies of this world have been unable to break up that unity. Just how is such a thing possible?

[3] It is possible because they have come out of mystic Babylon with her babble of religions and they are no longer a part of this split world, though they are still in it. Jesus said in prayer to God: "They are no part of the world just as I am no part of the world. Sanctify them by means of the truth; your word is truth." Then he prayed for their unity in the very midst of this world: "In order that they may all be one, just as you, Father, are in union with me and I am in union with you, that they also may be in union with us, in order that the world may believe that you sent me forth." (John 17:16, 17, 21, *NW*) It is by the divine truth that they are sanctified or set apart more and more from this world of confusion. Such sanctification is part of the pure, undefiled religion: "to keep oneself unspotted from the world."

---

3. Why is such present-day unity possible, and so what is it that unites them with one another?

This religion is a form of worship based on truth. So that which unites them with one another and with Jehovah God and his Son Jesus Christ is their common worship of the one Most High God and their common allegiance to the everlasting kingdom of his Son Jesus Christ.

⁴ For the time being they speak different native tongues, but they all have one language which they everywhere speak and understand in common. It is the "pure language" of the truth about God and his purpose and theocratic government. The Bible is the textbook of the pure language. God promised to bestow it upon his remnant of spiritual Israelites after delivering them from mystic Babylon and before destroying Satan's "earth" and its nations. In a warning to Christendom, which is unfaithful Jerusalem's modern counterpart, he said: "Therefore wait ye for me, saith Jehovah, until the day that I rise up to the prey; for my determination is to gather the nations, that I may assemble the kingdoms, to pour upon them mine indignation, even all my fierce anger; for all the earth shall be devoured with the fire of my jealousy. For then will I turn to the peoples a pure language, that they may all call upon the name of Jehovah, to serve him with one consent. The remnant of Israel shall not do iniquity, nor speak lies; neither shall a deceitful tongue be found in their mouth; . . . I will make you a name and a praise among all the peoples of the earth, when I bring back your captivity before your eyes, saith Jehovah." (Zephaniah 3:8, 9, 13, 20, AS) Under the power and guidance of this "pure language" the remnant and the good-

---

4. What language do they all now speak in common, and so whom do they worship with one consent?

will people out of all the doomed nations call on Jehovah's name for salvation through Christ and unite "with one consent" in serving him. All are Jehovah's witnesses.

⁵ Revealing that this "great crowd" of associates of the remnant would unite with them in the one worship despite their different national extractions and native languages, John says: "Look! a great crowd, which no man was able to number, out of all nations and tribes and peoples and tongues, standing before the throne and before the Lamb, dressed in white robes, and there were palm branches in their hands. And they keep on crying with a loud voice, saying: 'Salvation we owe to our God, who is seated on the throne, and

___

5. How does The Revelation show that the associates of the remnant unite with them in worship, and how is there now "one flock"?

A view of Theocracy's Increase Assembly of Jehovah's witnesses at Yankee Stadium, New York city, N. Y., July 30 to August 6, 1950, which was attended by over 80,000 members of the remnant and "great crowd" of many languages from some 65 lands, and with a public meeting of 123,707 in attendance.

to the Lamb.' " Who are these? "These are the ones that come out of the great tribulation, and they have washed their robes and made them white in the blood of the Lamb. That is why they are before the throne of God, and they are rendering him sacred service day and night in his temple, and the one seated on the throne will spread his tent over them. . . . And God will wipe out every tear from their eyes." (Revelation 7:9, 10, 14-17, NW) They are the "other sheep" of the Right Shepherd, and he has brought them into unity with the remnant of his "little flock", so that there is now "one flock, one shepherd". —John 10:16, NW; AS; Luke 12:32.

⁶ This unity in the "pure language" and in worshiping Jehovah God with one consent they will carry with them through the great tribulation of Armageddon and across the threshold of God's new world, consisting of "new heavens and a new earth". The new heavens of God's creation are to consist of the righteous new heavenly ruling powers, Christ Jesus with his "bride" of 144,000 members. The new earth is to be, not a new earthly globe, but the righteous earthly subjects of the King living under a new social arrangement.

⁷ The spiritual remnant and their fellow survivors, the "great crowd", have different destinies. But this does not divide them, no more than the new heavens and the new earth are divided but are inseparably united. The remnant are the last ones of the called and elected "bride" of Christ. Hence after they have finished their temporary

---

6. How will they carry their unity into the new world, and what are the new heavens and the new earth to be?
7. Does their having different destinies divide them, and what are their respective destinies?

post-Armageddon work on earth, they must finish their earthly course and lay down their human lives as Christ Jesus has demonstrated for them. They will not sleep in death the way dead mankind has done, but they will participate in the "first resurrection" and so will be changed instantaneously, "sown a physical body, . . . raised up a spiritual body" and putting on immortality and incorruption. As members of his glorified "bride" they will be united forever with their Bridegroom in the "new heavens" and will reign with him for a thousand years for the special blessing of all families and nations on earth. (Revelation 20:6 and 1 Corinthians 15:44-54, *NW*) On the other hand, the "great crowd" of Armageddon survivors have an earthly destiny. Their hope according to God's promise is eternal life in the "new earth" with Paradise restored to earth and eventually encircling the entire globe.

8 The first thing Noah did after emerging from the ark with his family into the postflood earth was to build an altar and renew the pure worship of Jehovah God on the earth. Bearing the true religion through the battle of Armageddon, the remnant and "great crowd" will unitedly start the worship of the one true God in the cleansed earth. As survivors they will have witnessed Jehovah's vindication of his name and universal sovereignty over the Devil's combined wicked world. As a result of Jehovah's victory at Armageddon there will be none on earth who will not know he is the Most High and Almighty God: "For the earth shall be filled with the knowledge of the glory of

---

8. What will they unitedly start first thing after Armageddon, and what visible Kingdom representatives will the remnant leave behind?

Jehovah, as the waters cover the sea." (Habakkuk 2:14, *AS*) When the spiritual remnant pass off the visible earthly scene, it will remove the last of the heirs of the kingdom of the "new heavens". But they will leave behind other visible representatives of the kingdom of Christ Jesus and his joint heirs. These will be men designated as "princes in all the earth".

⁹ To Christ Jesus the King it is prophetically said: "Instead of thy fathers shall be thy children, whom thou shalt make princes in all the earth." (Psalm 45:16, *AS*) Many of these will be men out of the great crowd of Armageddon survivors, who have proved faithful during this "time of the end" in preaching the Kingdom gospel and in caring for the welfare of Jehovah's people. For their dependability today under adverse conditions in this world, he will advance them then to princely responsibility of various kinds in the "new earth". But the prophecy indicates that faithful men of old, Jehovah's witnesses of times before Christ, will also be made such princes. How will this be possible? By giving these an early resurrection from the dead to human life in the "new earth", that is, a resurrection in advance of the resurrection of the remainder of mankind in the graves. They will include such men of faith in Jehovah as are named in Hebrews, chapter eleven, Abel, Enoch, Noah, Abraham, Isaac, Jacob, Moses, Daniel, and others of proved faith.—Hebrews 11:35-40; Daniel 12:5, 13.

¹⁰ Jesus foretold not only the first resurrection

---

9. Whom will the King make princes in all the earth, and how?

10. Of whom will there then be a resurrection, and with what purpose, and hence what will the King come to be called?

of the members of his bride to immortal heavenly life but also the resurrection of all mankind for whom he died and who are in the memorial tombs. John's vision vividly showed how they will come forth in God's due time from the sea and the common grave of mankind or "Hades", in response to the command of Christ Jesus, Jehovah's anointed King. (John 5:28, 29, *NW;* Revelation 20:11-13, *AS*) Jesus' purpose is to give them eternal perfect human life in compensation for the perfect human life which he laid down in sacrifice and the value of which he as High Priest presented to Jehovah God in heaven. Hence "his name shall be called Wonderful, Counsellor, Mighty God, Everlasting Father", that is, toward ransomed mankind.—Isaiah 9:6, *AS*.

[11] He will judge them, not according to their past conduct during the regime of Satan the Devil when they were born as sinner descendants from Adam, but according to their course of action under his thousand-year kingdom. Past unrighteousness will, of course, have hindering effects, but to the willing and obedient the King will extend his help. Those who then take up the clean religion then taught and who render sincere worship to Jehovah and prove themselves obedient subjects of his reigning King will, by the close of the thousand years, be raised to perfect freedom from sin and imperfection. Those uplifted men and women will have the pristine perfection of the innocent Adam and Eve in Eden.

---

11. On what basis will they be judged, and to what will the obedient subjects attain by the close of the thousand years?

[12] Will they now go the way of Adam and Eve or will they stay loyal to God and his Christ? How can they go the way of Adam and Eve when there is no forbidden tree of knowledge of good and evil and when the original Serpent is not there? Ah, but the Serpent will make his reappearance, according to the vision at Revelation 20:1-10. He and his demons have been reserved inactive in the abyss during the uplift work of the Kingdom during the thousand years. Now they will be released to test the fully instructed and perfected human race of the "new earth". This time, however, they will not be unborn in Adam's loins and subject to his course. Each one will be there because of the ransom sacrifice of the "Everlasting Father", Jesus Christ. Each will be on his own responsibility and will determine just his own destiny by his individual choice of action. Those individuals who follow Adam and Eve's example and yield to the misleading by the original Serpent and his demons will be destroyed, being cast into the "second death" symbolized by the "lake of fire". Christ Jesus now immortal and no longer human cannot die a second time to redeem these from the second death, and so they are annihilated. This accomplished, the Serpent and his demons who induced the desertion of these from the side of Jehovah's universal sovereignty will be destroyed with this same annihilation. Thus Christ Jesus the Seed of God's woman will crush the Serpent and all his demon and human brood forever, and the Edenic promise at Genesis 3:15 will have its final, complete fulfillment.—Revelation 20:12-15, *NW*.

---

12. How will the integrity of all on earth be tested then, and how will Genesis 3:15 have its final, complete fulfillment?

[13] Almighty God has declared authoritatively that the new heavens and the new earth are to remain before him for all eternity. (Isaiah 65:17; 66:22-24) That means there will be loyal men and women on earth who will resist Satan and his demons at that most crucial moment in all their lives. As respects these the Serpent will fail absolutely in this restored Paradise, and mankind will not be driven out of it again. The Serpent and his brood will be the ones to be destroyed out of it, and faithful men and women of integrity toward Jehovah God the Universal Sovereign will stay in this Paradise. On these he will pronounce his approval and bestow the right to eternal life in the "new earth", to be sustained by all the fruits and life provisions of the beauteous global paradise. In this way through Christ "he hath swallowed up death for ever; and the Lord Jehovah will wipe away tears from off all faces". (Isaiah 25:8, AS) "As the last enemy, death is to be destroyed." "And death [through Adam] will be no more, neither will mourning nor outcry nor pain be any more. The former things have passed away." (1 Corinthians 15:26 and Revelation 21:4, NW) Mankind will thus become children of Jehovah God the Creator through his only-begotten Son Jesus. As such they will be members of his faithful universal theocratic family. Since Christ Jesus is the chief one of God's heavenly organization which is his symbolic woman, and since they receive everlasting life in the new world through Jesus, they will thus, too, be visible earthly children of God's "woman".

---

13. Will mankind again be driven out of paradise, what will be destroyed as the last enemy, and whose children will mankind become?

[14] At that stupendous achievement of divine power the Most High God will have united all living creation under him forever. Yes, "then the Son himself will also subject himself to the one who subjected all things to him, that God may be all things to everyone." (1 Corinthians 15:28, *NW*) Jehovah God will be acknowledged to be supreme, and all loyal, obedient creatures will forever continue worshiping him unitedly through his most devoted Son Christ Jesus, "who, although he was existing in God's form, gave no consideration to a seizure, namely, that he should be equal to God. No, but he emptied himself and took a slave's form and came to be in the likeness of men. More than that, when he found himself in fashion as a man, he humbled himself and became obedient as far as death, yes, death on a torture stake. For this very reason also God exalted him to a superior position and kindly gave him the name that is above every other name, so that in the name of Jesus every knee should bend of those in heaven and those on earth and those under the ground, and every tongue should openly confess that Jesus Christ is Lord to the glory of God the Father." —Philippians 2:5-11, *NW;* Revelation 5:13, *NW.*

[15] Catch that sublime vision of the entire universe united at last in a perfect bond which will hold for eternity, the bond of the one worship of the universal heavenly Father because all his children love and adore him above all. False religion has long denied his existence or has misrepresented him as a repellant God, fiendish,

14. Who will thus be united under the Most High God, and through whom will they unitedly worship Him?
15. As against false religion, how does true religion present God, and how does the vision of his purpose accomplished vindicate him?

vengeful and responsible for all the suffering, imperfection, sorrows and calamities of humankind. But true religion, fully enlightened by the revelations from his Holy Scriptures of truth, presents him as the very personification of love, summed up in these heart-warming words, "God is love." (1 John 4:8, 16) The glorious vision of the full accomplishment of his loving purpose at his own appointed time completely vindicates him of all the reproachful aspersions which Satan and his diabolical religion have hurled at Jehovah God. It exalts him before all the universe as the Supreme and Eternal One, faultless in wisdom, power, justice and love; a God whose eyes are too pure to look upon sin and wickedness in any part of his universe and who is fully able to make a clean, happy universe; a God worthy of the gratitude, affection and worship of all creatures with all their heart, mind, soul and strength.

[16] We can love a God like this. Drawn to Jehovah by his matchless loving-kindness, we want to worship and adore such a God as He is. In the light of his wondrous revelations of truth it is now our privilege to do so without delay, together with all those who worship him with spirit and with truth. This is the true religion for which you have longed and which alone will unite all creation that lives; just as the last psalm says: "Let everything that hath breath praise Jehovah." (Psalm 150:6, *AS*) Everlasting life in the righteous, peaceful, free world under Jehovah God and his Christ—this is what the clean, undefiled religion gains for obedient mankind.

---

16. What is it now our privilege to do without delay, and what does the clean, undefiled religion gain for obedient mankind?

How to Follow Up Your Reading of This Book

NOW that you have read the book you will want some practical suggestions so as to benefit from this information and have it work to your good. Here they are: start a study (without obligation) with the one who left the book with you, or any one of Jehovah's witnesses. Or, feeling you are able, and desire to do so, now that you have read it through, why not aid your friends, neighbors and relatives to have and enjoy this knowledge as you do? Study it with them, reading first the question, then discussing the paragraph, and lastly reading the paragraph aloud as the final comment. Thus your own happiness, knowledge and understanding will increase.

Additional information too can be gained by obtaining other literature published by the Watchtower Society. An especially interesting booklet is *Religion Reaps the Whirlwind*. It answers such questions as: Where does one go at death? Can one gain life for a deceased loved one? What is the Bible teaching on the trinity? the true church? the keys of heaven? What place do images have in worship? These, and many others that arouse just as much interest, are of concern to every honest-hearted person whatever his faith, or lack of it, may be.

All thinking persons are concerned about obtaining eternal life and in overcoming problems encountered in the pursuit of it. So none can afford to be complacent and indifferent about the serious times in which we find ourselves today. You, dear reader, realize this more fully now, having had your eyes of understanding enlightened and your mind made free of the bondage of this old world, which is due to end shortly. Also, you will want to see your fellow human so favored with this knowledge and become free, and get in line to be a part of the incoming righteous new system of things. You have taken a step in the right direction by reading this book. Don't stop here! Continue your search for truth, go forward to a more abundant life, help others now, and gain life that is life indeed.

Religion Reaps the Whirlwind will be sent to you for 5c a copy. Bound volumes, such as *"The Truth Shall Make You Free"*, *"The Kingdom Is at Hand"*, *"Let God Be True"*, *"This Means Everlasting Life"*, and others, can be obtained for 50c a copy. Send for them now. For ordering above see addresses on last page.

SUBJECT INDEX

INDEX TO SCRIPTURES CITED

THE WATCHTOWER

Man, with his false religions and present world political setup, his modern medical and scientific advancements, has brought no real hope of a cure or remedy for the perilous and perplexing times in which we are now living.

In sharp contrast, the Bible reveals God's purpose of fulfilling your desires for relief by removing this present ungodly system of things. The new system of things to be set up is Jehovah's kingdom; and the magazine dedicated to heralding to you the announcement of its establishment is *The Watchtower*. By strict adherence to Bible prophecy it points out the only way of salvation and entrance into a new world system. It does not privately interpret prophecy, but calls attention to physical facts, sets them alongside prophecy, and you see for yourself how well the two match, how accurately Jehovah God interprets his own prophecy.

A full year's subscription for this 32-page journal, published semimonthly in large print, may be had for $1.00. Take advantage of this enlightening, hopeful journal by subscribing now! Available in 36 languages.

WATCHTOWER BIBLE EDITIONS

New World Translation. Outstanding among Bibles is the *New World Translation of the Christian Greek Scriptures* ("New Testament" only). It is an entirely new translation from the original language, based upon the most ancient and reliable manuscripts. Accuracy, uniformity, clarity, and up-to-date language mark this excellent work. Bible study aids without equal make this an indispensable help to sincere searching students of God's Word. Size 7 5/16" x 5" x 1". $1.50.

American Standard Version of 1901. Clear-face, readable type; self-pronouncing, cyclopedic concordance; footnotes; maps. Bound in light-brown leatherette, it measures 7⅞" x 5⅛" x 1⅜". $1.50.

Authorized Version or *King James Version* of 1611. Bound in attractive maroon leatherette, it is 7¼" x 5" x 1⅜". It features copious marginal references, an index of names, expressions and their meanings, and a concordance. $1.00.

The Emphatic Diaglott ("New Testament" only). $2.00.

Any of above will be sent postpaid at contribution shown.
For ordering above see addresses on last page.

Chief Office and Official Address of

WATCH TOWER BIBLE & TRACT SOCIETY
WATCHTOWER BIBLE AND TRACT SOCIETY, INC.
INTERNATIONAL BIBLE STUDENTS ASSOCIATION
is
124 Columbia Heights, Brooklyn 2, New York, U. S. A.

Addresses of Branch offices:

America (U.S.), 117 Adams St., Brooklyn 1, N.Y. **Australia,** 11 Beresford Road, Strathfield, N.S.W. **Austria,** Liechtensteinstr. 24, Vienna IX. **Bahamas,** Box 1247, Nassau, N. P. **Belgium,** 28 Ave. Gen. Eisenhower, Schaerbeek-Brussels. **Bolivia,** Casilla No. 1440, La Paz. **Brazil,** Rua Licínio Cardoso 330, Rio de Janeiro. **British Guiana,** 50 Brickdam, Georgetown. **British Honduras,** Box 257, Belize. **British West Indies,** 21 Taylor St., Woodbrook, Port of Spain, Trinidad. **Burma,** P.O. Box 62, Rangoon. **Canada,** 40 Irwin Ave., Toronto 5, Ontario. **Chile,** Moneda 2390, Santiago. **China,** P.O. Box 1903, Shanghai. **Colombia,** Calle 21, No. 16A-43, Bogotá. **Costa Rica,** Apartado 2043, San José. **Cuba,** Calle D No. 206, Almendares, Marianao, Havana. **Cyprus,** Box 196, Famagusta. **Denmark,** Sondre Fasanvej 54, Copenhagen-Valby. **Ecuador,** Casilla 4512, Guayaquil. **Egypt,** Post Box 387, Cairo. **El Salvador,** Apartado 401, San Salvador. **England,** 34 Craven Terrace, London, W. 2. **Finland,** Vainamoisenkatu 27, Helsinki. **France,** 3 Villa Guibert, Paris 16e. **Gambia, B.W.A.,** Box 115, Bathurst. **Germany (U.S.Zone),** Am Kohlheck, (16) Wiesbaden-Dotzheim, Hesse. **Gold Coast, B.W.A.,** Box 760, Accra. **Greece,** 16 Tenedou St., Athens. **Guatemala,** 11 Avenida Norte No. 8, Guatemala. **Haiti,** Post Box B-185, Port-au-Prince. **Hashemite Jordan Kingdom,** P.O. Box 18, Beit-Jala, Via Beirut, Amman. **T. Hawaii,** 1228 Pensacola St., Honolulu 14. **Honduras,** Apartado 147, Tegucigalpa. **India,** 167 Love Lane, Bombay 27. **Israel,** P. O. Box 994, 10 Hechalutz St., Haifa. **Italy,** Via Monte Maloia 10, Monte Sacro, Rome 742. **Jamaica,** 151 King St., Kingston. **Japan,** 1 Toyooka-Cho, Shiba-Mita, Minato-Ku, Tokyo. **Lebanon,** P.O. Box 1122, Beirut. **Liberia,** c/o G. Watkins, 17 Johnson Street, Monrovia. **Luxembourg,** 95 Rue Eugene Welter, Luxembourg-Howald. **México,** Calzada Melchor Ocampo 71, México 4, D.F. **Netherlands,** Koningslaan 1, Amsterdam-Z. **Netherlands West Indies,** Breedestraat 12, Otrabanda, Curaçao. **Newfoundland, Canada,** Post Box 521, St. John's. **New Zealand,** G.P.O. Box 30, Wellington, C. 1. **Nicaragua,** Apartado 183, Managua, D.N. **Nigeria,** West Africa, P.O. Box 695, Lagos. **Northern Rhodesia,** Box 5, Lusaka. **Norway,** Inkognitogaten 28 B., Oslo. **Nyasaland,** Box 83, Blantyre. **Pakistan,** 15 Ilaco House, Victoria Road, Karachi 3. **Panama,** Box 274, Ancon, C. Z. **Paraguay,** Río de Janeiro y Esq. Mary Lyons, Asunción. **Peru,** Pasaje Velarde 165, Lima. **Philippine Republic,** 104 Roosevelt Rd., San-Francisco del Monte, Quezon City. **Puerto Rico,** 704 Calle Lafayette, Pda. 21, Urb. Hip., Santurce 34. **Sierra Leone,** Box 136, Freetown. **Singapore 15,** 33 Poole Road. **South Africa,** 623 Boston House, Cape Town. **Southern Rhodesia,** P. O. Box 1462, Salisbury. **Surinam,** Princestraat 35 Boven, Paramaribo. **Sweden,** Luntmakaregatan 94, Stockholm Va. **Switzerland,** Allmendstrasse 39, Berne 22. **Thailand,** Box 67, Bangkok. **Turkey,** P.K. 2077, Istanbul. **Uruguay,** Joaquín de Salterain 1264, Montevideo. **Venezuela,** Ave. Prin. del Paraíso 27, Quinta Savtepaul, Paraíso, Caracas.